SO-BMU-731

GOVERNORS STATE UNIVERSITY LIBRARY

3 1611 00319 9004

Even More Great Ideas for Libraries and Friends

Sally Gardner Reed and Beth Nawalinski

of Friends of Libraries U.S.A.

GOVERNORS STATE UNIVERSITY
UNIVERSITY PARK
IL 60466

Neal-Schuman Publishers, Inc.

New York   London

Published by Neal-Schuman Publishers, Inc.
100 William St., Suite 2004
New York, NY 10038

Copyright © 2008 Friends of Libraries U.S.A.

All rights reserved. Reproduction of this book, in whole or in part, without written permission of the publisher, is prohibited.

Printed and bound in the United States of America.

The paper used in this publication meets the minimum requirements of American National Standard for Information Sciences—Permanence of Paper for Printed Library Materials, ANSI Z39.48-1992.

Library of Congress Cataloging-in-Publication Data

Reed, Sally Gardner, 1953-
    Even more great ideas for libraries and friends / Sally Gardner Reed, Beth Nawa-
linski of Friends of Libraries U.S.A.
        p. cm.
    Includes index.
    ISBN 978-1-55570-638-8 (alk. paper)
    1. Friends of the library—United States—Case studies. 2. Library fund rais-
ing—United States—Case Studies. 3. Libraries and community—United States. I.
Nawalinski, Beth, 1972- II. Friends of Libraries U.S.A. III. Title.

Z681.7.U5R45 2008
021.7—dc22
                                                                2008032541

Z
681.7
.U5
R45
2008

Dedication

For the Friends of the Ilsley Public Library in Middlebury, Vermont, with whom I had the great pleasure of working from 1985 to 1993. They taught me the true value of Friends and I owe them more than I can ever repay.

Sally Gardner Reed

For Tom, who encouraged me to find the job of my dreams, gave me two wonderful children, and who reminds me often to slow down and enjoy life.

Beth Nawalinski

Contents

Chapter 2. Selling Books   67

Chapter 3. Programs for Services and Outreach   91

List of Figures

Chapter 1. Raising Money for Libraries

Chapter 2. Selling Books

Chapter 3. Programs for Services and Outreach

Chapter 4. Advocacy and Public Awareness

Chapter 5. Building Membership in Friends

List of Contributors

American Library Association
American University Library (Washington, DC)
Arapahoe Library District
Blackstone Branch Library of the Chicago (IL) Public Library
Caldwell County (NC) Public Library
Canton (MI) Public Library
Chestatee (GA) Regional Library
Cornell University Library (Ithaca, NY)
Friends of Berks County (PA) Public Libraries
Friends of Bryant Library (Roslyn, NY)
Friends of Ferguson Library (Stamford, CT)
Friends of Irving (TX) School Libraries
Friends of Libraries U.S.A.
Friends of the Alpine (TX) Public Library
Friends of the Canton (MI) Public Library
Friends of the Cleveland Heights–University Heights (OH) Public Library
Friends of the Dublin (CA) Library
Friends of the Dundee Township (IL) Public Library District
Friends of the Elkins Park (PA) Free Library
Friends of the Fargo (ND) Public Library
Friends of the Freeman (TX) Public Library
Friends of the Georgetown (TX) Public Library
Friends of the Hedberg Public Library (Janesville, WI)
Friends of the Henderson (KY) Public Library
Friends of the Houston (TX) Public Library

Friends of the Hunterdon County (NJ) Library System
Friends of the Huntington (IN) Public Library
Friends of the J. V. Fletcher Library (Westford, MA)
Friends of the Johnson County (KS) Library
Friends of the Joseph T. Simpson Public Library (Mechanicsburg, PA)
Friends of the Lake Oswego (OR) Public Library
Friends of the Lawrence (KS) Public Library
Friends of the Leesburg (FL) Library
Friends of the Libraries at the University of Memphis (TN)
Friends of the Library and Scharchburg Archives (Kettering University, Flint, MI)
Friends of the Little Elm (TX) Public Library
Friends of the Mansfield (TX) Public Library
Friends of the Medford (OR) Library
Friends of the Mineola (TX) Public Library
The Friends of the Minneapolis (MN) Public Library
Friends of the Multnomah County (OR) Library
Friends of the Newfields (NH) Public Library
Friends of the Northside Independent School District Libraries
    (San Antonio, TX)
Friends of the Northville (MI) Public Library
Friends of the Novi (MI) Public Library
Friends of the Old Dominion University Library (Norfolk, VA)
Friends of the Oradell (NJ) Library
Friends of the Pasco County (FL) Public Library
Friends of the Plymouth (MI) Public Library
The Friends of the Saint Paul (MN) Public Library
Friends of the South Pasadena (CA) Public Library
Friends of the Stark County District Library (Canton, OH)
Friends of the Tippecanoe County Public Library (Lafayette, IN)
Friends of the University of Arizona Libraries (Tucson, AZ)
Friends of the Wardsboro (VT) Library
Friends of the Waterloo (IA) Public Library
Friends of the Webster Groves (MO) Public Library
Loveland (CO) Public Library
Oxford (NC) Public Library
Peninsula Friends of the Library (Palos Verdes, CA)
Rochester (NY) Public Library
Salt Lake City (UT) Public Library
San Antonio (TX) Public Library Foundation
State Library of North Carolina (Raleigh, NC)
University Library System at the University of Pittsburgh (PA)

University of Cincinnati (OH) Libraries
Washington University (St. Louis, MO)
www.ilovelibraries.org
Wyndham Robertson Library at Hollins University (Roanoke, VA)
Wyoming State Library (Cheyenne, WY)
Z. Smith Reynolds Library, Wake Forest (NC) University

Preface

We at Friends of Libraries U.S.A. are pleased to bring you this new collection of great ideas from libraries and Friends groups at public, academic, and school libraries across the country. Raising money and public awareness can make an incredible difference, and the ideas presented in this book demonstrate that doing so can be both fun and effective.

Even More Great Ideas for Libraries and Friends is the sequel to *101+ Great Ideas for Libraries and Friends*. Like its predecessor, it provides information on how to replicate success in fund-raising, program development, advocacy, and bookselling, as well as on how to ensure that you have an effective Friends group with lots of members!

You'll find ideas for author programs and library anniversary celebrations. You'll get the information you need to raise money through an amazingly successful book sale or an antiques appraisal event; and you'll learn how to get single, large donations by making "the ask." You'll get great tips on how to hold "virtual meetings," as well as on how to increase the membership of your Friends group.

Large or small, libraries of all kinds—academic, public, school, or special—can benefit from the success of colleagues and cohorts everywhere. Why spend time and energy trying to come up with the perfect fund-raising idea when some other library or Friends group has already done it? Why write your own bylaws if you can use the samples in this book as your guide?

Sharing information and ideas is what libraries and Friends are all about! It's been our good fortune to learn about hundreds of ideas that make many of America's libraries better, and we are confident that these ideas will also help you make *your* library better. For ease of use, we've divided this book into six chapters:

- Chapter 1, "Raising Money for Libraries," shows just how creative and lucrative fund-raising can be. The Gilfeather Turnip Festival in Wardsboro (VT), for example, not only raises money but also increases the library's recognition level—and the festival grows each year! Friends in Georgetown (TX), and Friends in Michigan describe how they make money for the library through author events. Whether it's a trivia competition or the sale of historic photos, the ways in which you can engage the community and increase revenues seem limitless.

- Chapter 2, "Selling Books," covers an activity worthy of its own chapter because selling books is such a traditional way of raising funds—and it has the added benefit of recycling. Here you will find ways to improve the annual on-site book sale, and you'll get some great tips on how to sell books online —a terrific way to expand your target audience to include the entire world. Ongoing book sales—in the library lobby or in a Friends' bookstore—bring in the bucks. In addition, you'll also find ways to donate the books that just won't sell.

- Chapter 3, "Programs for Services and Outreach," will show you ways to turn tired public programs into ones that generate excitement and participation. Find out how to jazz up your "one city, one book" program by adding a musical performance, as the Friends of the Stark County District Library did in Canton, OH. Or, take a page from the University of Cincinnati's book and celebrate the scholarly and creative works of faculty and staff—the way to do it can be found here. In addition to public programs, you'll get new ideas for thanking library staff members (as is done in Canton, MI) and creating a "People's University"—a big success in Minneapolis, MN.

- Chapter 4, "Advocacy and Public Awareness," shares important and high-profile programs, celebrations, and outreach efforts designed to highlight the important contributions libraries make on campuses and in their communities. Ideas for creating a buzz about libraries and increasing public awareness of their importance range from anniversary celebrations to highlighting and promoting special alumni collections. Find out in this chapter how North Carolina used the Public Library Association's "Smartest Card" promotion to develop their own statewide campaign. Discover how to highlight the value of your Friends group by participating in National Friends of Library Week. Here, too, you will find a complete tool kit from the American Library Association's advocacy office so that you can wage your own local campaign. Libraries are important and essential; ideas included here will help you get the word out.

- Chapter 5, "Building Membership in Friends," is based on the premise that without Friends groups that have large and active memberships, libraries would be much poorer. Building and maintaining strong membership, however, has been a daunting task for many Friends groups. Luckily, there are some who've been very successful in this endeavor, and they have shared their strategies with us. We even have a number of excellent membership brochures to share with you. Whether it's special incentives—such as those offered by the Friends of the Tippecanoe County Public Library in Lafayette, IN—or special categories—such as those promoted by the Friends of the University of Arizona Libraries in Tucson—you'll find new ways in this chapter to bring in more members and more membership dollars.

- Chapter 6, "Organizational Effectiveness," shows that while it may not be sexy, making sure your group is functional is the best way to create a solid foundation for success. Groups that function well attract new members, foster higher levels of creativity, raise more money, and have more fun than those that don't. It's important for groups to have a clear set of bylaws, a solid committee structure with clear charges, and a plan for the future. In this chapter, you will find all of this from both academic and public library groups, along with tips for keeping volunteers motivated and for surveying members to determine their level of satisfaction. In this chapter, you'll also find a sample "Memorandum of Understanding" between the library and the Friends, so mutual expectations can be set and misunderstandings won't have a chance to ruin a beautiful relationship.

We at Friends of Libraries U.S.A. believe that the most important thing library supporters can do to help their libraries is to learn to become great advocates and to raise money to complement the library's budget. In *Even More Great Ideas for Libraries and Friends*, we are giving you the tools you need to maximize citizen, student, and faculty support. In addition to good ideas for fund-raising and advocacy, we provide lots of good ideas for keeping your Friends group strong. Strong Friends mean strong libraries!

Chapter One

Raising Money for Libraries

Friends of Libraries U.S.A. surveyed its members recently and found that in 2006 Friends groups raised, on average, over $50,000 for their libraries. Wow. Through effective advocacy, Friends can work to ensure that operational funding by the city or campus administration stays strong, but there will always be projects, start-up collections, and services that are not normally covered by the annual budget.

Luckily, Friends and library supporters have found ways to bring in the extra money that can take a library from good to great. In addition, fund-raising has always been a way of "friend-raising" and library promotion, too. Every time there is a book sale, an author event, a cookbook printed, or photographs published, the library enters the public spotlight. Not only that, but when people give to the library, they invest in it. Donors become stakeholders and will likely come to the library's defense if the budget is threatened or if a bond issue needs passing.

In this chapter you'll find lots of ideas and sample graphics. They are yours to use, copy, modify, or stimulate your own new great idea—which, hopefully, will find its way into the next edition of this book!

1-1   Raising Money for Sundays

Local funding for Sunday library hours at the J.V. Fletcher Library, Inc., in Westford (MA) was cut from the library budget, so the Friends decided to raise funds to restore Sunday hours. Taking a cue from the Shrewsbury (MA) Friends, who had waged a similar campaign, they solicited local corporations, organizations, and individuals. Friends contacted local businesses in person, by telephone, and by mail, asking for donations of $650 per Sunday. They promised publicity for Sunday hours sponsors, including postings in the library each week as to who was sponsoring that specific Sunday.

How It Worked

- In May, the Friends started collecting prospective business names. The volunteer committee contacted businesses by phone, in person, and by mail. Person-to-person contacts were the most effective, but the group had a limited number of volunteers comfortable with making personal contacts. Therefore, in October, they also mailed a letter announcing the campaign to their membership. The campaign deadline was December 31.
- They worked with the local media to get a feature article in as many of the papers as possible. A discussion of the campaign appeared numerous times in the *Library Latest* weekly feature of the local paper. The local access cable station ran notices of the campaign.
- Donors were promised publicity in the media, on a bookmark that would be handed out throughout the season listing all sponsors, and on posters displayed in the library every week thanking the particular sponsor of that Sunday.
- Although businesses and a foundation contributed, they were surprised by the number of local families who decided to sponsor a Sunday on their own.
- The library director was a key member of the volunteer team that carried out the campaign. She attended all the meetings and helped to produce the campaign materials (letters, posters, and bookmarks) and thanked sponsors directly after receiving donations.

Results

The Friends raised more than $11,000 and restored the regular season of 16 Sundays (January through April). In addition, the campaign generated a significant amount of publicity, including feature articles in the local papers. The campaign also raised the profile of the Friends, producing a very tangible contribution and probably contributing to the increased membership they experienced following the campaign.

DIRECTOR
ELLEN D. RAINVILLE

RE: SPONSORSHIP OF LIBRARY SERVICE

Dear

We are asking your help in making the J. V. Fletcher Library the best it can be, and in making the community of Westford a better place!

Specifically, we are asking your help in opening the J. V. Fletcher Library one (or more) Sunday(s) during January through April of 2007.

The townspeople of Westford would have a favorite service restored that was lost through budget cuts and we can promise you high visibility and publicity for your generosity! Sponsor's names will be listed in our e-newsletter, in our Westford Eagle weekly by-line, on bookmarks, on a poster at the building entrance, on the library web site, in our Annual Report and in press releases and other media. In addition, we plan to publicize your generosity on our local cable station. Finally, your sponsorship would be tax-deductible.

Over 225,000 customers visit the Fletcher Library each year, with Sunday being one of the heaviest days of use. This past year, library circulation increased 10% over the prior year, cresting 330,000 items. Therefore, your support of our Sunday season would gratify thousands of users.

The cost of funding one day of Sunday service is approximately $650 for staffing and facility costs. Your pledge to sponsor one or more Sundays would be a tax-deductible gift payable to the Friends of the J. V. Fletcher Library, Inc. and could be made in 2006 and/or 2007.

We hope you will consider this attractive civic-minded opportunity and be available for a personal visit to share the promotional and publicity materials that would market your business to the many customers who use and support the J. V. Fletcher Library. Please feel free to contact Library Director Ellen Rainville at 978-692-5557 or erainville@mvlc.org for further information.

Very Truly Yours,

Sally Harris
President, Friends of the J. V. Fletcher Library, Inc.

50 MAIN STREET • WESTFORD, MA 01886-2599 • TEL. (978) 692-5555 • FAX (978) 692-0287 • www.westfordlibrary.org

Figure 1-A   Library Sunday Hours Restoration Appeal Letter

Library Sunday Hours Restoration
Pledge Form

All gifts are made out to: "Friends of the J. V. Fletcher Library, Inc." and are tax-deductible. Please fill out the information below for your acknowledgment and your tax letter.

Pledge Amount: _____ Date: _____ (for your records)

--✂Cut Here---

I pledge to give $_____ for _____ Sunday(s) ($650.00 per Sunday)

❑ I would like to pay _____ in 2006.

❑ I would like to pay _____ in 2007.

❑ My check is enclosed

Name: _____

Address: _____

City: _____ State:_____ Zip:_____

Phone : _____

E-mail:_____

All Contributions are Welcome!

Thank you!

Please return to:
J. V. Fletcher Library
ATTN: Ellen Rainville, Library Director
50 Main St.
Westford MA 01886

This campaign is made possible
by the
Friends of the J. V. Fletcher Library, Inc.

Figure 1-B   Library Sunday Hours Restoration Pledge Form

ADVOCACY GIFT

DONOR: _____

J. V. FLETCHER LIBRARY SUNDAY PLEDGE DONATION FORM

DONOR INFORMATION:
Today's Date:_____
Donor's Name:_____
Address: _____
Telephone: _____
Contact Name:_____

ADVOCACY GIFT
Amount of Donation:_____
Number of Sundays: _____
Other:_____

SPECIAL INSTRUCTIONS
STAFF COMMENTS: _____
_____

STAFF CHECKLIST:	**DATE**	**BY WHOM**
Check Routed/Deposited to FOL:	____/____/____	FOL Treas._____
Check Memo Line says SUNDAY GIFT		
cc of *Sunday Pledge Form* attached to Deposit:	____/____/____	Director _____
Thank You, FOL Mbrship, Magnet		
and *Certificate of Recognition* sent:	____/____/____	Director _____
Company Name and Sponsorship added to		
Sunday Pledges EXCEL spreadsheet:	____/____/____	Director _____
Company Name and Sponsorship added to:	____/____/____	Director _____

Website	Cable	Press Releases
E newsletter	Annual Report	Cable TV

Final letter sent with cc of publicity items: ____/____/____   Director _____

COMPLETION DATE: ____/____/____   _____

Figure 1-C   Library Sunday Hours Restoration Donation Form

ENSR Corporation
2 Technology Park Dr.
Westford MA 01886

RESTORED SUNDAY HOURS CAMPAIGN:
DONOR ATTRIBUTION

Dear ENSR Corporation:

December 11, 2006

We would like to thank you once again for your generous funding of Restored Sunday Hours at the J. V. Fletcher Library, and ask you to provide correct attribution for our bookmarks, posters and on-going publicity.

We have your Donation information as: ENSR Corporation

Please indicate the following:

☐ This information is correct

☐ This information is incorrect and should be the following:

_____

☐ I wish my gift to be ANONYMOUS

☐ I wish my gift to be attributed to _____

(e.g. a Private Donor, a Grateful Reader, a Library Supporter -- you provide the language)

Please return this form in the provided SASE by December 22, 2006 or email me with your specific language at erainville@mvlc.org. Please email your business logo if you wish this to appear on our posters! Thank you again for your civic-minded sharing and generosity of spirit!

Very Truly Yours,

Ellen D. Rainville, Library Director
Encl: SASE

Figure 1-D   Library Sunday Hours Restoration Donor Attribution

1-2   Ts & Bs!

Because the small town of Mineola (TX) needed a new library and tax support was nonexistent, the Friends of the library decided to raise the awareness and use of the existing library so that fund-raising would be easier. Where to begin? The group decided that everyone likes to eat and shop, so they created their Ts (teas) & Bs (spelling & tasting bees) program.

How It Worked

- The Friends began their year of promotion with a Valentine Tea, followed by a Rotary Club Spelling Bee, and finished the year with their main fund-raising event, a Tasting Bee.
- Because public awareness was deemed as important as fund-raising, they decided not to charge a fee to attend the first two activities in the first year of the Ts & Bs events.
- For the *Valentine Tea*, the Friends pooled their "proper" tea services of crystal and china and gathered recipes for tea cookies and treats. A member who worked for a neighboring travel agency was invited to speak about her experiences of taking tea while traveling in England. She also discussed the proper etiquette involved in the ceremony.
- Later in the spring, the Rotary Club hosted their annual citywide *Spelling Bee* and agreed to donate all proceeds this year to the Mineola Library. To support the effort, the Friends entered a team and came home with the "Gold!"
- The final event for the year was the *Tasting Bee* held in November. One group of the Friends established a Country Store featuring handmade items for sale. Another group created a silent auction for the event. One member made recipe cards for all the dishes and also designed and printed a "program" list of all the dishes served. The Friends established a food committee to oversee the food, service, and cleanup.
- A price of $7.00 per person was established for this event. Some tickets were given away to local dignitaries, such as the mayor and the president of the chamber of commerce, to encourage their attendance.
- Members of the Friends provided all the food, table decorations, and serving items. They held the Tasting Bee in a local church activity center. All types of foods were accepted for tasting—in the end there were 51 assortments of delicious food on hand.
- The Country Store proved a great success with such items as homemade aprons, needlework, woodwork, and holiday decorations donated to sell.

Local merchants donated approximately 50 items for the silent auction, and it was very successful as well.

Results

The first two activities raised the profile of the library and of the Friends immeasurably so that by the final event the room capacity of 200 was met. The Friends raised $4,000 for the new library and are already planning their next series of events.

Figure 1-E   Country Store at the Tasting Bee

Figure 1-F   Tasting Bee Program (Outside)

To Purchase recipes circle your selections and take this card to the cashier in the country store
$1.00 per recipe
All proceeds benefit the library

BREADS:
Hotdog Bread Sticks
Green Chili Cornbread Muffins

SNACKS & APPETIZERS:
Cold Black Bean Dip
Ham Pinwheels
Kosher Sweet Pickles
Party Pinwheels
Pinwheels
Ritzy Peanut Snack
Roasted Almonds with Coriander and Chile
Texas Caviar

SIDES:
Allison's Potato Casserole
Angel Hair Flans
Autumn Fruit Salad
Autumn Succotash
Broccoli Casserole
Broccoli Salad
Broccoli Slaw with Cranberries
Five Cup Salad
Fruit Salad
Green Bean Salad
Hashbrown Potato Salad
Layered Salad
Nacho Salad
Spanish Rice

Soups:
Butternut Squash and Apple Bisque
Roasted Tomato Basil Soup

ENTREES:
Chicken-Broccoli Casserole
Chili and Ham Cups
Crunchy Sausage Casserole
Glazed Pork Loin with Cranberry Chutney
Italian Sausage Lasagna
Lacquered Salmon
Low-carb Beef Stew
"Mom Hid the Veggies" Sausage Casserole
Mom's Jalapeno Hash
Porcupine Meatballs
Poppy Seed Chicken
Triple Mustard Chicken Salad
Sausage Casserole
Spinach, Egg and Cheese Bake
Taco Stew

COOKIES AND DESSERTS:
Almond Macaroons
Brownie Bourbon Balls
Chocolate-apricot Thumbprint Cookies
Chocolate Peanut Butter Cheesecake Bars
Chocolate-Peanut Butter Chip Squares
Crisco Pound Cake
Hershey Bar Pie
Key Lime Coconut Snowballs
Pumpkin Pie Bars
Southern Scalloped Pineapple

Figure 1-G   Tasting Bee Program (Inside)

1-3 Raising Money with Historical Photographs

The Friends of the Oradell (NJ) Library came across two boxes of historical photographs taken between 1933 and 1934. The photos, taken for property tax reevaluation, included every building standing in the town. The Friends encouraged residents to come to the library and find the photo of their home. The Friends framed copies of the pictures and sold them for $35 each. The Friends also sold photos of the town's historic structures, some no longer in existence. After a successful initial drive, the Friends sent out reminder postcards to the residents who had not already purchased a photo of their home. During the holiday season, they offered note cards with photographs of individual homes.

How It Works

- Find historic photographs of your town. This is not as intimidating as it may seem. They might not be photos of houses but, perhaps, photos of well-known landmarks. The library itself or a local historical society may have a collection of photos.
- Catalog the original or copied photograph for easy retrieval and organization.
- Brainstorm ideas to reach the public—in a smaller town, this might include contacting residents directly.

Results

The cost to copy each photograph using a color ink jet printer and photo paper and to frame it was approximately $12, and each sold for $35. The Friends raised over $10,000 for the library over the course of two years. The money was used to build an Oradell History Archive Room as part of a major library renovation. The fundraiser attracted the attention of the community and brought local residents into the library.

"Our Home" Notepaper

Custom made for you by —

Our Home at 866 Amaryllis Avenue, Oradell, New Jersey
As it looked in 1933

The Friends
of the
Oradell
Library

12 cards for $10.00

Fill out your order form here —
◆ Your address
    ◆ Choose your address style
        ◆ Choose your type style
Orders usually take one week

Our Home Greeting Cards

Figure 1-H   Historical Note Card Sign Posted in the Library

Friends of the Oradell Library
375 Kinderkamack Road
Oradell, New Jersey 07649

Oradell

Permit

This Oradell home stood at 165
Kinderkamack Road. It was destroyed by
fire, but yours was not. (See other side.)

Address

The Oradell Library Archives probably has a picture of your home taken around 1933. Come in and see what your home looked like 70 odd years ago.

Framed computer prints are available for $35 including its history – including, most cases, when it was built and by whom.

Unframed print, without history are $25.

They make a nice family present or a thank you gift for thoughtful a neighbor.

Stop at the library and check out our files. We have other pictures including our churches, schools, stores, and almost any building in town in the early 1930s.

Sponsored as a fund raiser by
The Friends of the Oradell Library

Figure 1-1   Historical Photograph Postcard Mailed to Home Owners

1-4   Trivia at the Library

The Friends of the Little Elm (TX) Public Library present a trivia contest each year that has been gaining in momentum in terms of both participation and raising money for the library. Eight to ten member teams compete and test their genius in areas such as history, geography, fine arts, entertainment, and super trivia. Monetary prizes and a traveling trophy are awarded to the winning team.

How It Works

- Approximately 50 tables ($120 to $250 each) are sold to sponsored teams of contestants.
- Each table has a book that is purchased and donated by the team at the table.
- The Friends place small items around the table that relate to the theme of the book. These items may be taken by the team members at the end of the contest.
- Each seat at each table has a place mat containing the names and levels of sponsors.
- Sponsors may purchase tables, donate money, or donate items such as food, books, or logistical support materials.
- The Friends also award door prizes as participants enter the event venue. Each table is decked out with a basket of popcorn and a pizza (donated by local businesses).
- Food is sold throughout the event, and no food is allowed to be brought in by the participants.
- All individual attendees are encouraged to join the Friends of the Library with a minimum donation of $10.00.
- The contest itself is very simple. Questions are asked, and correct answers are tracked by team and projected on a screen. At the end of the evening, a trophy is awarded to the team that has answered the greatest number of questions correctly. This trophy is held for a year and then returned.

Results

This event has a history of earning between $10,000 and $15,000 for the library. It is an annual event that has become a highly anticipated part of the civic fabric in Little Elm.

Figure 1-J   Trivia Contest Participants

᪲᪲ ᪲᪲

1-5   Youth Basketball Clinic

The Friends of the Newfields (NH) Public Library began hosting a basketball clinic for children in their community several years ago. So far they've been joined for the day by professional basketball star Dwight Davis and local athletes to provide practice advice and instruction. The costs are low for participation, with discounted fees for multiple-child families. In addition, several scholarship opportunities are available for local residents.

The clinic, open to all boys and girls 6 to 16 years old from any state and town, focuses not only on basketball skills but also on the values of academics, community service, and character. Participants get practice advice and are led in scrimmages and instruction by Davis, as well as by many local current and former basketball players and coaches.

Even without a star like Dwight Davis, a community with access to college "stars" or even high school "stars" could hold a similar clinic for children in their area.

How It Works

- Six to eight volunteer coaches are recruited to help with the day's event.
- The entry fee includes a custom-printed T-shirt, pizza lunch, drinks, autographs, and trading cards.
- Partnerships are developed with several local businesses to help defray the costs of the shirts, food, and promotional materials.
- A timeline for publicity and promotion is developed:
  - The first notices go out in the Friends' quarterly newsletter in September.
  - Registrations are sent to all students at the five local elementary schools in early October.
  - Press releases go out in mid-October.
  - Posters are distributed to all local libraries, ice cream shops, and stores throughout October.
  - The clinic takes place the first weekend in November.
- Budgeted expenses have averaged around $800, with the largest cost being that for the T-shirts.

Results

After their costs, the Friends typically net around $1,000 and have between 40 and 50 participants. Their business sponsors pay for the pizza lunch, and they have been able to negotiate a discount on the T-shirts from a local vendor. In addition to the money they raise for the library, the Friends also receive advance coverage and day-of-event coverage from the local media and even had an article written about the clinic in the sports section of the *Boston Globe*.

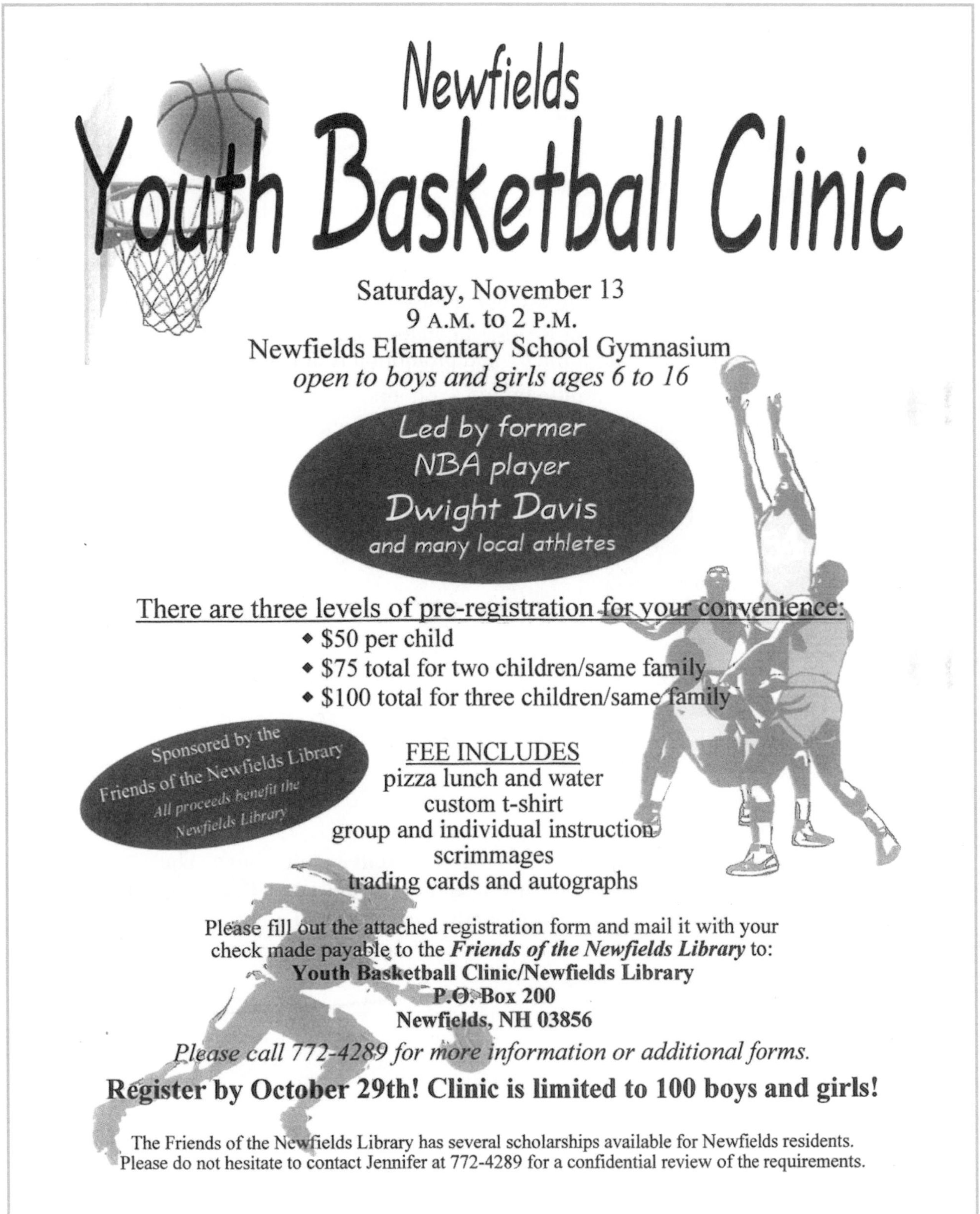

Newfields
Youth Basketball Clinic

Saturday, November 13
9 A.M. to 2 P.M.
Newfields Elementary School Gymnasium
open to boys and girls ages 6 to 16

Led by former
NBA player
Dwight Davis
and many local athletes

There are three levels of pre-registration for your convenience:

- ◆ $50 per child
- ◆ $75 total for two children/same family
- ◆ $100 total for three children/same family

Sponsored by the
Friends of the Newfields Library
*All proceeds benefit the
Newfields Library*

FEE INCLUDES
pizza lunch and water
custom t-shirt
group and individual instruction
scrimmages
trading cards and autographs

Please fill out the attached registration form and mail it with your
check made payable to the *Friends of the Newfields Library* to:
Youth Basketball Clinic/Newfields Library
P.O. Box 200
Newfields, NH 03856

Please call 772-4289 for more information or additional forms.

Register by October 29th! Clinic is limited to 100 boys and girls!

The Friends of the Newfields Library has several scholarships available for Newfields residents.
Please do not hesitate to contact Jennifer at 772-4289 for a confidential review of the requirements.

Figure 1-K   Basketball Clinic Flyer

1-6 Read-a-Thon in Rochester (NY)

To raise money to help support "Teen Book Festival (TBF) LIVE!: The Greater Rochester Teen Book Festival," the youth services librarians held Read-a-Thons at several libraries and schools throughout the Rochester area. During Teen Read Week, they planned simultaneous Read-a-Thons across three counties.

Read-a-Thons took place at public libraries and school libraries. Teens registered ahead of time to be readers. As with Walk-a-Thons, teens sought sponsors. Instead of sponsoring miles walked, donors sponsored the number of hours that teens would read. Sponsors could donate a dollar amount per hour read or a flat amount.

Teens gathered at their Read-a-Thon locations with comfy pillows and blankets in hand. Libraries provided books, magazines, and munchies. Each Read-a-Thon was scheduled to last a minimum of four hours, with a lunch break provided. Some libraries had pizza and other snacks donated. Each location also provided reading incentives. Books and other items were given away as door prizes. In addition, the two teens who raised the most money across all of the Read-a-Thons received a variety of Teen Book Festival items and gift certificates to spend at the Festival.

How It Works

- Select a date and decide on number of adult chaperones needed for the day of the Read-a-Thon.
- Create all needed materials (sponsor logs, envelopes for collecting money, donation receipts, and handouts explaining the fund-raiser and the organization or event to benefit from the Read-a-Thon). You might be able to find a local office supply store to donate the materials (folders, envelopes, paper).
- Partner with area schools that have active teen groups. These teens will be collecting money on behalf of the organization, so they need to be teens who are known and trusted.
- Send information and reader packets to partners. Allow around two months for readers to seek sponsors.
- Seek donations from local restaurants for pizza lunch and beverages for readers.
- Work with librarians to provide reading materials and to allow time for readers to check out books before and after Read-a-Thon.
- Keep track of readers as they register, and follow up with them as you get closer to the Read-a-Thon.

- Set a deadline for all money raised to be turned into either a partner school or the library. One month beyond the Read-a-Thon is perhaps the longest you would want to allow.
- Have fun!

Results

The greater Rochester area had six simultaneous Read-a-Thons with approximately 50 teen readers. These teens raised $2,500 total. Local newspapers came to some of the locations and ran special articles on the Read-a-Thons and on the Teen Book Festival. The money raised paid for the hotel stays for Festival guest authors. The best part was that the teens literally took ownership of their Festival!

the Book

**Second Annual
Greater Rochester Teen Book
Festival**

*Our Mission is to foster a community effort
to celebrate and promote reading by
connecting teens and authors.*

www.teenbookfestival.org

*Saturday, March 31, 2007
10:00 AM - 5:00 PM
Fairport High School*

2007 Committee Members

*Stephanie A. Squicciarini
Teen Book Festival Chair
Fairport Public Library*

*Beth Puckett
Minerva Deland School*

*Chris Daily
Brockport-Seymour Library*

*Christine Attinasi
Ontario Public Library*

*Christine McGinty
Newark Public Library*

*Diane M. Thibault
Central Library of Rochester and Monroe
County*

*Elizabeth Woolever
Rochester Public Library, Charlotte Branch*

*Geri McMahon
Johanna Perrin/Martha Brown Middle
Schools*

*Jennifer McLaughlin
Martha Brown Middle School*

*Karen Hultz
Irondequoit Public Library*

*Lisa Ferri
Fairport High School*

*Lisa Osur
Honeoye Falls- Lima High School*

*Mary Rinaldo
Gates-Chili High School*

*Olivia Durant
Webster Public Library*

Roberta Voekl

Ogden Farmers' Library

*Sharyn L. Johnson
Monroe #1 BOCES*

*Toni Baller
Barker Road Middle School, Pittsford*

*Trish Warren
Webster Thomas High School*

Dear Fellow YA Literature Enthusiast:

Thank you for agreeing to host a TBF LIVE Read-a-Thon at your library! You will be helping us reach our financial goal so that together we can bring a really amazing day to our teens and the entire Greater Rochester Area. On behalf of the entire TBF Committee and all the teens that asked us this past April to do it again...thank you!

We hope that you will be able to partner with your school or public library. With the theme for Teen Read Week 2006 being "Get Active @ Your Library," this is a perfect time for us to work cooperatively as our teens also take an active role in making TBF LIVE a reality.

Enclosed is a **LIBRARIAN TIP SHEET** that will help as you continue to plan your Read-a-Thon event. Also included is a copy of the information card on the Festival. Every reader will be given these cards to give to potential reading sponsors. You can use this information as you make contact and work with your partnering librarian(s). Please also look through the sample **READER PACKET**. This is everything your readers will be given to help with their fundraising efforts. **Please contact me as soon as your event is scheduled so I can customize the reader letters with your specific Read-a-Thon date and time information and inform local media of the different events.**

In addition to the items mentioned above, enclosed you will find the following:

- Five copies of a Read-a-Thon **REGISTRATION FORM** –for your library, for your partner library or libraries, and one to consolidate names onto a master list
- Two copies of the Read-a-Thon **READING LOG** – use this to track the time each reader spends reading and to calculate the total time
- Extra **SPONSOR LISTS** should your readers get lots of sponsors (YAY!) and need more space
- Blank **TBF LIVE Sponsor/Donation Forms** should anyone else (public, library staff, etc) wish to contribute to the Festival apart from the Read-a-Thon
- **READ-A-THON Prize** Entries: every reader will be entered into a prize drawing (prizes yet to be determined)

If you have any questions or concerns regarding any of this material or anything pertaining to the Read-a-Thon or TBF LIVE, please contact me. If your Read-a-Thon is planned for a day other than October 21st, I will try my best to either be there or give you contact information should you need to get a hold of me during your event.

Thank you again for hosting a Read-a-Thon. The Festival Planning Committee knows the amount of work involved and we are all very grateful! We hope that you and your teen readers join us at the Festival as we celebrate books and reading and get to know the authors that help make it all happen!

With heartfelt gratitude,

Stephanie A. Squicciarini, MLS

Figure 1-L   Read-a-Thon Librarian Thank You Letter

Second Annual Greater Rochester Teen Book Festival
READ-A-THON

TIP SHEET FOR LIBRARIANS

General:

- Select a FOUR (minimum) hour reading block dedicated to reading
- Require readers to arrive 30 minutes prior to official start of Read-a-Thon to allow time to get settled and allow 30 minutes at the end of the reading time to allow for finalizing log sheets and giving readers final instructions (for example, a 10:00am-3:00pm overall Read-a-Thon time would allow for official reading 10:30am-2:30pm)
- Plan for a few reading "chaperones" (i.e. partner public/school librarians)
- Only allow readers you or your partner know/trust to register...no need to open this to everyone (contact past summer reading participants, TAB/TAG members, volunteers, etc)

Registration:

- Keep a Registration Log and encourage in-person registration (need to give readers info packets)
- Limit number of readers to what would be comfortable in your Meeting Room/Library
- Give each reader the packet of information provided (includes a letter with details, TBF Information Card, Sponsor Envelope for collecting pledges, and donation receipts to give to sponsors)
- Encourage readers to bring blankets, pillows, beanbags, etc to allow for comfy reading
- School and Public Librarian should communicate as new readers are added or removed and confirm with each other the final list of readers day or two prior to Read-a-Thon
- Call all readers a few days before the Read-a-Thon to confirm and remind readers to bring own reading material or come 15-30 minutes early to check out books from collection

Refreshments:

- Contact local pizza places for donations or discounts
- Have water, juice, lemonade, etc. (Note: Purchasing juice boxes/small water bottles will allow use of leftover beverages for future programs)
- Ask staff or parents to donate snacks
- Ask readers to bring their favorite snack

Day of Read-A-Thon:

- Set up meeting room to allow for easy changing to accommodate readers moving about
- Have extra circ staff working to accommodate readers checking out books if you have not set the arrival time prior to library opening
- Check out a cart or two of books to an internal card so that patrons are not looking for books that are being read during the Read-a-Thon
- Have issues of magazines available for readers
- Have teens sign in (on Reading Log provided)
- Announce rules of the day
- Have readers/chaperones log the time reading begins (on Reading Log)
- Have readers complete door prize entry forms (prizes provided by TBF Committee and any supplemental prizes you may wish to give)

▸ ⸱ Thank You ⸱ ◂▸ ⸱ Thank You ⸱ ◂▸ ⸱ Thank You ⸱ ◂▸ ⸱ Thank You ⸱ ◂

Figure 1-M   Read-a-Thon Tip Sheet for Librarians

the Book

SECOND ANNUAL GREATER ROCHESTER TEEN BOOK FESTIVAL
*Our Mission is to foster a community effort to celebrate and promote
reading by connecting teens and authors.*

*Thank you for sponsoring the Teen Book Festival Read-a-Thon! We are very proud
and excited that our teens are working to bring young adult authors into the area.
The money raised by this Read-a-Thon will be used in its entirety to help underwrite
the Second Annual Greater Rochester Teen Book Festival (TBF LIVE!) on
March 31, 2007. Here is some info about TBF LIVE!*

Why a Teen Book Festival?
Teens can often be overlooked in libraries, with much attention, money, and resources
given to children and adults. Caught in the middle of budgetary constraints, this is a
unique opportunity to dedicate an event to teens, to encourage and celebrate their
reading, and to demonstrate their value to and within communities. And to have FUN!

The goals of the Teen Book Festival are to:
- Connect teen readers to award-winning authors.
- Educate, enrich, inform, and entertain local teens and other Festival
  participants.
- Enhance reading and literacy skills.
- Encourage interaction between aspiring writers and established authors.
- Socially bring together teens who have a common love of reading.
- Support, promote, and celebrate the educational and recreational benefits of
  recreational teen reading.

How will the Festival work?
- After a kickoff keynote speaker, there will be four 30-minute"breakout"
  sessions allowing smaller groups to interact together with the authors.
- Authors will each present four times, allowing attendees to get to know four
  different authors throughout the day.
- Local teen talent will perform throughout the Festival.
- The Festival will conclude with a special autographing session, with Lift
  Bridge Books on hand with book selections from all guest authors for
  purchase.

Why is financial support needed?
Funds raised will help cover Festival expenses including author honoraria, travel, and
meal expenses as well as publicity materials. Entry into the Festival will be *free*! The
Rundel Library Foundation is the Fiscal Agent for the Second Annual Greater
Rochester Teen Book Festival and is a 501(c)3 non-profit organization. As such, all
donations to the Festival are tax-deductible.

Checks for pledges can be made out to: <u>The Rundel Library Foundation</u>.

Figure 1-N   Read-a-Thon Information Card for Readers

1-7 Hill Country (Georgetown, TX) Authors Series

The Friends of the Georgetown (TX) Public Library hold quarterly author events at their new library. Their objectives are to introduce local authors to their community of 42,000 residents and to raise funds for the Friends, which will eventually benefit the library.

For The Hill Country Authors Series, the Friends solicit authors in central Texas, so they do not have to pay travel expenses. At this point, the authors invited do not charge a speaker's fee, but the Friends present them with one of their book bags——specially hand painted by a talented member of their group and uniquely designed with the author's name, the date, and the event.

How It Works

- The committee consists of six volunteers plus the person who does the artwork.
- Committee meetings begin six weeks before an event, and promotion and ticket sales start approximately four to five weeks in advance.
- To coordinate and make the work easier, the volunteers follow a task list that they have created.
- The art work for the promotional materials, tickets, and programs is produced by a creative volunteer from the Friends.
- The program is promoted via e-mail to Friends of the Library members and to local book club members, via Public Service Announcements run by local radio stations and newspapers, and by bookmarks (with library hours and information printed on the reverse side) and flyers placed at the circulation desk and at local businesses.
- Tickets are $13 in advance and $15 at the door. They are sold at the Friends' bookstore as well as by some Friends' board members. Ticket sales are tracked in order to estimate the attendance.
- The Friends serve desserts prepared in the library's cafe in a buffet format. Additional volunteers are recruited as necessary to serve desserts at the event.

Results

The first event attracted more than 180 people. The Friends were surprised and thrilled! They cleared about $1,400. Expenses were limited to catering charges; simple table decorations using books from the Friends' bookstore; and paper supplies for tickets, posters, bookmarks (advertising), and programs distributed at the event.

FOL AUTHORS LUNCHEON TASK LIST
KAREN MAC INERNEY, MAY 2, 2007

CATEGORY	TASK	WHO	DUE DT.	COMPLT
Pre-plan	Select tentative date	chr		
Pre-plan	Find author	chr		
Pre-plan	Reserve venue	chr		
Pre-plan	Get committee members	chr		
Pre-plan	Choose menu	comm		
Pre-plan	Set price	comm		
Pre-plan	Choose author gift (book bag)	comm		
Pre-plan	Arrange for gift (artist painting name/date)	ML		
Pre-plan	Print name tags	DB		
Post event	Collect comm. Members' expenses	chr		
Post event	Turn in comm. Members' expenses	chr		
Tickets	Design/Print tickets	Art		
Tickets	Design/print Sales Record Sheet	chr		
Tickets	Set up procedure w/SHP to sell tickets	chr		
Tickets	Pick up tkt sales $$ from SHP Wkly	LB		
Tickets	Record ticket sales names in Excel file	LB		
Tickets	Track ticket Sales	LB		
Tickets	Make up tkt packets for Bd. Mem. To sell	ML		
Publicity	Design/Print flier	Art		
Publicity	Design/print bookmarks	Art		
Publicity	ID book clubs	Comm.		
Publicity	Send flier to book clubs via email	Pub/ML		
Publicity	Send flier to Wmson Co. Libraries	CS		
Publicity	Send flier/email to outlying newspapers	CS		
Publicity	Contact Wmson Co. Sun-article	ML		
Publicity	Put notice in Wmson Co Sun Calendar	CS		
Publicity	Put notice in AAS Wmson Co section Calendar	CS		
Publicity	Put book marks in local stores	TK,JA,PG		
Publicity	Put book marks at Circ Desk, SHP	ML		
Publicity	Send Sun Rays 'Around Town' notice	Pub		
Publicity	Send email to FOL list	chr		
Publicity	Ask Judy Fabry to publicize in column	Pub/ML		
Publicity	Sun City NRO newsletter	ML		
Publicity	Design poster for library lobby	ML		
Set Up	Make table signs	ML		
Set Up	Put out table signs	ML		
Set Up	Determine room layout/set up	Comm.		
Set Up	Review layout/set up plan to caterer	ML		
Set Up	Determine table decorations	CL,TK,CS		
Set Up	Det. Extra table needs-n.tags signing, selling;tkts	comm		
Set Up	Design/print program	Art		
Set Up	Determine who sits at Head Table	Comm.		
Set Up	Write check for Author	Treas		
Set Up	Take new memberships post discussion	VP		

Figure 1-O   Author Luncheon Task List

of the
Georgetown Public Library

presents

The Hill Country Authors Series

Featuring Julie Kenner

National bestselling author Julie Kenner's first book hit the stores in February of 2000, and she's been on the go ever since. Her novel Aphrodite's Kiss was a USA Today bestseller, and Carpe Demon: Adventures of a Demon-Hunting Soccer Mom was a Book Sense Summer Paperback Pick. She lives in Georgetown, Texas, with her husband, daughters and three cats.

Author of Demons Are Forever:
Confessions of a Demon-Hunting Soccer Mom

Wed - August 1, 2007 - 2:00pm
Georgetown Public Library - 402 W Eighth Street
Community Room, 2nd Floor

Enjoy Scrumptious Desserts
by the
Red Poppy Café

Tickets $13.00 ~ ($15 at the door)
on sale at Second Hand Prose
2nd floor, Georgetown Library
or call Louise Beyer 512-635-3447

The Friends of the Georgetown Public Library is a 501(C) (3) organization.

Figure 1-P   Author Luncheon Flyer

1-8   Annual Book & Author Luncheon Fund-Raiser

In 1987, representatives from four area Friends groups (Plymouth, Canton, Northville, and Novi, MI) met to discuss pooling their resources and hosting a fund-raiser to benefit their four libraries. Together they decided on a book and author luncheon held at a central location.

The four groups divided into committees and have generally remained in charge of the same duties over the years (one representative from each group):

- Friends of the Plymouth District Library provide the table decorations.
- Friends of the Canton Public Library secure the author and do the printing.
- Friends of the Northville Public Library take care of the facilities—rental, menu, contacts, and so forth.
- Friends of the Novi Public Library manage the ticket sales.

The groups split the profits equally and use the monies for various programs in their respective libraries.

How It Works

- The four committees begin meeting in January to plan the event for April or May, depending on when an author may be available. They have had some notable authors over the years, generally from Michigan or its immediate surrounding area. They have never paid an author to appear; however, they have had to pay transportation on occasion.
- The Friends have loyal people who have attended each luncheon over the past 20 years. Many in their libraries look forward to this event each year. The profits are never huge, but the day itself is lovely. Working with other groups has been most enjoyable and gets the Friends visibility in the newspapers and within their communities.
- They hold the event at a local country club with a pretty setting, great food, and impeccable service. The Canton representative acts as the hostess for the event. The centerpieces are given to the person at each table whose birthday is closest to the author's.
- The "head table" consists of the guest author, the directors of the four libraries involved, and two committee members. The directors are always invited guests and are thanked for all they do to encourage and motivate the various Friends groups. The groups report that without the directors' cooperation, they could never be as successful as they are.

Friends of Plymouth, Canton, Novi and Northville Libraries

present

Death's Door

by

Steve Lehto

*A Michigan Author
*A Michigan Notable Book for 2007
*A Michigan Story

Annual Book & Author Luncheon

May1, 2007

Previous Guests

Linda Lang Bartell	1987
Neal Shine	1988
Tony Spina	1989
S.K. Wolf	1990
Lucy Taylor	1991
Ruth Langan	1992
James Hynes	1993
Charles Baxter	1994
Jillian Karr	1995
Nicholas Delbanco	1996
Judith Guest	1997
Mort Crim	1998
Jack Driscoll	1999
George Cantor	2000
Brian Lewis	2001
Devin Scillian	2002
B.J. Campbell	2003
Keith Famie	2004
Rochelle Riley	2005
Tim Kiska	2006

Friends of Plymouth, Canton, Novi and Northville Libraries

Death's Door
by Steve Lehto

Subtitled "The Truth

Behind Michigan's

Largest Mass Murder",

Mr. Lehto's book gives

us the long-awaited

answers. What really

happened that tragic

Christmas Eve in 1913

when more than 70

people were crushed to

death in a panic to flee

The Italian Hall in tiny

Calumet, Michigan?

Figure I-Q   Book & Author Luncheon Brochure (Outside)

1-9 Silent Auction Adds Dollars to Book Sale

The Friends of the Library and Scharchburg Archives (FOLA) at Kettering University (Flint, MI) holds an annual Book Sale & Silent Auction. Auction items are donated by area businesses, Kettering University employees, and FOLA members. Books are received from Kettering employees and FOLA members and from library withdrawals. The Book Sale & Silent Auction is a two-day event (Thursday and Friday). The Silent Auction concludes on Friday with a "ringing of the bell" at 1:30 p.m., and the Book Sale ends at 3:00 p.m. on Friday.

How It Works

- The Book Sale Committee gets volunteers from the community, Retired and Senior Volunteer Program participants, and FOLA members.
- Six months before the event, a group of committee members begins calling for donations for the Silent Auction and will continue to call and accept donations until two weeks before the sale. They begin to design and produce publicity items.
- Three months before the event, they start inventorying the auction items collected, sorting the books for the Book Sale, and promoting the event in earnest.
- Two months before the event, the committee starts recruiting volunteers.
- One month before the event, they begin creating the catalog of the auction items (they usually have over 150 items by this time). Every item is listed.
- One week before the event, they print the catalog.
- At event time, all auction items and books are transported to the Kettering University cafeteria, where they are set up for viewing.

In past years they have had an evening Gala or Preview with an entry fee that includes food and a year's membership to FOLA. The FOLA members get in free that evening. The Preview includes preview of auction items, first chance to look at and purchase books, and live entertainment (usually a piano concert).

The library staff usually head the Book Sale & Silent Auction committee and do most of the paperwork and gathering of information and items. *All* library staff help out at the actual event—even if they are not on the committee.

Budget

Friends of the Library and Scharchburg Archives purchases the supplies for the Book Sale & Silent Auction. The budget is approximately $300 of which most goes to printing costs of promotional materials and catalogs.

Results

The FOLA Book Sale & Silent Auction raises approximately $5,000 a year. The FOLA board hopes to increase that level in the future. Approximately 300 people attend the event. The Book Sale & Silent Auction has become a community building event with publicity generated in both the university and the Flint area communities.

KETTERING
UNIVERSITY

Campus
Center
Sunset Room

General Information:
810-762-9840

Auction Items:
810-762-7817

Email:
ldifilip@kettering.edu

This event has been sponsored by the
Friends of the Kettering University
Library and Scharchburg Archives

KETTERING UNIVERSITY LIBRARY'S 5TH ANNUAL

BOOK SALE
&
SILENT AUCTION

March 8 & 9, 2007

Book Sale
Thursday 8:00 A.M. - 5:30 P.M.
Friday 8:00 A.M. - 3:00 P.M.

Auction bidding will end Friday at 1:30 p.m.

Special Friends only sale Wednesday, March 7
4:00 - 7:00 p.m.

Donations of books or auction items can be sent to:

Kettering University Library
1700 West Third Avenue
Flint, MI 48504

Figure 1-R   Kettering Book Sale and Silent Auction Flyer

1-10 Friends of the University of Arizona Libraries Raise Over $100,000 in Partnership with Basketball Coach

Arizona Wildcats head coach and Naismith Memorial Basketball Hall of Famer Lute Olson teamed up with the Friends of the University of Arizona Libraries for a dinner and book signing of Lute's memoir, *Lute! The Seasons of My Life.* The book, written with David Fisher and with a forward by John Wooden, details Lute's personal life and his courtship of his wife Christine Toretti as well as the years spent with his first wife, Bobbi Olson.

Coach Olson is one of just 24 head coaches in the National Collegiate Athletic Association (NCAA) history to win 700 or more games. He owns a career record of 741–256, which adds up to a winning average of .743. Coach Olson has also guided Arizona to 18 consecutive 20-win seasons (the longest active streak in the nation) and is one of only four coaches in NCAA history to record 27 or more 20-win seasons.

How It Worked

- Sponsorship levels were determined and named appropriately to match the event
  - NCAA Champion: $5,000+ donation ($3,800 tax deductible), which included a sponsor table with eight complimentary dinner tickets, eight autographed copies of the book, acknowledgement of sponsorship at the event, recognition in the printed program, and inclusion in pre-event press releases.
  - Final Four: $2,500+ donation ($1,900 tax deductible), which included four complimentary dinner tickets, four autographed copies of the book, acknowledgement of sponsorship at the event, recognition in the printed program, and inclusion in pre-event press releases.
  - Elite Eight: $1,000+ donation ($700 tax deductible), which included two complimentary dinner tickets, two autographed copies of the book, acknowledgement of sponsorship at the event, recognition in the printed program, and inclusion in pre-event press releases.
  - Sweet Sixteen: $500+ donation (100% tax deducible), which included acknowledgement of sponsorship at the event, recognition in the printed program, and inclusion in pre-event press releases.
- Committee members contacted potential donors, eliciting one NCAA Champion, two Final Four, ten Elite Eight, and four Sweet Sixteen donors.
- The committee contacted and reserved the Tucson Country Club with space for cocktails and dinner, the ability to show a video, and a setup that would accommodate comfortable chairs on a stage for the guest of honor and the interviewer. *(Text continues on p. 34.)*

Figure 1-S   Sponsorship Information Card

Figures 1-T & 1-U   Bookmark Promoting the Event (Front-*Left* and Back-*Right*)

- Promotional materials were developed, including bookmarks, invitations with a response card, and an information card with details about sponsorships.
- The University of Arizona President and Dean of Libraries were invited to speak during the event.
- Attendees could submit questions in advance for Lute to answer during the program.
- The program featured dinner, a video of Lute's career, and a talk by Lute's wife.
- Tickets were $150 per person and included dinner, drinks, and a signed book.

Results

Despite pouring rain, the event attracted 210 people and raised over $100,000. This included an outright gift of $25,000 from the Olson family and an additional matching challenge donation, offered by Lute's wife, Christine Olson, on behalf of the Olson family.

"LUTE! THE SEASONS OF MY LIFE"

FRIENDS OF THE UNIVERSITY OF ARIZONA LIBRARIES

PLEASE RESPOND BY OCTOBER 2, 2006

PLEASE PRINT

NAME: _____

ADDRESS: _____

CITY: _____ STATE: _____ ZIP: _____

EMAIL: _____

$150 PER PERSON ($50 PER GUEST TAX-DEDUCTIBLE)

$1200 TABLE OF 8 ($400 PER TABLE TAX-DEDUCTIBLE)

■ TOTAL AMOUNT-$150 X _____ TICKETS = $_____

❏ CHECK ENCLOSED MADE TO "UAF/FOL"

❏ BILL CREDIT CARD AS FOLLOWS:

❏ MASTERCARD ❏ VISA EXPIRATION DATE: _____

NAME AS IT APPEARS ON CARD:

_____

NUMBER

___ - ___ - ___ _____

SIGNATURE: _____

HOST:

1. _____

GUEST'S NAMES:

2. _____

3. _____

4. _____

5. _____

6. _____

7. _____

8. _____

NUMBER OF VEGETARIAN PLATES: _____

FRIENDS OF THE UNIVERSITY OF ARIZONA LIBRARIES

Figures I-V & I-W   Response Card Included with Invitation (Front-*Left* and Back-*Right*)

1-11 Taste of the Heights (Cleveland Heights, OH): A Friends Culinary Collection

The Friends of the Cleveland Heights–University Heights Public Library in Ohio raises money primarily through used book sales. However, when the main library was to undergo a complete renovation and there would be no place to store and sort books, they decided to become involved. The Friends board was concerned that during the renovation they would lose members as well as community awareness and support. They needed a way to keep the Friends active and visible during the construction, so they decided to publish a cookbook.

How It Worked

- To make the cookbook distinctive, the Friends decided to inform the potential buyers about the history of the library and created a historical report to include.
- Members' recipes were solicited through the group's newsletter and on their Web site. The Web site also had a recipe form to fill out and submit online. Other recipes were dropped off at the Friends' office or received by e-mail and snail mail.
- An effort was made to contact well-known individuals in the community and the surrounding area to provide their favorite recipes. Many members of organizations, authors, local government employees, and businesspeople contributed recipes
- Volunteers from the Friends membership and board performed all of the work in obtaining recipes and preparing and typing the cookbook. All recipes were transcribed on home computers and then transferred into publishing software. A hard copy was printed, and volunteers proofed all the pages. Volunteers also researched and wrote the historical material.
- A graphic artist (a Friends officer) prepared the digital copy for the printer.
- The historical photographs were obtained through the courtesy of Cleveland Heights Historical Center at Superior Schoolhouse.
- Local bookstores carried the cookbook during the holiday. A local organization, Heights Arts, also carried the book. In addition, the library sells the cookbooks at the service desk.
- The printing cost was their only expense.

Special Note: The Friends began working on the cookbook in March 2005 and planned for it to be completed in time for the library opening celebration in October 2006. As it turned out, they needed all of that time. They had to extend the collec-

Figure 1-X   Front of Cookbook

tion of recipes in order to have enough to create a comprehensive book. The printing became a problem when the printer changed his turnaround time quite drastically, so be prepared for the unexpected!

Results

The release of the cookbook coincided with the public opening of the fully renovated library. The book had a prominent place in the main lobby. Approximately 7,000 people attended the celebration, and many stopped and admired and bought the cookbook. During the winter holidays, the Friends sold books through local bookstores and at holiday boutiques. The Friends are now working to place cookbooks in other areas. In the first six months, they sold about $2,500 worth of books.

಄ ಊ

1-12   What's It Worth? A Collectibles and Antiques Appraisal Raises Money for Libraries

Each spring, the Friends of the Elkins Park (PA) Free Library do something special to raise money for their library. They have had wine and cheese receptions, cook and cookbook author events, garden experts, a Renaissance Afternoon with appropriate music and refreshments, and a performance by an a cappella boys' singing group. Their most recent spring celebration was a takeoff of the *Antiques Roadshow*, called "What's It Worth?"

The appraisers and others presented brief workshops on how to determine the worth of objects. Local restaurants and stores contributed food without charge to encourage attendance. Money was raised by charging participants per object evaluated.

How It Worked

- The library was closed on a Sunday afternoon to make its space available for the event.
- With date, time, and location secured, the Friends started contacting appraisers and dealers. They worked to ensure a variety of interests were represented—coins and stamps, jewelry, maps, books and prints, fine arts and paintings, and so on. One volunteer agreed to make the dozens of calls necessary to secure the experts. In the end, eight experts agreed to provide their services free of charge!
- The Friends worked ahead of time to manage logistics for the day. They developed color-coded signage for the different types of collectors.

What's It Worth?

Find out at the Elkins Park Free Library
Sunday, April 18, 2004   **1:00 PM – 6:00 PM**

Bring that piece you've been wondering about
Is it trash or treasure?

Meet experts in various fields, including 18/19th c. art,
stamps/coins, men's accessories, books, trains, decorative arts

Light refreshments, collectors' corner, crafts people

Admission: $15.00/person with one piece for evaluation
                  $25.00/person with 2 pieces
                  $10.00 to attend and browse

We strongly encourage advance registration:

What's It Worth?
Name:_____ Address:_____
Phone:_____ Number attending:___ Check enclosed:_____
Item(s) for evaluation:_____

Plese make checks payable to :
Friends of the Elkins Park Library
563 E. Church Rd., Elkins Park, PA 19027

Additional information: call 215-635-3648, or visit www.elkinsparklibrary.org

Figure 1-Y   Flyer/Invitation for What's It Worth?

- Floor watchers were appointed to help with traffic flow on the day of the event.
- The Friends' greeter at the door asked those entering where they heard about the event, so the Friends could improve promotions in the future.
- A "Collector's Corner" was set up in the Children's Room where experienced individuals gave informal talks on their areas of expertise throughout the afternoon.
- Local businesses were contacted to provide prepared food for the event and were thanked prominently for their support at each table of food that they sponsored.
- The neighboring Auxiliary Police managed traffic and parking for the event.

Results

When it was over, all the appraisers commended the Friends on their degree of organization, and each said he or she would like to return again. Within three days of the event, the local newspaper published a full front page of photos describing the event!

The Friends charged $10 in advance and $15 at the door for attending, and the fee included one item for evaluation. Each additional item evaluated was $10. The event raised approximately $1,700 for the library and untold publicity for both the library and the Friends!

৩১ ৬৩

1-13   Gilfeather Turnip Festival in Wardsboro (VT)

It's hard to imagine how an ugly vegetable could become the key ingredient in the signature event of the Friends of the Wardsboro (VT) Library, but that's what happened. Many towns have festivals celebrating almost everything: pumpkins, apple pies, maple syrup, and garlic. But Wardsboro has a product that originated there—the Gilfeather® turnip. So, five years ago, the Friends launched the Gilfeather Turnip Festival, an annual, all-day event that celebrates the famous turnip and its role in the history of this small town (population under 900).

Each year the festival grows, but the essentials include lunch featuring Gilfeather Turnip Soup made in cauldrons in the Town Hall kitchen; organic farmers vending fruits and vegetables; crafters selling their wares; continuous showing of a video on the turnip's history, along with a display of historical photos; a tasting table, where everyone can sample turnip dishes; a Friends booth selling the Turnip

Cookbook along with books, postcards, aprons, T-shirts, turnip seeds, and the like; musicians playing country music; and turnip decorating for children.

Postevent evaluations help the group make plans for next year's festival, and fortunately new ideas keep popping up. A new edition of the cookbook is in the works, and the search is on for something special for children: Could a Giant Turnip rise from the pumpkin patch? Is there a vegetable counterpart for Santa Claus? Each year's festival brings a few surprises.

How It Works

- Find local farmers who will grow the turnips (or other native produce) needed and will either donate them or sell them at wholesale prices. Turnips are needed for soup and other dishes, for selling, and for carving or decorating.
- Sign up volunteers for the following tasks: making soup, bringing in cooked turnip dishes, baking and bringing in other items for lunch, serving lunch, and supervising the tasting table.
- Arrange for a volunteer to handle publicity. This will include writing articles and arranging pictures for local publications. This person must work months in advance to get the event listed in regional and state magazines, for example, that require considerable lead time. Contact radio and television stations. Arrange for posters to be distributed in stores in surrounding towns.
- Find a local musician or group that is willing to perform during the time the festival runs, or arrange for some other form of entertainment.
- Contact local crafters, organic farmers, and other vendors who might be willing to rent space and sell their wares. Try to line up as much local produce, including maple syrup and jams and jellies, as possible. Be sure to have plenty of gourds and pumpkins.
- Arrange for volunteers to sell Friends' products at a table that will also distribute fliers about the organization, will advertise future events, and will urge people to join the organization.
- Put someone in charge of children's activities. Find someone who will do face painting, especially with some vegetable overtones. Get the local school involved by working with the art teacher on some turnip project or by getting some new ideas for kids' activities from the staff.

Results

The money raised from the Gilfeather Turnip Festival increases each year, as does the attendance. Weather causes the attendance figures to fluctuate. In 2003, 75 people

Figure 1-Z   Gilfeather Turnip Cooks

Figure 1-AA   Gilfeather Turnips

attended and the Friends raised $732. In 2006, approximately 125 people attended and $1,233 was raised. The number of turnips used for cooking or sold as produce also increases each year, with 400 turnips on order for 2007.

Local newspapers, specifically the *Brattleboro Reformer* and the *Deerfield Valley News*, have been generous in their coverage, both with pre- and postevent stories. The *Reformer* came through with a full-color picture on page one in its coverage in 2005. Vermont Public Radio sent down a reporter from Colchester, who interviewed Friends as they stirred pots of turnip soup and arranged exotic turnip dishes on the tasting table; the segment was broadcast later in the day. A widely read online magazine, *Heart of New England,* asked for an article, picture, and the recipe for Greg Parks' famous soup.

≈◎ ◎≈

1-14   Library Cats in Berks County (PA) Help Raise Funds and Awareness for Libraries

"The Library Cats of Berks County (PA)" is a project much like the Cows of Chicago but on a much smaller scale. Foot-high resin cats were purchased from a local hardware store by county libraries, and the individual libraries then sought local artists to transform the cats into works of art. Each artist's vision was unique. Some libraries had as many as ten or more artists create cats and submit them to the library. Submissions included "Mercat" (half mermaid, half cat), Billy the Kid-ty, Cool Cat (dressed in a spiffy suit decorated with musical notation), and Mosaic cat (covered with small pieces of ceramic and glass).

The cats were collected and put on display at a local art center (includes gallery space, classes, etc.) for one month. A poster of pictures of the cats was created and displayed in the gallery with a poster explaining the connections among books, libraries, and cats. Copies of the unframed posters were for sale and could be ordered by filling out a form provided at the gallery. The ultimate goal of the project was to offer for auction as many cats as the local libraries were willing to sell. The money bid on each cat was paid to the library that originally owned the cat. Some libraries actually chose to keep their cats and not have them included in the auction.

Catalogs, which were smaller copies of the posters, were available at the gallery showing which cats could be bid on. Bid sheets were provided for pre-auction bids. Three days after the gallery exhibition, the Friends sponsored the cat auction. In addition to the cats provided by the libraries, items donated by the Friends board were also auctioned off. Free refreshments were provided by the Friends. The Friends of Berks County Public Libraries created the project, oversaw the process, paid for the gallery, and ran the auction.

How It Works

- Create a timeline. The project in Berks County was announced in April and completed on December 3, the date of the cat auction.
- Find a source for the resin cats. This group purchased cats from a local hardware store for $11 each, paid for by the libraries.
- Decide on the number of cats you would like completed. The Friends of Berks County Public Libraries did this project countywide, which meant that 23 libraries were involved and 40 cats were created.
- Create a list of rules and an application form for the artists to fill out and submit. Make the application forms available at all libraries.
- Publicize the project with posters as well as articles in the local newspaper and your library or Friends newsletter. Don't forget your Web site, too!
- Contact local art organizations, and publicize the project with them. In Berks County, many local artists volunteered to create cats without being asked by the libraries or Friends.
- Review submitted applications, and select the artists to design the cats. Each artist provides the materials and time for the project. The artist receives no remuneration.
- Find a local gallery to display the cats for the public to view.
- Collect the cats.
- Display the cats in the gallery where a "*cat*alog" is available along with bid sheets for absentee bidders.
- Collect the bid sheets, and move the cats to the auction site.
- Hold the live auction. Provide free light refreshments for the attendees.
- Clean up the auction space.
- Write checks for the amount of money each library's cat(s) earned.
- Celebrate!

Results

Hundreds of people viewed the cats at the gallery, and the administrators of the art center were thrilled with the response to the exhibit. From the pre-auction bids received, the Friends sold one cat to a bidder from Michigan and others to folks outside the immediate Berks County area. In other words, the group received a great deal of word-of-mouth publicity as well as that provided by the posters in the libraries and ads that were placed in local newspapers.

The group raised a total of $4,400, which was less than their expectation but not bad for a first effort. People loved the whole concept, and some traveled a distance to attend the auction. The auctioneer donated his services and was one of the group's staunchest supporters. People have been asking when the group plans to repeat the project. *(Text continues on p. 47.)*

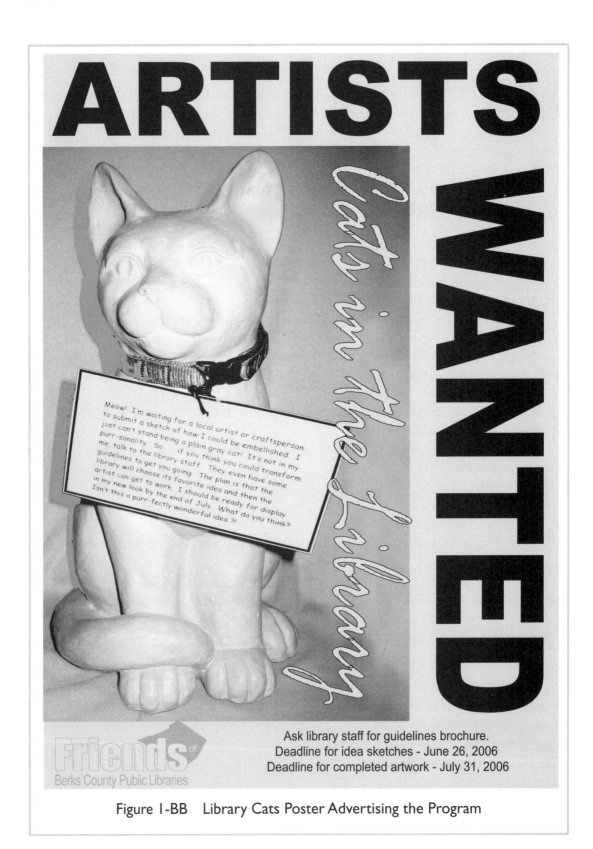

Figure 1-BB   Library Cats Poster Advertising the Program

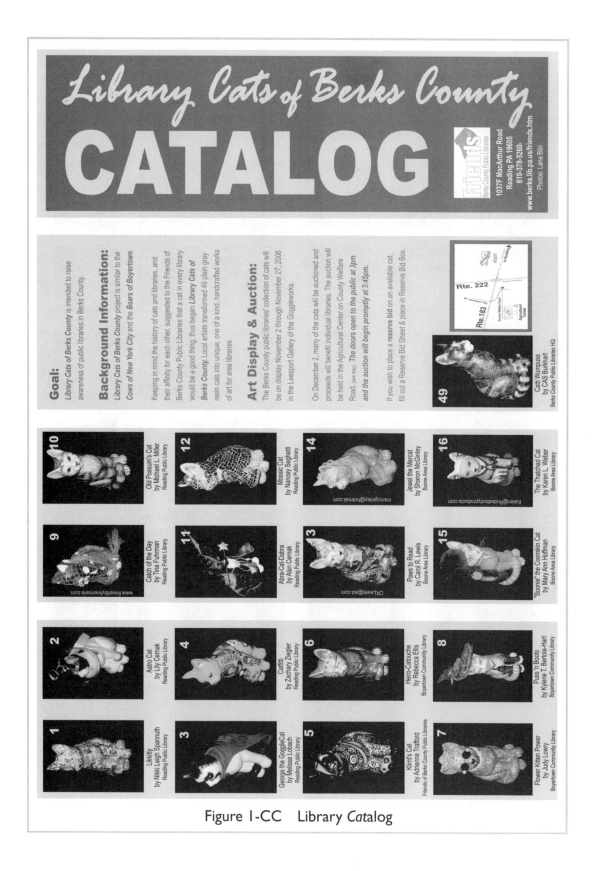

Figure 1-CC   Library Catalog

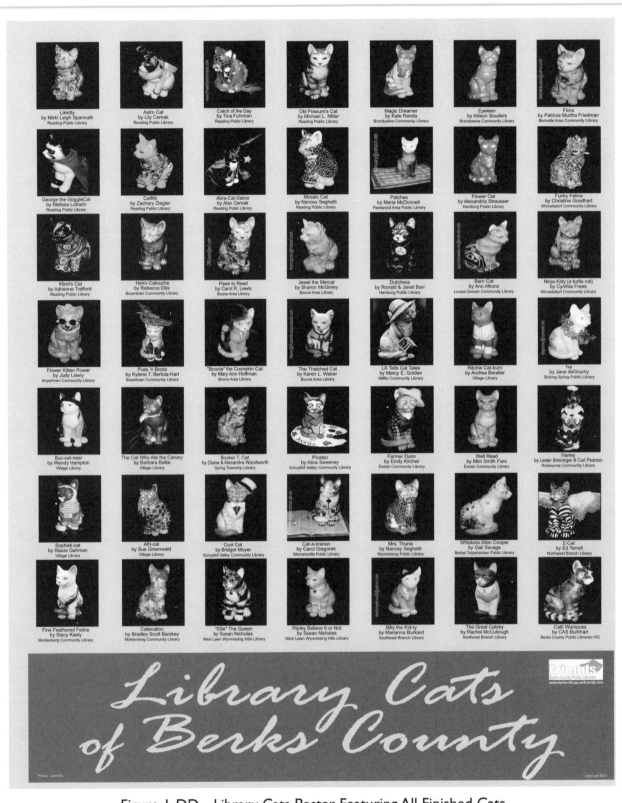

Figure 1-DD   Library Cats Poster Featuring All Finished Cats

The Friends continue to sell cat posters, and some of the cats were actually purchased by patrons and then turned over to their home library. So the library got the profit and also the cat for display. About one-third of the cats were not auctioned off because the libraries wanted to keep them.

෴ ෴

1-15 Gifts of Books and Materials

Cornell (NY) University Library welcomes and encourages gifts of materials and funds. Indeed, the library relies heavily upon donors to help sustain its growth, and many of the library's most valuable resources and special collections originated in this way. Gifts of money, books, periodicals, equipment, and other research materials contribute to the library's development. Gifts at all levels are much appreciated, as are bequests and other planned gifts, endowments, and larger contributions.

How It Works

In preparation for receiving gifts of books or other materials (referred to as gifts-in-kind), the library encourages donors to provide a list of materials, including titles, publication dates, and general conditions. Because of the complex nature of Cornell's library system, it is often necessary to impose certain conditions upon acceptance of gifts. If gifts are accepted, it should be understood by the donor that upon receipt the university becomes the owner of the material. As such, the library reserves the right to determine its retention, location, cataloging treatment, and other considerations related to its use, maintenance, or removal. They ask donors to also consider giving a minimum of $1,000 per 100 volumes donated to help expedite processing as well as defray costs of maintaining the material given to the library.

Appraisal

The library encourages donors to consider, for their own interest, obtaining a professional appraisal of their gifts for income tax purposes. Such appraisals are the responsibility of the donor and should be made, if possible, before the gifts are transferred to Cornell in order to establish their fair market value. The Internal Revenue Service considers the library to be an interested party, which therefore precludes appraisals made or financed by Cornell. For this reason, donors must bear the costs of appraisals, but the costs may be deductible expenses. As income and estate tax laws are subject to frequent revision, Cornell recommends that donors discuss gift-in-kind appraisals with their attorneys. The library is willing to help by suggesting appropriate professional appraisers who might be consulted or by arranging for third-party appraisals after receipt of the gift in the library. The acceptance of a gift that has been appraised by a disinterested party does not in any way imply endorsement of the appraisal by the library.

Acknowledgment

The library acknowledges all gifts it receives. The Cornell University Division of Alumni Affairs and Development will send the donor a receipt and a signed copy of IRS form 8283. They also provide gift and/or class credit for gifts-in-kind that include an appraisal or valuation by the donor.

⤳ ⤵

1-16   Have a Heart, Give a Book

Friends of Irving (TX) School Libraries (FISL), whose members include library media specialists, Irving Independent School District (ISD) staff, and community liaisons and leaders, was organized with the mission to establish home libraries for the over 30,000 students throughout Irving ISD. With the help of librarians from all levels, including prekindergarten, kindergarten, elementary, middle school, and high school, FISL developed a list of classic, timeless, cross-gender books for each grade level, prekindergarten through grade 12, to provide to the students of Irving ISD.

Irving's socioeconomic breakdown includes at least 60 percent or more students at the poverty level. In many of these homes, no library exists.

Without a true source of funding to purchase books to establish home libraries, the group determined that a community book drive was the best route to fast funding. FISL scheduled the drive to coincide with February's National Book Lover's Month, and the campaign was held throughout the month. Using the Salvation Army Angel Tree Program as a model, FISL designed a program to place pink trees containing red hearts with book titles in local businesses throughout the community.

The book titles were from the list of predetermined titles. Members of the community could take a heart off the tree with a selected book title, purchase the book, and bring it back to the business to place in a drop box. A large bookstore in town created display tables and provided phone order services for the month.

How It Worked

- Plans for creating the trees, covering boxes, making hearts, and getting the trees into businesses began in January. Using the theme of hearts and valentines, FISL chose the design of bright pink trees with red hearts.

Hi, my name is _____, and I am a librarian for Irving ISD. You recently received a letter from our library director, Caroline Kienzle, asking you to participate in the FRIENDS OF IRVING SCHOOL LIBRARIES Campaign, "Have a Heart, Buy a Book." Have you received the letter?

If YES, they have received the letter…
Great! Then you know a little about our campaign. We are asking your business to consider placing a tree in your lobby or office area. We will bring a wooden pink tree with hearts attached. Your employees (and patrons – if applicable), can then take a heart with a recommended book title, purchase, and return the book to you. We have boxes available for collection.
Would you be willing to help out the Friends of Irving School Libraries by placing a tree in your business?

If YES, they will place a tree in their business…
Thank you so much. We will bring the tree to your business and set it up. What time is convenient for you?
    FYI: We will pick up the books and add more hearts to the tree as needed.

If "I have to speak with someone else"…
I understand. Let me call you back on _____ (1-2 days), and we can discuss your company's participation. Is there a time that is good for you? Also, you might want to check out our website at www.irvingisd.net/libraryfriends. This website does a great job of explaining FISL. There is also a picture of the tree on the website.

If No, they are not interested…
Thank you for your time. Please keep us in mind in the future as we will have a spring membership drive for businesses to join Friends of Irving School Libraries.

If No, they have not received the letter…
Let me quickly tell you a little about our project. Friends of the Irving School Libraries or FISL, have the goal of building a home library for each child in the district by giving them a book each year. In order to achieve this goal, FISL will be sponsoring "Have a Heart, Give a Book: Loving Literacy" throughout the month of February. "Have a Heart, Give a Book" is a campaign designed similar to the Angel Tree program in that trees with hearts are placed in local businesses. The hearts will have recommended book titles. Community members will be able to take a heart and return their purchase to a designated location at the business. In her letter, Mrs. Kienzle ask that you please consider placing a tree in your business to give employees and/or members of the community an opportunity to participating in providing books for children.
Would you be willing to help out the Friends of Irving School Libraries by placing a tree in your business?

If YES, they will place a tree in their business…
Thank you so much. We will bring the tree to your business and set it up. What time is convenient for you?
    FYI: We will pick up the books and add more hearts to the tree as needed.

If "I have to speak with someone else"…
I understand. Let me call you back on _____ (1-2 days), and we can discuss your company's participation. Is there a time that is good for you? Also, you might want to check out our website at www.irvingisd.net/libraryfriends. This website does a great job of explaining FISL. There is also a picture of the tree on the website.

If No, they will not be able to participate…Thank you so much for your time. Please keep us in mind in the future as we will have a spring membership drive for businesses to join Friends of Irving School Libraries.

Figure 1-EE   Have a Heart, Give a Book Phone Script

- A tree was designed and developed and a prototype made. Utilizing the services of librarians, spouses, and friends from throughout the school district, volunteers began to saw, hammer, and paint wooden trees to go into the community.
- While the trees were being constructed, another team of volunteers and librarians set to work getting the trees placed in local businesses. The Irving ISD Director of Learning Resources sent out letters to local businesses and a variety of partners in education.
- Ten different librarians in the district followed up the letter with a call to establish a relationship. The librarians were provided with a script, a contact log, and information about the book drive.
- FISL set pick up and delivery times. Volunteers collected boxes and covered them to serve as book drops for the participating businesses.
- The residents of a local retirement community affixed the labels with the predetermined book titles to over 1,000 hearts. The labels also included information for donations and listed the FISL Web site address.
- Irving librarians and other volunteers from the school district delivered 25 trees to businesses, churches, and community centers. They also placed specially designed flyers and replacement hearts at each location.
- Volunteers collected the boxes at the end of the month.

Results

In their initial book drive, FISL received 532 books as well as $2,500 in donations from corporate sponsors. One local car company provided 310 copies of *The Cat in the Hat* for the district's kindergarteners. The Have a Heart, Give a Book book drive gave the Friends a powerful head start in reaching their goal to create home libraries for all the district students and proved a catalyst for the establishment of Friends of Irving School Libraries.

1-17 Phone-a-Thon and Honor with Books: Two Programs with a Happy Synergy

The American University Library in Washington, DC, regularly holds a phone-a-thon to call parents of current students. Students are callers on behalf of the university as a whole, but what made the overwhelming difference one year in terms of getting donors to designate specifically to the library was the program offered. For the library, the callers pushed the Honor with Books program. The students of parents who donate $100 are "honored" with a personalized bookplate placed in a new book added to the library's collection in a chosen subject. The donors chose the subject, and the collection development staff picked out an appropriate title from the school's incoming books.

How It Works

- The American University Annual Fund campaign has a phone-a-thon and paid student callers set up. When school is ready to begin in the fall, a library representative meets with the phone-a-thon callers to discuss what's happening at the library, and they provide a phone script to get them comfortable with the Honor with Books procedure and language. This could also work with a volunteer corps armed with a phone script and numbers to call. It is great to have students do the calling, because the funding directly impacts their library experience.
- When the library gets notice of a pledge, the information is routed to the collection development manager, who picks out an appropriate book (according to the donor's subject wishes) from the new arrivals. A staff member places a bookplate in the book and sends the donor a thank you letter with the title of the book and a sample bookplate.

Results

The American University Library had over 200 parents take advantage of the naming opportunity. Although not everyone fulfilled their pledges, the library raised over $12,000 in one year. An added bonus—the majority of the donors were new donors to the library!

1-18   Endowment Plaque

Public recognition of significant library donors is a great way to thank them for their support. It's also a great way to encourage others to follow suit. The Canton (MI) Public Library has had great success with a prominently displayed plaque.

How It Worked

- The minimum amount to be on the endowment plaque was $1,000 (payable over five years). The background of the plaque has "thank you" written in many languages. The Friends purchased it from a local Ann Arbor (MI) company for $1,500, and it hangs next to the interior exit doors of the library. Many of the gifts were given "in memory of" or "in honor of" people.
- A matching plaque was made for additional donations received after the initial campaign concluded. It hangs on the other side of the doors.
- The Friends hosted an upscale unveiling/thank you party for the charter donors. It was held on a Friday night after the library service hours. It was glamorous, with catered appetizers, wine, and lavish flower arrangements. The Friends hired a harp player, a stringed quartet, and other musicians, which were stationed around the library.

Figure 1-FF   Endowment Plaque

Results

The Friends' initial drive in 2002, called the Charter Endowment Fund, raised about $30,000 over a three-month period and resulted in the first plaque. This plaque is engraved and unable to be changed.

The Friends have since placed a companion plaque on the other side of the main doorway. It is similar in looks, but names are added as new donations come in. The Friends have raised an additional $181,000 with this plaque.

಄ ಄

1-19   Build for the Future: Campaign Naming Opportunities

The Friends of the Leesburg (FL) Library were officially organized over 50 years ago, but there has been a strong citizen support base for the local library since 1892, when a library opened in a little store on Main Street. Almost 115 years later, the City of Leesburg began construction of their first building specifically designed to be a library. When the budget was set ($6,000,000) and the plans developed, it was clear that an additional 1,700 square feet would be needed to ensure that the library could meet all its service needs.

In addition, the Friends wanted to provide funding for art in the Children's and Young Adult sections of the library and to create a sculpture garden. These plans would cost an additional $320,000, but the Friends had only about $63,000 in their account. The Friends pursued an aggressive grassroots fund-raising campaign and a capital campaign that included naming opportunities for various rooms, areas, and installments of furnishings for the library.

Results

By the opening of the new City of Leesburg Public Library, the Friends had raised over $700,000! The library plans were increased by 2,000 square feet. The Friends commissioned two original bronze sculptures and provided the funds for dynamic indoor art for the Children's and Young Adult departments.

One of the sculptures was of Annie Oakley (and her dog Dave), who used to winter in Leesburg. Library Director Barbara J. Morse said, "I suspect that the bronze sculpture will become polished by the touch of many young hands as they reach out and touch the person of Annie and pet the head of her dog, Dave."

THE LEESBURG LIBRARY
Build for the Future Campaign-Naming Opportunities

The new library will have numerous naming opportunities - appropriate for those wishing to recognize a business or organization, to honor a family, or memorialize a loved one. The richness of the architectural plan provides a range of opportunities from large, impressive public spaces to smaller parts of the building with their unique and personal meanings.

PACESETTING GIFTS[1]
The Lobby/Courtyard $1,000,000
Meeting Room $500,000
Adult Reading Area $250,000
Local History/Genealogy $250,000
Reference & Collection $250,000

LEADERSHIP GIFTS[2]
Children's Collection $100,000
Young Adult Room $100,000
Technology Lab $100,000
Staging Area/Outdoor Programs $100,000
Florida Reading Room $100,000
Children's Story Room $50,000
Circulation/Service Desk $50,000
Family Reading Garden $50,000
Friends' Bookstore .... (Celebrating the Friends' 50th year Anniversary) $50,000

MAJOR GIFTS[2]
Music Collection Area $25,000
Audio Book Collection Area $25,000
Video/DVD Collection Area $25,000
Library Landscaping $25,000
Café/Coffee Shop $25,000
Study Rooms/Tutoring Center $15,000
Self Check Out Stations $15,000

SPECIAL GIFTS[3]
Public Access Computer Stations .... $2,500 ea
Reading Tables and Chairs .... $1,500 ea
Special Display Area/Cases .... $1,000 ea
Lounge Chairs .... $1,000 ea
Study Carrels .... $1,000 ea

COMMUNITY GIFTS[3]
Adult Collection Shelves .... $500 ea
Children's Collection Shelves .... $300 ea
Young Adult Collection Shelves .... $300 ea
Large Inscribed Bricks .... $500 ea
Small Inscribed Bricks .... $50 ea
Chairs .... $100 ea

GIFT RECOGNITION
[1]Gifts of $500,000 and above will permanently and gratefully acknowledged by an individual recognition plaque displayed prominently in the sponsored area with a portrait.

[2]Gifts of $10,000 will be permanently and gratefully acknowledged by an individual recognition plaque displayed prominently in the sponsored area.

[3]All gifts over $1,000 will be gratefully acknowledged by donor level on a plaque in keeping with the design of the building on a wall in the meeting room.

If you are interested in making a donation or a pledge, or if you would like a member of Friends of the Leesburg Library to contact you, please call the Library Director at (XXX) XXX-XXXX.

The Internal Revenue Service has determined that the Friends of the Leesburg Library is a Section 501(c)3 charitable organization.

Figure 1-GG   Leesburg (FL) Public Library Naming Opportunities

1-20   Making "The Ask": Reaching Potential Donors in Your Community

The typical mission of a library foundation is to raise significant money for the library. This money is often used to build an endowment fund, support a capital campaign for a building, or perhaps establish special programs or services. While a foundation's fund-raising may be ongoing, there will no doubt be times when it engages in an organized campaign with a large monetary goal in mind.

Before the campaign can begin, much background work must be done. A case statement must be developed outlining the reason for the campaign and what will result from its success. Based on the need, a monetary goal for fund-raising must be set, and, finally, potential donors need to be identified.

Potential donors can be those who have shown generosity previously—either by giving to the foundation or by donating to similar community services in the past. They might be persons who are personally known to board members and have the ability to donate a significant gift. They may be library volunteers or regular patrons who, again, have the means to make a large gift.

Once you've identified prospects, determine the amount of money you'll ask for. This can be based on past donation history, knowledge of their financial ability to give, or significant interest they've exhibited in the library.

Once this background work has been completed, it's time to make "the ask." Some people are quite comfortable asking for money but for many, this is a daunting task. For those who are comfortable and for those who are rookies (and feel a little trepidation), it's important to perform this step correctly. Other than asking someone well known to the solicitor, following a three-step process is usually best.

First: The Letter

Send a letter to all potential donors who are not good personal friends or relatives explaining that a capital campaign is being undertaken for the library and why. Tell the prospects why you are writing—because you believe they will support your cause and because they have shown support for the library in the past (as donor, patron, or volunteer if this is the case). If they were recommended by another as a potential donor, let them know that you are writing because Jane Doe thought they would be interested in this campaign. Once you've outlined why you are writing to them (and to them specifically), let them know that you will be following up with a phone call to set up an appointment to speak to them about this important initiative.

Next: The Phone Call

For many, making the phone call is the hardest part. If this is true for you, you might want to write up a short script and practice beforehand. Refer back to the letter you sent, and anticipate and be prepared for some immediate reactions that aren't positive. If a prospect says that he or she is too busy to meet right now, suggest that you meet in a couple of weeks. If the prospect says he or she can't make any commitments without speaking with a spouse, express your understanding and promise to call back later in the week to set a time when they can both meet with you. If the prospect says he or she believes public libraries should be supported with public tax dollars, express your agreement but remind the prospect that some important services, programs, collections, and building concerns are not being addressed by tax dollars. Tell all prospects that their support is needed to ensure that the library achieves excellence.

The important thing to remember is that you are doing this because you believe in the importance of the library. Let the prospect know you are volunteering your time because of this. Most people are flattered to be asked to be part of a capital campaign, and your persistence will show them the level of your commitment.

Finally: The Meeting

The meeting should be a little easier than the phone call. If the potential donor has agreed to meet with you, he or she obviously has some level of interest. Be sure to bring the case statement with you, along with a library staff member if you anticipate questions you can't answer. Again, let the prospect know that you are volunteering and that you have already committed to the campaign financially (because, of course, you have!). Once you've gone over the case for the campaign and answered questions, it's time to look the potential donor straight in the eyes and say, "I am asking that you consider a gift of $xx,xxx." Your background work has determined the amount to suggest. If you don't suggest a specific amount, you are likely to be given less—perhaps far less—than you had planned, and it's hard to move up significantly from there. Be prepared to discuss pledges and payment plans or to accept a check on the spot.

This is a very broad overview of the process. More information is available at the following Web sites:

- www.grassrootsfundraising.org
- http://www.aspca.org/site/PageServer?pagename=ih_lib_makingtheask
- http://www.unitedwayelpaso.org/Making_the_Ask.pdf

1-21 Making "The Ask" for Large Donations: Sample Letters to Get You Started

Making "the ask" for large donations is an important part of raising a significant amount of money. Those who give the large donations set the tone (and the success) for meeting your fund-raising goal. Writing a letter to potential donors is the first step in the asking process, and it's an important one.

Making the ask involves determining who your potential large donors are and how much they might be able and willing to give, writing an initial contact letter, and following up with a phone call to set up an appointment. Finally, it involves visiting the potential donor to go in detail about the campaign and to make "the ask."

After you have identified those in the community who have the likelihood and means to make a large donation, and once you've determined how much they might give, you need to make initial contact with them. This contact is generally done by letter unless the person you plan to contact is a close personal friend or relative (then you can go straight to the phone call or visit).

The best person to write this initial contact letter is someone who the recipient will know or know of. The letter should be direct, short, and personal. It should explain that you are volunteering to raise money for an important capital campaign, what the campaign is for, and that you yourself have already made a pledge in support of the campaign.

What follows are sample letters to your potential donor—one for a public library campaign and one for an academic campaign.

Dear Linda,

I am writing to let you know that the Smith Library at DSU has a wonderful opportunity to expand its nationally renowned Barrymore Collection. Until recently, the private letters that Tracy Barrymore wrote to her mentor and confidante, Lucille Edwards, have been in private hands.

We've received word that the owner is willing to sell this collection to us. As a consequence, the Smith Library Foundation is embarking on a campaign to raise $150,000 for its purchase. I'm sure I don't have to tell you how important these letters are and how they will permanently enrich our existing collection. As the recognized repository for the Barrymore papers, the Smith Library simply cannot afford to let this collection go to another library or, worse, to another private collector.

Because I know how much our research collection matters to our institution now and for the future, I have volunteered to work on this campaign and I have already made a personal pledge to this fund-raising effort. You've always been a leader in championing both DSU and the Smith Library, so I am confident that you will want to be involved as well.

I would like to have the opportunity to discuss the details of this acquisition with you in person and to solicit your support as a leadership donor. I will call you in the next week or two to see if we can schedule a time to meet. It's not often one has an opportunity to help in acquiring such a unique collection of letters that will add infinitely to the quality and cache of the Barrymore Collection. I look forward to discussing the details with you.

Sincerely yours,

Joe Wilson

Dear Phil,

I am excited to let you know that the Smithville Library Foundation is embarking on a large-scale fund-raising campaign to help support a new addition to our library. Our city government has challenged us to raise $1,000,000 or approximately 10% of the total cost for the addition. An ambitious goal, but one that we believe is achievable.

As you may know, the library was built in 1977 and has been well loved and used by our community. Although many changes have been made over the past 30 years to accommodate a growing collection, various (and constantly changing) audio/visual formats, and vital computer technology, the present facility can no longer adequately address this continuing growth in use and materials. It's time for an addition to this beloved facility.

That's where you come in! I know how much you support the quality of life in our community. You have shown yourself to be a generous contributor for a variety of worthy projects and I believe you'll want to be supportive of this one as well. I am so convinced that our library is the very center of Smithville's cultural and intellectual well-being that I have made my own pledge to this effort and I have offered to volunteer my time as well.

I would like to meet with you sometime in the near future at your convenience to go over the details of this important campaign and to ask you for your support with a leadership gift. I'll give you a call in the next week or two to set a time. Maybe we could go to lunch?

I appreciate in advance your willingness to meet with me and, again, I am confident that you'll want to be a part of this exciting effort.

All the best,

Susan Smith

1-22 Making "The Ask" for Large Donations: The Visit—The (Almost) Last Step

Now that you have identified potential donors in your community and written an initial contact letter, it's time to visit them. This really should be the most exciting part of making "the ask," because, if you have been granted the opportunity to visit with a prospect, then you can rest assured that he or she is positively inclined to hear more about the library project and knows that you will be asking for a gift. There is no guarantee that you will get the donation you are hoping for, or any donation at all, but at least the potential donor is receptive.

There are a few things you will want to have with you when making the visit. First, you will want to bring a case statement with you along with any other pertinent information that will help answer questions about the project and the campaign. Putting together a kit of materials is critical. The case statement kit should include (but not necessarily be limited to) the following:

- Executive summary of the project—what you are planning to do and why it is needed.
- Architectural renderings if the campaign is to support a building project.
- Budget for the project, including how much will be derived by fund-raising, how much by city or administrative support, how much by grants, and so forth.
- General information about the library.

Being armed with concrete information will help bolster your courage if you need it. So will bringing along a partner who knows the details of the project, such as the library director or the president of the trustees. Obviously, if you are asking for a leadership gift, you will want your partner to be of high ranking status. Bringing along someone from technical services, for example (even if he or she is on the building committee), may send the message to your prospective donor that he or she isn't important enough for the "big guns."

You will know in advance exactly how much you hope this person will give. Part of the capital fund-raising background work includes determining who might give, how much each might give, and how many gifts at different levels will be needed in order to reach your goal. Those who you hope will give at the highest levels are the "leadership" givers, and this is the kind of donor you are now visiting.

Once you and your partner have discussed the project with your prospect, answered any of his or her questions, and showed how much enthusiasm you have for the project (making sure you say that's why you're volunteering to raise money and why you have already made a gift yourself), it's time to actually make "the ask."

For many, this is the hard part, but don't blink. Look the person straight in the eye and say, "Laura, this is so important for the library's future. I know you have a keen interest in this city and its future. To help us reach our fund-raising goal, we'd like you to consider a gift or pledge of $100,000." Then close your mouth and wait. It may be an uncomfortable moment if there is hesitation, but that's okay. It won't last long.

Donors will make a variety of responses, and you should be prepared for all that you can think of. Hopefully, you'll get an immediate, "sure, let me get my checkbook!" But it's more likely you'll get one of the following:

- I need some time to think this over or discuss it with my partner.
- That's more than I'm able to contribute at this time.
- Thank you for thinking of me for this project. I was interested in hearing about your plans, but my giving is focused on the new opera building at this time.

If you are told the donor needs more time, that's fine—it's a lot better than a no, but be sure to ask when you should check back. If the response is that you're asking for too much, don't back down right away, but remind him or her that you would be happy to accept a pledge paid out over the next three years. If that doesn't work, then you can ask for a lower amount that you've predetermined in anticipation of this possibility. It's always best to ask for a specific amount rather than leaving it up to the donor, because, if you do, you are very likely to get less (and sometimes far less) than you were hoping for.

If you get a polite "no," be respectful of the reason given. For example, "Yes, I've donated to the opera campaign as well. I understand that timing isn't the best for two important facilities, but in this city it's hard to find the right time. We're really growing, and it's wonderful for Smithville. Understanding that you give priority to the opera, do you think it would be possible for you to consider, instead, a gift of $50,000.'We can accept a pledge over three years if that would help. The library really needs your help at this time. We'd like to count on you."

In the end, you may get what you asked for, something less, or nothing at all. Nevertheless, once you leave you still have at least one more contact to make with the person you visited. Be sure, no matter the size of the gift (if any) or the reception you get, you must immediately send a thank you letter. Cultivating potential donors will serve you now and in the future. Good luck!

కా ఆ

1-23   Sample Promotional Materials

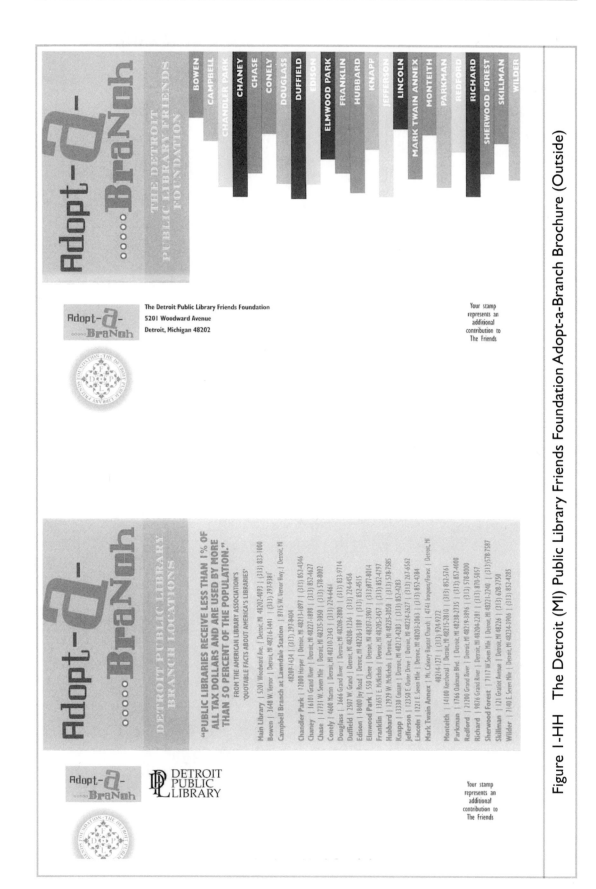

Figure 1-HH   The Detroit (MI) Public Library Friends Foundation Adopt-a-Branch Brochure (Outside)

Adopt-a-BraNch

In return for their investment, donors will be offered benefits unique to Adopt a Branch sponsors, as listed below. Additionally, as a Detroit Public Library Friends Foundation member you will be invited to participate in select opportunities such as architectural tours of the library buildings, rare book events, previews of our ever-popular Used Book Sale, and free or reduced-price admission to our friends programs.

Best of all, being an Adopt a Branch sponsor entitles you to both a Federal tax deduction and an educational credit on your State of Michigan return. Call The Friends at (313) 833-4048 for more information.

LEVELS OF SPONSORSHIP

BIBLIOPHILE | $1,000
EACH $1,000 ANNUAL CONTRIBUTION PROVIDES ONE BRANCH WITH:

A year of programming in support of children's literacy, as well as educational activities designed to entertain and inspire. This includes, but is not limited to, story hours, puppet shows, and seasonal craft activities (including supplies). As the donor, your company name will be prominently featured on marketing materials and signage, as well as attached to the program name (The XYZ Company Story Hour). Additionally, your name and company affiliation will be listed as an Adopt a Branch sponsor in The Friends' annual Donor Report.

BIBLIOMANE | $2,500
EACH $2,500 ANNUAL CONTRIBUTION PROVIDES ONE BRANCH WITH:

All of the programs listed above, with $1,000 of your contribution allocated to the acquisition of children's literature and materials for adult book discussion groups. Books purchased through your sponsorship will be affixed with bookplates inscribed with your name or company logo.

BIBLIOSOPH | $5,000
EACH $5,000 ANNUAL CONTRIBUTION PROVIDES ONE BRANCH WITH:

All of the programs listed above, plus a computer terminal dedicated for homework assistance. Your company name and logo will be displayed at the terminal for one year.

BIBLIOTECH | $10,000
EACH $10,000 ANNUAL CONTRIBUTION PROVIDES ONE BRANCH WITH:

All of the above, plus an engraved brass plaque acknowledging your generosity, displayed above the branch's circulation desk for the year of your sponsorship.

Adopt-a-BraNch

YES! I WOULD LIKE TO SUPPORT THE LITERARY INITIATIVES OF THE FRIENDS BY ADOPTING A BRANCH:

Name _____

Company Name _____

Address _____

City/State/Zip Code _____

Home Telephone _____

E-Mail Address _____

☐ Enclosed is my check for $ _____

☐ Please charge my (VISA or MasterCard) in the amount of: _____

Card No. _____ Exp. Date _____

Signature _____

I WOULD LIKE TO DESIGNATE MY GIFT FOR THE LIBRARY BRANCH LOCATION OF:
_____

I WOULD LIKE MY SPONSORSHIP LISTING TO READ AS FOLLOWS:
_____

Contributions to The Detroit Public Library Friends Foundation are tax deductible as provided by Federal Law and also qualify for a special tax credit against your State of Michigan income tax. Charitable Solicitation License no. MICS 5086.

PLEASE MAIL THIS FORM TO:
The Detroit Public Library Friends Foundation
5201 Woodward Avenue
Detroit, Michigan 48202
Telephone: (313) 833 4048 | Fax: (313) 832 7606

THANK YOU FOR YOUR SUPPORT!

Figure 1-11   The Detroit (MI) Public Library Friends Foundation Adopt-a-Branch Brochure (Inside)

I have always imagined that Paradise will be a kind of library.
-Jorge Luis Borges, author

Make a PLANNED GIFT TODAY to build the Library of Tomorrow!

THE FRIENDS
OF THE SAINT PAUL PUBLIC LIBRARY

ABOUT THE FRIENDS

Our Mission

THE FRIENDS EXPANDS the Library's capacity to serve Saint Paul's many communities. The Friends:
- Increases use of the Library through public awareness & cultural programming;
- Advocates for strong public funding of the Library;
- Provides private funding to enhance Library services.

Through this work. The Friends serves as a national model for its unique, comprehensive support of the Saint Paul Public Library.

Our Vision

THE FRIENDS WILL PROVIDE the necessary support to ensure that the Saint Paul Public Library is among the foremost library systems in the United States.

Our Values

THE FRIENDS IS GUIDED in its work by:
- Creative, innovative and entrepreneurial approaches to challenging issues;
- Inclusivity and integrity in all its activities;
- Responsible stewardship of its resources in perpetuity.

THE FRIENDS *of the* SAINT PAUL PUBLIC LIBRARY
325 Cedar Street, Suite 555, Saint Paul, MN 55101
(651)222-3242 ● www.thefriends.org

SECURE THE FUTURE *of our* PUBLIC LIBRARY

OUR GOAL:
To provide at least 10% of the Saint Paul Public Library's resources each year.

TO ENSURE THE GOAL IS MET, WE NEED to increase endowments supporting the Library from the current $14 million to $25 million. When you remember The Friends of the Saint Paul Public Library in your will or estate plan, you will provide a lasting legacy for high quality Library resources and become a member of the John & Myrtle Briggs Circle.

Join the John & Myrtle Briggs Circle

DR. JOHN BRIGGS, A SAINT PAUL internist and heart specialist, and his wife, Myrtle Briggs, were avid users of the Library. When Mrs. Briggs became an invalid, Dr. Briggs made frequent trips to the Library to select books for her. When they died, the Briggses left their entire estate of $1.8 million to benefit The Friends. It is the foundation upon which the work of The Friends rests. Make a planned gift to The Friends today, and you will further the profound legacy of John & Myrtle Briggs in providing for the future of the Saint Paul Public Library.

A BRIGHT FUTURE

PUBLIC LIBRARIES HAVE ALWAYS relied on private funding in order to offer top quality services. Throughout the years, the generous contributions of private citizens in Saint Paul have supplemented public resources to ensure that we have fine Library facilities and collections. The Friends works closely with the Library staff each year to determine the Library's most urgent needs.

WHEN THE ORGANIZATION WAS formed in 1945, then Library Director Perrie Jones said,

WHAT WE NEED IS SOME COMMUNITY LIBRARY SPIRIT, AND PEOPLE TO GENERATE ENTHUSIASM FOR LIBRARIES AS THE BEST FREE THING IN TOWN.

MORE THAN 60 YEARS LATER, the Public Library is still the best free thing in town and with your help, The Friends of the Saint Paul Public Library will ensure the Library's bright and promising future.

Figure I-JJ   The Friends of the Saint Paul (MN) Public Library Planned Giving Brochure (Outside)

ABOUT PLANNED GIFTS

PLANNED GIVING INCLUDES a variety of financial arrangements allowing you to give to a charitable organization. The most common form of planned gift is a:

○ **Bequest in your will**

A bequest in a will can include many types of gifts, including:

○ **Cash**
○ **Stocks and bonds**
○ **Real Estate**
○ **Personal Property**

In addition to a bequest in a will, there are many other forms of planned gifts, including:

○ **Trusts**
○ **Annuities**
○ **Life Insurance**
○ **Individual Retirement Accounts**

UNRESTRICTED GIFTS ARE PREFERRED because they give The Friends the ability to build endowment funds and respond to the changing needs of the Library. Designated gifts will be accepted that are consistent with the mission of The Friends and the Saint Paul Public Library.

The John & Myrtle Briggs Circle

MORE THAN SIXTY MEMBERS of the John & Myrtle Briggs Circle have already chosen to make a lasting commitment to The Friends with a provision in their will or estate plan. The Library has benefited greatly from The Friends' endowments and gifts established by these individuals. Through the generosity of John & Myrtle Briggs Circle members, The Friends has provided:

● **Funding for tens of thousands of Library books and materials**

● **Free, award-winning literary and music programs**

● **Support for renovating and constructing new Library buildings**

● **Community outreach programs**

JOIN OUR CIRCLE

"Many years ago, we added The Friends to our planned gifts. We're happy to support Saint Paul's Library system to assure that this cornerstone of democracy will continue in the future. We value the personal satisfaction of giving back to the community."

— *Bob and Bobbi Megard,*
Members of the John & Myrtle Briggs Circle

A RICH HISTORY

THE FRIENDS OF THE SAINT PAUL PUBLIC LIBRARY IS DEDICATED to supporting public library services in Saint Paul. Formed in 1945, the nonprofit membership organization has provided extensive aid to the Library over the past 60 years, making possible better services, expanded collections, and many special community outreach projects. In the last decade, The Friends has provided the Library with increasing amounts of assistance up to $2 million annually, including support to purchase approximately 200,000 new books for the Library. From 1997 to 2000, The Friends raised nearly $6 million in private funds as part of a campaign to renovate Central Library. In 2002, The Friends was honored as the best Library Friends group in the nation.

WHEN YOU MAKE A GIFT

Once you decide to make a gift, allow us to suggest the following language for your will: *I give to The Friends of the Saint Paul Public Library, 325 Cedar Street, Suite 555, Saint Paul, MN 55101 , _____ percent of my residuary estate (or, the sum of $_____ , or a description of property, securities, etc.) for its endowment funds.*

Building the Library of Tomorrow Today!

I'd like to know more about making a planned gift and joining the John & Myrtle Briggs Circle:

Name (s)

Address

City, State, Zip

Daytime Phone Number

Evening Phone Number

E-mail Address

○ Please contact me about including The Friends in my will or estate planning.

○ Please send me additional information about estate planning.

○ I have already included The Friends of the Saint Paul Public Library in my estate plan and would like to know more about the John & Myrtle Briggs Circle.

PLEASE RETURN FORM TO:
The Friends of the Saint Paul Public Library
325 Cedar Street, Suite 555
Saint Paul, MN 55101-1055

For more details on planned giving or the John & Myrtle Briggs Circle, please contact Mark Mallander at The Friends, 651/222-3242 or mark@thefriends.org.

Figure I-KK The Friends of the Saint Paul (MN) Public Library Planned Giving Brochure (Inside)

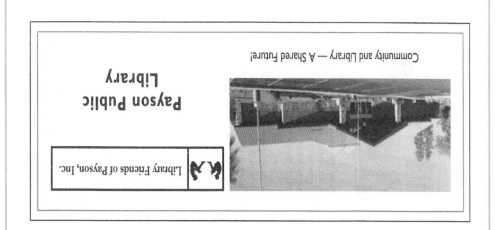

Payson Public
Library

Library Friends of Payson, Inc.

Community and Library — A Shared Future!

Library Friends of Payson, Inc.

P.O. Box 13, Payson, AZ 85547-0013

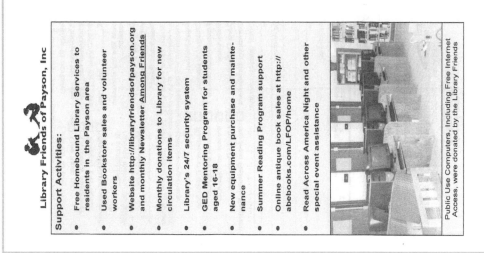

Library Friends of Payson, Inc

Support Activities:

- Free Homebound Library Services to residents in the Payson area
- Used Bookstore sales and volunteer workers
- Website http://libraryfriendsofpayson.org and monthly Newsletter Among Friends
- Monthly donations to Library for new circulation items
- Library's 24/7 security system
- GED Mentoring Program for students aged 16-18
- New equipment purchase and maintenance
- Summer Reading Program support
- Online antique book sales at http:// abebooks.com/LFOP/home
- Read Across America Night and other special event assistance

Public Use Computers, Including Free Internet Access, were donated by the Library Friends

Figure 1-LL   Library Friends of Payson (AZ), Inc., Memorial Gifts Brochure (Outside)

A Long History of Giving

About Our Organization

The Library Friends of Payson, Inc., is a private, non-profit corporation whose mission is to provide financial and community support to the Payson Public Library.

Our involvement follows a grassroots activist tradition that originated in 1921 with a group of ranch wives who formed the **Payson Women's Club.** These dedicated ladies established the first Library in Payson.

As our community has grown, the Library has also grown. Each expansion was made possible only by the devoted work of volunteers and the financial support of the community.

The Library is part of the Gila County Library District, which provides limited funding for personnel and services. The Town of Payson also provides operating expenses, but **we still depend heavily upon community support.**

Payson's First Library, established by the Payson Women's Club

A New Home in Rumsey Park

In 2002, we moved into our beautiful new Library in Payson's Rumsey Park. In a fundraising effort spanning nearly two decades, the Library Friends raised funds to furnish the new building with state-of-the-art facilities, saving the Town and taxpayers nearly **half a million dollars.**

Continuing Commitment

Payson Public Library is busier than all the other Gila Country AZ Libraries *combined,* with nearly **200 new users each month.** Without the community's continuing support, it would be unable to provide the residents of Rim Country with the level of service we have come to expect.

Our long term goal is to donate $3000 each month to augment the Library's limited budget for new material. We currently donate only $1000/month, **so we need your help now.**

Please consider our many flexible gift plans, and choose the one that fits your budget. *All gifts are 100% tax-deductible,* and every dollar counts.

THANK YOU!

Main Circulation Desk in the new Library Building

Library Friends Donation Form

Please fill out the information below, including the range of years. If no number of years is specified, we will assign your donation a range of 1 year.

I pledge to donate: I prefer to pay in:

- ☐ $250/year for ___ yrs   ☐ One lump sum
- ☐ $500/year for ___ yrs   ☐ Quarterly payments
- ☐ $1000/year for ___ yrs   ☐ Monthly payments
- ☐ $___ for ___ yrs   ☐ Semi-Annual payments

I would like my donation to benefit:

(If applicable):
☐ I would like my donation to be made 'In Memoriam' for _____

- ☐ Building Fund
- ☐ Wherever most needed
- ☐ Restricted Fund*

*For **Restricted Fund Only**, please specify the purpose of your donation. If you choose more than one category, your donation will be equally divided among them:

- ☐ Adult Fiction
- ☐ Children's Books
- ☐ Young Adult Books
- ☐ Reference
- ☐ Core Collection
- ☐ Computer Equipment
- ☐ Other (please specify): _____
- ☐ Large Print Books
- ☐ Southwest Collection
- ☐ Movies DVD/VCR
- ☐ Books on Tape/CD
- ☐ Music Collection
- ☐ Summer Reading Program

Name _____

Mailing Address _____

Phone _____

Email (optional) _____

☐ Please contact me regarding donations via wills/trusts/real estate

Library Friends of Payson, Inc.

P.O. Box 13, Payson, AZ 85547-0013
E-mail: library_friends@hotmail.com
Website http://libraryfriendsofpayson.org

Payson Public Library
328 N. McLane Road, Payson AZ 85541
Phone 474-9260   Fax 474-2679
Mon, Wed, Fri 9a-6p
Tues, Thurs 9a-7p
Sat 10a-4p
Closed Sunday

Figure I-MM   Library Friends of Payson (AZ), Inc., Memorial Gifts Brochure (Inside)

Chapter Two

Selling Books

Annual or semiannual used book sales have been a staple fund-raising event for Friends for years—and with good reason. It is no exaggeration to claim that millions of dollars are raised each year for libraries through these sales. They are a wonderful way to bring book lovers together, recycle books into the hands of new owners who will read and appreciate them, and raise a good deal of money!

Although book sales are traditional for Friends, there are, increasingly, new twists to get profit from books that are culled from the collection or donated for the purpose. Online sales of books are gaining in popularity, and now new companies are popping up everywhere to sell used books via the Internet for Friends groups who don't have the staff or volunteer time to do it themselves.

In this chapter, you'll learn about in-library book shops and ongoing sales as well as ways to expand and change the way you operate a sale as they did in Hunterdon County (NJ), where they recently raised over $90,000! You'll get tips on handling overly aggressive booksellers and ideas for letting your public know just what kinds of books and materials you are looking for to increase the number of salable donations. You'll even find out what one group does to get rid of their leftover books without making a midnight trip to the landfill.

While Friends are doing a lot of innovative things to raise money for libraries, book sales continue to be basic . . . and lucrative!

2-1 Ongoing Book Sale, on the Honor System

The Peninsula Friends of the Library, an all-volunteer group, serves the Palos Verdes Library District in California. The Friends run two major book sales two weekends a month, each at a different site. These sales net the Friends group substantial returns.

Because of an overflow of salable books, the Friends have taken over a portion of the parking garage at the main library site where the overflow is available to the public any time during normal library operating hours. There are no volunteers on site during this time, so the Friends have devised an honor system that works quite well.

How It Works

- Each book or other medium item is clearly marked with a price.
- Signs give directions on how to purchase these items.
- Envelopes are provided in which to place the cash.
- The purchaser puts the cash into the envelope and seals it.
- The purchaser then places the sealed envelope under the door to the locked sale area.
- Several times a week, a managing volunteer collects the envelopes.

Results

The benefits of the honor system are twofold. Peninsula Friends of the Library are able to serve the population by providing sale items for more hours than just the scheduled sales. In addition, they sell more books and media, adding greatly to the monthly income from books sales.

2-2 Online Book Sales Raise More Money for Libraries

When a Friends' volunteer at the Freeman (TX) Library started selling books for their library about ten years ago, hardback books sold for $1. After a while it became clear that a lot of the books that passed through their hands were worth considerably more than that, so they decided to increase their prices. However, because of the high dollar value of some of the books and the limited exposure they would receive at the library, the Friends decided in 2002 to try selling on the Internet.

How It Works

The Friends selected books they felt would have more than local interest and were of probable high value and started selling them on Half.com, a site now owned by eBay. They have since slowly switched the majority of their Internet inventory to amazon.com because of its greater popularity (meaning more potential customers looking at their books).

Results

The outcome of their venture in Internet selling has been a substantial amount of income that would not have been generated had they limited sales only to the library. What is significant about Internet selling is that the book inventory is exposed to a vastly greater buying public for 24 hours a day, 7 days a week.

They started slowly in online sales, making only a few thousand dollars in the first year. By the end of their last fiscal year, however (May 31, 2007), their gross sales were a little more than $18,000.

While this may not appear significant compared with amounts generated by large central city libraries, it has to be considered in context. The Freeman Library is one of some 25 branch libraries in Houston, so it is not a big player in the larger scheme of libraries and Friends organizations. The Internet sales were about 30 percent of total sales for the year (the rest generated by their bookstore) and were thus a substantial contribution to the total income.

⊷ ⊷

2-3   Used Bookstore

In 2000, the Canton (MI) Public Library underwent a large expansion project. The Friends lobbied for a used book sale room and were successful. The Secondhand Prose Used Bookstore measures approximately 28 by 38 feet in a lovely setting with two nice windows overlooking a pond and green area. One side of the room is filled with compact moveable shelving, allowing the Friends to accommodate approximately 10,000 books.

The opposing wall contains shelving for special collections such as Nearly New, Collectibles, and Oprah books. The Friends charge double for these, because the market will bear their higher prices. The Friends also sell games and puzzles. The largest shelving on the wall consists of six runs of shelves from floor to ceiling that are labeled "New This Week." This has been their most successful idea as it helps frequent shoppers to zero in on what they haven't already seen.

How It Works

- The book crew consists of 40 to 50 book sales volunteers and a cull/sort/ shelving (CSS) crew of six dependable volunteers. The CSS crew comes in on Friday, Monday, and Tuesday to take the donations from the outside donation shed, sort and cull them, and place them on book carts in the shop's storage room. The storage room houses eight book carts, has a door to the exterior of the back of the building with direct access to the donation shed, and a long counter that runs along one wall that the book carts are stored under.

- The shop is closed on Tuesday mornings so the volunteers can move items from the "New This Week" shelves to the regular moveable shelves. They then place the new donations on the "New This Week" shelves. Booksellers especially like this feature. All books are divided by genre and are arranged in alphabetical order by author.

- The volunteers work in two-hour shifts. The Friends hold quarterly meetings for all bookstore volunteers to update them on any new happenings, as well as produce a quarterly newsletter just for bookstore volunteers.

- The bookstore is open for Friends members only on Tuesday afternoons, from 2:00 to 8:00 p.m., so that members get first pick of the new books donated that week, thus increasing their membership on a regular basis. (Members of the Friends of Canton Public Library now number approximately 375.) Except Tuesdays, the bookstore is open each day from one hour after the library opens to one hour before it closes.

Honoring Their Volunteers

The name of each book crew member who volunteers during the month is placed in a container. At the end of each month, a name is drawn, and the winning volunteer receives a $25 gift certificate to a local restaurant. It's a nice perk and appreciated by all.

Results

The Secondhand Prose Used Bookstore brings in between $50,000 and $60,000 per year. The biggest day of the week is always Tuesdays, when the members-only two-hour sale usually nets between $600 and $700. According to the Friends coordinator, it takes much less time and energy to run the bookshop than the three big book sales they used to hold.

2-4   One Used Book Sale = $90,500 Raised!

With only six weeks until their next book sale, the Friends of the Hunterdon County (NJ) Library System decided to host the "best ever" used book sale to benefit their library. The group quickly geared up to make major adjustments to reach their goal.

How It Worked

Planning:

- The ten-member committee held its meetings with the objective of organizing an event that would exceed the previous year's results.
- They added a fifth book collection drive in a previously "uncollected" region of the county. Book drives took place on five consecutive Saturdays. After only two drives, it was apparent that the number of donated items was going to exceed the previous year by nearly 50%.
- As a consequence, additional floor space for the sale was needed. The Friends worked with the local National Guard Armory to add to the 6,000 square foot space previously allotted. The armory personnel agreed to offer a second building on the property—a large motor pool/storage garage—effectively doubling the space they had before.

Implementation:

- Friends members and armory personnel cleaned the sales areas.
- Armory personnel networked with other armories in the area to borrow the additional 50% tables they would need.
- The county library provided a wish list of books and other media before the first day of sorting so they could cull books from donations that would be suitable for the library.
- Friends volunteers ran book collection drives, sorted books into 45 Fiction and Nonfiction categories, set up the sales floors, priced materials, and collected payments during the sale.

Innovation:

- Lighting in the garage was insufficient. The Friends networked with the county 4-H group to borrow some of their lights, which were strung on bright yellow cords.
- Book babysitting: The Friends rented a truck and parked it between the two armory buildings. Two volunteers checked purchased books at the

truck so that customers could enter the second building unencumbered and shop some more.

- Book parking spaces: Individuals, families, and book dealers who selected more books than they could carry were given a parking space to place their books.

Other new and older traditions:

- The Friends hold an "Exclusive Private Book Sale Preview," which is limited to 50 members of the Friends (first come, first served). Each individual pays $50 to attend this three-hour, Friday afternoon sale. This preview sells out.
- All inventory not sold over the course of the event is donated to other nonprofit organizations or wholesaled to booksellers.
- Bulk Buyer Buddies (volunteers) take books to customers' parking spaces.
- Rare and specially priced books are sold in the Book Boutique, separate from the rest of the books.
- The Kid's Corner is in a separate room for younger customers and their parents.

Community and volunteer involvement:

- The committee and cochairs, along with a "staff" of over 200 volunteers, gave more than 5,000 hours to make the event a success.
- The Boy Scouts and county 4-H groups became involved for the first time.
- Several young men and women completed their community service sentences working at the event and ended up continuing to volunteer after their required hours were met.

Results

The Friends of the Hunterdon County Library raised $90,500 during the course of a three-day weekend! In addition, $11,520 worth of items entered the library's collection before the sale began.

NOTE: Each building has its own checkout. You must pay in one building before proceeding to the next. Please take purchases to your car or check them at our Book Babysitter before entering the next building. (Not responsible for loss or theft.)

Thank you for your cooperation & support of our Book Sale!

2005 BOOK SALE CATEGORIES & PRICES
Very special items are in the BOOK BOUTIQUE located in Bldg A, Section C
Audio Books, CDs, Cassettes, LPs, Computer Software in Entrance Room of Building B

CATEGORY	Bldg	ROW	CATEGORY	Bldg	ROW
Animals	B	1	Large Print	A	A1
Anthologies	A	C1	Movie Tie-Ins	A	A1
Arts & Entertainment	B	1	Mysteries & Thrillers (A-K) (L-Z) (Author name)	A	5-7
Biography	B	1	New Jersey	B	3
Business & Finance	B	2	Non-Fiction (General)	B	3
Children & Young Adult (Books & Videos)	A	Kids Rm	Old & Interesting	A	C
Classics	A	8	Parenting & Childbirth	B	3
Collectibles & Decorative Arts	B	1	Philosophy/Religion/Inspiration	B	4
Computers & Software	B	2	Plays & Poetry	A	A1
Cookbooks	B	1	Popular Authors (Clancy; Clark, Mary H; Cussler; Grisham; King; Koontz; Patterson, J.; Roberts, N/Robb; D. Steel)	A	10
Crafts & Hobbies	B	1	Recent Releases, Best Sellers, Book Clubs, Book Awards, Volunteer Favorites	A	A2
Diet/Fitness/Beauty	B	2	Reference	B	3
Education/ Teaching/ Home Schooling	B	3	Romance	A	9
Fiction (A-K) (L-Z) (Author's Last Name)	A	1-4	Science Fiction & Fantasy	A	8
Foreign Language	B	3	Science/Nature/Environment	B	4
Gardening	B	3	Self-Help/Psychology	B	4
Health & Medical	B	2	Social Science/Anthropology/Urban Studies	B	4
History & Politics	B	2	Sports & Games	B	4
Holidays & Weddings	B	3	Travel	B	4
House & Car	B	3	Videos	A	B1
Humor	A	A2	Westerns	A	8

SATURDAY PRICE LIST

Hardbacks,	$2.00
Large & Trade Paperbacks	$2.00
Regular Paperbacks (Mass Market)	$0.50
Children's Hardbacks	$1.00
Children's Paperbacks/Mini Hardbks	$ .50
Romance Series Paperbks	10 for $1.00
(Avon, Harlequin, etc)	
Books on Tape or DVD	$5.00
DVDs	$5.00
Videos	$2.00
CDs	$2.00
Software/Comp. Games	$2.00
Records	$ .50
Cassettes	$ .50
Pamphlets/Tiny Hardbks	$ .50
Specially Priced Items/Sets	Price on Green Dot or Box

SUNDAY PRICE LIST (HALF PRICE DAY!!)

Hardbacks,	$1.00
Large & Trade Paperbacks	$1.00
Regular Paperbacks (Mass Market)	$ .25
Children's Hardbacks (50¢ ea.)	3 for $1.00
Children's Pprbks/Mini Hdbks (25¢ ea)	5 for $1.00
Romance Series Paperbks	5 for $ .25
(Avon, Harlequin, etc)	
Books on Tape or DVD	$2.50
DVDs	$2.50
Videos	$1.00
CDs	$1.00
Software/Comp. Games	$1.00
Records (25¢ ea.)	5 for $1.00
Cassettes (25¢ ea.)	5 for $1.00
Pamphlets/Tiny Hardbks	$ .25
Specially Priced Items/Sets	½ of Price on Green Dot or Box

Enjoy a treat from the Food Tent sponsored by:
The Hunterdon County Employee Appreciation Committee

Figure 2-A Book Sale Handout (Front with Guide)

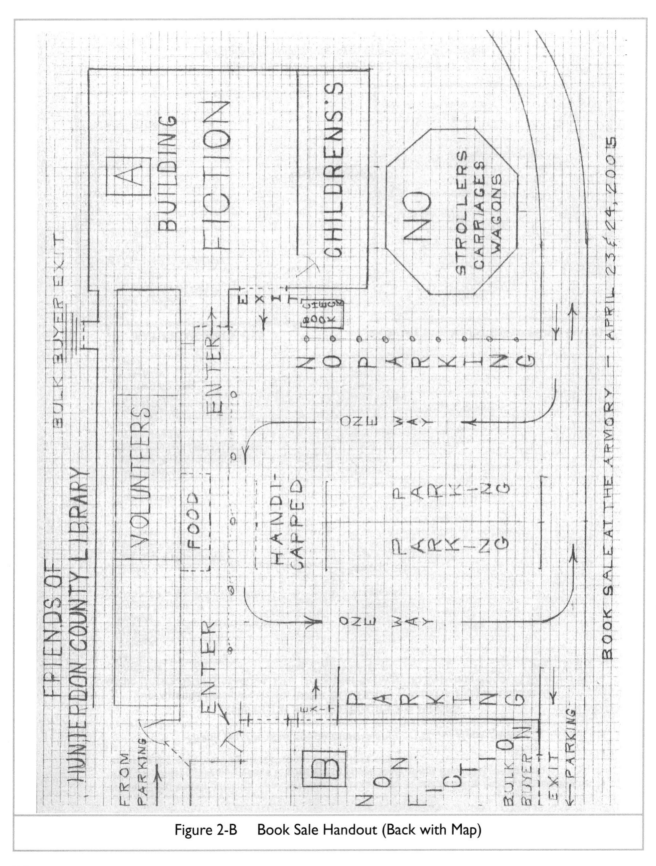

Figure 2-B   Book Sale Handout (Back with Map)

2005 BOOK SALE VOLUNTEER OPPORTUNITIES

Check ☑ all areas where you can help. You will be contacted to confirm dates/availability. Thanks!

☐ **BOX PICKUP (2/21 – 4/9)** – Get empty boxes at ShopRite & other identified stores daily (usually by 9 AM) & transport them to the Armory. Check day(s) available: ☐Mon ☐Tues ☐Wed ☐Thu ☐Fri ☐Sat

☐ **BOOK PICKUP (3/7 – 4/9)** – Need volunteers to pick up donations from Hunterdon County residents who are physically unable to bring donations to us. A van or truck is helpful, but not required.

☐ **SATURDAY BOOK DRIVES (3/12 – 4/9)** – Volunteers help patrons unload cars and load donations onto truck for delivery to the Armory. Help is also needed to unload the books at the Armory late Saturday after each book drive.

PLEASE CHECK ☑ DATE(S) AND SHIFT(S) YOU CAN WORK:

☐ MARCH 12 North County Branch, Clinton	☐ MARCH 19 Headquarters Library, Rt 12	☐ MARCH 26 North County Branch, Clinton	☐ APRIL 2 Headquarters Library, Rt 12	☐ APRIL 9 East Whitehouse Fire Station, Whitehouse
☐ 9 AM – 1PM	☐ 9 AM – 1PM	☐ 9 AM – 1PM	☐ 9 AM – 1PM	☐ 9 AM – 1PM
☐ 12:30 – 3:15PM	☐ 12:30 – 3:15PM	☐ 12:30 – 3:15PM	☐ 12:30 – 3:15PM	☐ 12:30 – 3:15PM
☐ 3:30– 4:45 PM Help unload at Armory on Rt. 12	☐ 3:15 – 4:45 PM Help unload at Armory on Rt. 12	☐ 3:30 – 4:45 PM Help unload at Armory on Rt. 12	☐ 3:15 – 4:45 PM Help unload at Armory on Rt. 12	☐ 3:30 – 4:45PM Help unload at Armory on Rt. 12

☐ **BOOK SORTING (3/13 – 4/15)** – Monday thru Thursday, 9AM to 1PM at the Armory on Rt. 12. Scheduling is flexible, volunteer for a few hours, days, or every day. Volunteers sort the books into categories, pack them into boxes and stack the boxes. All are welcome, but we especially need sorters/packers who can lift a box of books (approx. 30 lbs) from the sorting table to a dolly.

☐ **LIBRARY BOOK COLLECTION (3/7 – 4/9)** – Weekdays – Volunteers transport donations from the library collection boxes to the Armory. Some packing and lifting of boxes is involved. A van or truck is helpful, but not required. Check the library most convenient for you.

    ☐ **Headquarters Library**   ☐ **North County Branch, Clinton**   ☐ **South County Branch, Ringoes**

☐ **BOOK SALE SET UP WEEK**: at the Armory on Rt. 12, Flemington. Need volunteers to move & unpack boxes, and set up the sale tables within the Armory. Some lifting is necessary. **Daily from 9AM – 2PM**. Please check date(s) available:

☐ Monday, April 18	☐ Tuesday, April 19	☐ Wednesday, April 20	☐ Thursday, April 21

☐ **BOOK SALE WEEKEND:**

Please check ☑ job(s) you are interested in:
☐ **Cashier** –Collect money for books purchased.
☐ **Pricer** –Assist Cashiers by pricing books of customers in line.
☐**Table Restocking** Restock the books on the tables during the sale.
☐ **Parking** –Direct traffic in the parking areas.

Please check dates and shifts you will work:	
☐ **Saturday, April 23**	☐ **Sunday, April 24**
☐ 7:15 AM – 12:30 PM	☐ 9:30 AM – 1:00 PM
☐ 12:00 PM – 5:15 PM	☐ 12:30 PM – 4:00 PM

Please complete and return this form by MARCH 7TH.

Be sure to include your e-mail ID if available. Mail to the address on the back.
Questions? Contact Mary Ellen Soldavin at (908) 996-4512 (marcnmel@msn.com)

Name _____   **Day Phone** _____

E-mail _____   **Eve Phone** _____

Join us – you'll have a GREAT time!

Figure 2-C   Book Sale Volunteer Sign-Up Form

2-5   How the Friends of the Houston (TX) Public Library Work with Booksellers at Their Book Sales

The issue of including booksellers at Friends group book sales is a hot topic everywhere. New technologies (blackberries, scanners, etc.) have empowered the sellers with access to information on a book's salability. Increasingly sellers are accused of aggressive tactics at the sales, and this conflict can hurt your sale in a number of ways:

- Members and the public have a less enjoyable experience.
- You can lose thousands of dollars in sales when booksellers stash or hoard books.
- The sale's integrity is questioned if people believe the stock to be picked over.

On the other hand, the purchases that booksellers make are often for hundreds or even thousands of dollars. The Friends of the Houston Public Library sincerely want to work with the sellers and not against them. To find a solution, the Friends compiled information from various sources, asked for input from members and booksellers alike, examined their procedures, and implemented a few changes

How It Works

A successful solution will be a combination of measures:

- Continue the established practice of limiting set-up purchases to $3 per hour, and do not allow dealers in during set up.
- Use a larger sorting area with wide access to re-sort and a knowledgeable volunteer to monitor the area.
- Use more volunteers for more efficient re-sorting.
- Provide a volunteer to tally the booksellers' purchases, seal them, and mark the packages to be paid for.
- Have policies posted clearly, and announce them in the newsletter.
- Have monitors throughout the sale to inform guests that anything stashed will be reshelved. The monitors should understand the issue and manage the floor aspects of encountering it. They will direct a tally volunteer to the booksellers' piles; they will know the policies and be able to explain them; and they will see that large stashes are returned to the re-sorting area.
- Maintain an organized "book keep" to accommodate more use.

The Friends' Policy Statement is posted at the sale entrance:

It is the goal of the Friends of the Houston Public Library to have a successful book sale that is enjoyable for everyone. When books are removed from the sale tables, we can't raise as much as we could for the Library, and our sale is compromised. We all want this sale to be the best it can be to help support our Library. Please know that the following policy will be in place at all of our Book Sales.

Stashed Books Will Be Returned to the Sale Tables

Books removed from sale tables and "stashed" will be returned to the sale tables. A "stash" of books is any unattended pile, bag, or box.

Sorting Area

We've set aside a large sorting area where materials may be sorted through. Unwanted materials can easily be returned to the sale tables from this area.

If You Are Making a Big Purchase

Use the sorting area and return unwanted materials promptly to the designated area so they can be reshelved. Any unattended piles of books will be returned to the sale tables. When you are ready to check out, wait in line, and ask for a volunteer tally to come to you.

Book Keep

A Book Keep is provided to store books you intend to purchase while you continue browsing.

Book Sellers Are Not a Part of Set Up

As always, our policy is that volunteers who help set up are allowed to purchase $3 worth of books for each hour of volunteer service. Book sellers are not a part of set up.

Results

Everyone—community members, everyday readers, and booksellers alike—are entitled to the best selection of books available. When you minimize the number of books that are off the table, you make the sale better for everyone.

2-6   Friend-to-Friend, a Free Book Program

Friend-to-Friend (F2F) is a free service of the Friends of Ferguson Library in Stamford (CT) in cooperation with their sister program, the Friends Used Book Shops. The Friends supply free, clean, quality used books to Stamford-serving nonprofit agencies.

The F2F's mission is to serve as a free community literacy resource by promoting the use and reuse of books in their community and to save from disposal perfectly good reading material that cannot otherwise be sold in the group's bookshops (duplicates, lack of space, specialized). All F2F books were first donated by the community. The group "redonates" them to nonprofit agencies. Since 2003, F2F has redonated over 50,000 items to more than 55 agencies.

How It Works

The following Frequently Asked Questions are distributed by the Friends to those interested in participating in the F2F program.

Q. Who is eligible for free books?
A. Nonprofit educational, civic, government, religious, community, and similar organizations that serve Stamford residents or are based in Stamford. Re-donation is strictly limited to agency, never private, use. Resale is strictly forbidden.

Since many agencies rely on F2F, and our stock is limited by what we get donated to us, we trust our customers, in consultation with the volunteers as to current resources, to use some quantity restraint with selecting books during any one visit so as to preserve variety for others. You may visit again any time.

Q. What kind of books are available?
A. F2F books are exactly the same stock as regularly priced books found in our Shops, on all subjects and for all age levels. Eligible customers can take as many books as needed from the Main Library F2F Re-Donation Room and up to ten regularly priced items from the Shops at each visit. Our stock is replenished daily, so visit often.

Regular customers with specialty interests may request that we save books especially for them. Since all stock is donated, we cannot fill orders for multiple copies or guarantee particular titles. Available stock is directly dependent upon what the community donates to us, so please remind friends and family members to donate their books, videos, and music to the Friends!

Q. If the F2F books are used, aren't they dirty and scuffed?
A. No. We use only cleaned, quality books in good condition for this service, the same standard as in our popular Shops. Minor imperfections are to be expected but since YOU can choose your own books, satisfaction is 100% guaranteed!

Q. How do I get my books?
A. We are open whenever the Library is open. Walk in. Go directly into the Shop and choose up to ten regularly priced books depending on availability, complete a yellow F2F Re-Donation Record, and leave it with a volunteer (or library staff if no volunteer is present). At the Main Library, if there is a volunteer available in the Re-Donation Room, you also may visit there and take as many books as you need, with no limits.

Call ahead assistance: If you have a special subject need (US frontier history unit, Spanish cooking, 19th c. American poetry, Halloween, etc.), please call ahead, as we may be able have appropriate items ready for your inspection when you arrive. This is more likely in connection to subjects than to specific titles.

Always record your selection. For EVERY visit, the customer must complete an F2F Re-Donation Record. This yellow sheet is available for self-service in the Shops and also in the Re-Donation Room. Please fill out this form COMPLETELY for every visit in order to keep F2F privileges. When you first visit, an acknowledgment letter from the receiving agency is requested for documentation purposes.

May I take the books with me? The customer generally carries out the order. We will help you load your car, if needed. In rare circumstances, we may be able to deliver large orders, involving many boxes of books, directly to the agency.

Q. I have used the F2F service once. May I use it again?
A. Yes. Use it as often as you need to, up to once a month, if desired. Keep in mind, however, that our program is based on donations, so subjects and titles are not predictable.

Q. I know of a nonprofit organization that could use your service. May I suggest that they call you?
A. Sure, and we'd really appreciate that if you do. Just have them contact us at: XXX-XXX-XXXX. Leave a message and we'll return the call as soon as we can.

Q. I'd like to get a selection of youth fiction, adult non-fiction, and board books for very young children. Is this OK?
A. Yes, any combination of materials is acceptable. All subjects and types are available.

Q. I live in Stamford but teach at a public school in the South Bronx. Can I still use your service?
A. Not at this time. Our mission and policy limit this program to agencies that serve Stamford residents.

Q. Once the books have been used, must they be returned?
A. No, they are "for keeps." We even urge you to give them to clients to take home, consistent with your program goals.

Q. Some of my clients are Spanish speaking. Can I find books for them?
A. Yes, we always have a respectable stock of foreign language books: Russian, French, Spanish, German, and some Asian languages. If you have readers with specific needs, please telephone us to discuss how we might assist you.

Q. My readers are domestic violence victims. They do not want to read certain types of mysteries, for instance. How can we make sure some disturbing books don't slip into the mix?
A. We are careful to ask about and screen appropriate reading materials for your group. When you call to make contact, mention any such concerns.

Q. I have a great idea for a community project. Can F2F become involved?
A. Yes, so long as you do the legwork for the project, and we just make the books available to you. Also, we need to clear the project, so make sure you call us in advance to discuss your idea.

To keep this valuable program going . . .
Please remind friends and family to donate their books, videos, and music to the Friends.

Donation Drop Off Locations:
Any Ferguson Library circulation desk or The Friends Used Book Shops

Larger Donations:
Main Library at back loading dock (off Spring Street) or Harry Bennett Branch donation drop box by exit door

Please pack in bags or boxes.

2-7   Price-Sorter Guidelines

The Friends of the Lawrence (KS) Public Library developed guidelines to help train and retain book sale volunteers. In this way their volunteers better understand expectations, and the Friends are better prepared for each upcoming book sale. Twice a year the Friends sponsor a volunteer breakfast. While sharing bagels and coffee, volunteers ask questions, get to know each other, and train new volunteers.

How It Works

- A committee of Friends board members and volunteers meet to outline and write guidelines.
- The Friends board approves the guidelines.
- The Friends hold a volunteer breakfast twice a year or as needed. A seasoned book sale volunteer facilitates the session.
- Some hands-on techniques can be used. Selected books are passed around and attendees are asked to decide the category to which they belong.
- Copies of the Price-Sorter Guidelines are handed out.

Results

By striving to better communicate with and prepare their volunteers, the Friends now run a leaner and more organized operation. Books are sorted, priced, and shelved for the next sale in an efficient manner. Each sale presents the Friends to the public as an organized and focused group, bound to support the library. Their competent demeanor reflects well on the library they serve.

৽৹ ৻৵

2-8   Soliciting Book Donations

If your Friends group receives box after box of nonsalable books, refer to the following examples for communicating your needs and policies to patrons and to the community at large.

FAQ's for ALD Staff
Book Donations From Patrons

Did you know that the Friends of the Arapahoe Library District will raise over $70,000 from the sale of used books this year? The Friends will sort through 60,000 books to find the treasures that stock our stores and our annual sale. While we appreciate the generosity of our patrons, we cannot accept all materials. Here are a few guidelines that will help us process the large number of donations we receive every week.

If a patron walks into the library with a reasonable number of books or materials to donate (**5 boxes or less**) say *Thanks* and take the books.
You can then have the courier take the donation to Koelbel Library, addressed to: Friends Book Donations, or contact Louise Richey in the Friends Foundation office at 303-LIBRARY for assistance.
For all larger donations (**anything over 5 boxes**) please get a name and phone number and forward the information to Louise.

What can be donated?
Most gently-used books and media are accepted on behalf of the Friends of the Library.

What cannot be accepted?
Magazines (including *National Geographic*)
Patterns and puzzles
Readers' Digest condensed books
Most encyclopedias, textbooks or reference books over three years old
Any items previously owned by other libraries
Empty cases for CDs, DVDs, etc.

Why can't these items be used?
Our experience is that these items simply do not sell and must be discarded. The Library District has to pay for recycling and that doesn't seem like a good use of taxpayer dollars.

Can you suggest another place that could use these items?
Goodwill Industries International will accept magazines, Readers Digest condensed books and encyclopedias. See www.**goodwill**.org for more information.

Where can I drop off my donations to the Library District?
Patrons are asked to bring donations to Koelbel Library at 5955 S. Holly Street in Centennial.
Books and media materials must be boxed in sturdy boxes. Please do not accept bags
Rev 06/07

Figure 2-D FAQs for Arapahoe Library (Englewood, CO) District Staff: Book Donations from Patrons

filled with books as our volunteers cannot handle these well. All large donations (anything over 5 boxes) must be coordinated with the Friends Office. The back door at Koelbel (near the garage) is most convenient during weekday business hours, and there is a door bell there patrons can ring to get into the building during regular library hours. Otherwise, they may leave up to **five** boxes at any of the branch libraries during regular library hours.

If there are a large number of boxes, will the library pick them up?
Yes. The donation pick up is coordinated through the Friends office. Take the patron's contact information, and send it to the Friends office. Patrons can also call the Friends directly at 303-LIBRARY.

What does the library do with these donations?
The materials are sorted and sold in order to raise funds to support programs and projects throughout the Library District. The Friends Again Used Bookstore at the Koelbel Library sells a majority of the books throughout the year, with smaller ongoing book sales at Smoky Hill and other branch libraries. The annual Used Book Sale in the fall raises thousands of dollars for library programs and services each year.

Why doesn't the library add these materials to the regular collection?
Unless an item is particularly rare, the cost in staff time to sort, catalog and process it exceeds its face value. We simply don't have enough staff to handle all of the donations. Please contact the Manager of Library Materials, at 303-LIBRARY for further clarification.

Is my donation tax deductible?
Yes. Library staff can sign and date a receipt for the donor. The donor establishes the value of his donation.

How do I make a donation (other than used items) to the Library District? Can I donate a book in memory of a loved one?
Contact the Friends Foundation office at 303-798-2444, x1020. We have many options available to make sure that a donation will benefit the Library District.

Patrons can also consider becoming a member of the Friends. (Brochures should be available at all branches.) Friends members receive discounts at the book stores and there are many volunteer opportunities available. Funds raised through Friends memberships are used for Library District programs and services each year.

Rev 06/07

Figure 2-D FAQs for Arapahoe Library (Englewood, CO) District Staff: Book Donations from Patrons *(continued)*

Friends of the Library Used Book Sale
Where Do All These Books Come From?

The public often asks where all the books in the sale come from. They are from the Salt Lake City Public Library's collection and from public donations. Librarians must carefully choose what is added to our collection of nearly 800,000 items. They select material in a broad range of formats which respond to the interest and demand of the public and provide a balance of ideas and concepts.

In 2006–2007, librarians expect to spend nearly $1.9 million on new materials. As new items are added, librarians must discard materials that are worn-out, damaged beyond repair, outdated, or no longer in demand. Those materials are sent to the used book sale where Friends volunteers spend hundreds of hours sorting and preparing them for sale.

Thousands of books are donated by the public each year. Donated items are always carefully reviewed to determine if they will be added to our collection. Approximately 10,000 gift books are added to library shelves annually. With the cost of a new book averaging a conservative $18.00, this amounts to $180,000 worth of books added to the library's shelves each year.

Books not added are sold at the used book sale. Book sale revenues are donated back to the library. If you have books in good condition you would like to donate, please think of the City Library. It is a great way to recycle your old books, share your favorite reads with others, and support the library at the same time.

∽ ∾

2-9 Sample Promotional Materials

Friends of the
Alpine Public Library

Re-Reads Bookstore
is a project of the Alpine Public Library
and is staffed by Friends of the Alpine
Public Library volunteers. All proceeds
from sales are used to supplement the
Library's operational budget.

Re-Reads Bookstore

Design & Construction

By Thomas Greenwood,
Architect, PLLC

Re-Reads Bookstore

Alpine Public Library
203 North Seventh Street
Alpine, Texas 79830
Phone: 432-837-2621
E-mail: alpinepl@brooksdata.net
Web: www.alpinepubliclibrary.org

Friends of the Alpine Public Library

Our Mission

In appreciation of the role the library plays in the
quality of life in the Big Bend area, the Friends of
the Alpine Public Library work to provide and
strengthen library services and support a varied
menu of programs for the citizens of our area,
consistent with the goals and objectives of the
Alpine Public Library and its Board of Directors.

Join the Friends!

Your membership in the Friends of
the Alpine Public Library is vital to
the support of many special projects
for the library, including Re-Reads
Bookstore.

Please complete the following information and return it with your tax-
deductible gift to the address below.
Your support is much needed and
greatly appreciated!

Name _____

Mailing Address _____

Phone _____

E-Mail (Saves postage!) _____

Select your membership category:

( ) $5 Senior Citizen (65+)
( ) $10 Single or Student
( ) $15 Family
( ) $25 Business
( ) $100+ Patron
( ) *Contact me about volunteering!*

Mail to:

Kathy Bork, President
Friends of the Alpine Public Library
1008 E. Nations
Alpine, TX 79830

Figure 2-E   Friends of the Alpine (TX) Public Library Re-Reads Bookstore Brochure (Outside)
—Logo Design by Jennifer DeGarmo; Brochure Design by Kari Langkamp

Architect Tom Greenwood describes the ideas and practical considerations that inspired his design of the Alpine Public Library's Re-Reads Bookstore.

I began the design of Re-Reads with the idea that the building would be constructed with volunteer labor using materials common to the ranch buildings of West Texas. Corrugated metal and exposed wood were commonplace building materials before the advent of pre-engineered metal buildings. Welded steel connections have long been a mainstay of ranch construction and I hoped to use the talent of local townspeople in the assembly of the building. Concrete is another material that is not out of place in West Texas. I wanted to use it as an exposed finished material on the structure.

The form of the building is reminiscent of the Quonset hut structures found throughout West Texas. The arched roof form mimics the roof found on the old rock Student Activity Center on the Sul Ross campus. The exposed post and beam structure is not typically seen in this area. However, I wanted to express the beauty of the 6x6 Douglas fir posts rather than covering the wood.

The corrugated siding on Re-Reads is non-galvanized to allow the metal to rust to a rich earth tone over time. It is also installed horizontally, rather than vertically, as is typically seen. The intent is to contrast the vertical Douglas fir posts with the horizontal lines of the siding.

"The corrugated siding on Re-Reads is nongalvanized to allow the metal to rust to a rich earth tone over time."

The functional requirements of the bookstore called for solid wall space for bookshelves on three of the four exterior walls. Clerestory windows offered a good solution for getting diffused daylight into the building. Acrylic panels are used in the windows to achieve a rice paper appearance.

The interior lighting is low-voltage cable lighting that uses MR-16 lamps. The parallel cables have transformers that step the voltage down to a level that is safe to touch. The light fixtures simply clamp on to the parallel cables and the lamps can be swiveled to direct the light as needed. Each light fixture has two pieces of art glass that flank the MR-16 lamps.

The batt insulation used in the building is made from recycled blue jean denim. The R-value is identical to fiberglass insulation, but it is much easier and more fun to work with. I found belt loops and shredded jean labels mixed in with the cotton.

L. T. Construction, of Fort Stockton, poured the concrete slab and did a fine job with the hard trowel finish and saw cutting. The porch along the south side of the Re-Reads has a rock salt finish that provides a pitted, nonslip surface.

In addition to Texana Homes and the other contractors, over a dozen volunteers worked to get Re-Reads to the current level of completion. There is still much work to do with the handicapped-accessible ramp, concrete steps, maple veneer plywood wall finishes, curved drywall ceilings, adjustable shelving, painting, and landscaping. I believe that when completed, the Re-Reads Bookstore will be a building in which our entire community can take pride.

Tom Greenwood and his family reside in Alpine, Texas. He generously donated his architectural services in the design of Re-Reads Bookstore.

Figure 2-F Friends of the Alpine (TX) Public Library Re-Reads Bookstore Brochure (Inside)
—Logo Design by Jennifer DeGarmo; Brochure Design by Kari Langkamp

MULTNOMAH COUNTY LIBRARY

The Friends' Library Store

Discover us as you explore downtown Portland

Offering high quality used books and unique literary gifts for book lovers of all levels

www.friends-library.org

Hours

Tuesday - Saturday   10 a.m. to 6 p.m

Location

The Friends' Library Store is located inside the Multnomah County Central Library located downtown on SW 10th and Taylor.

Trimet routes: MAX and trolley drop you right at our door. You can also reach us on any bus labeled "TO PORTLAND."

Multnomah County Central Library
& the Friends' Library Store

W Burnside

SW 10th Ave

SW Broadway

SW Morrison

SW Yamhill

SW Taylor

Pioneer Courthouse Square

MULTNOMAH COUNTY LIBRARY

FRIENDS OF THE LIBRARY

Friends' Library Store
801 SW 10th Avenue
Portland, Oregon 97201
(503) 988-5911
www.friends-library.org

Hand-selected, affordable titles and gifts for book-lovers

Volunteers with a passion for books help select the titles offered in the store at a fraction of their original price. You'll find:

• Hardcover editions straight off the *New York Times* Bestseller List

• Folio editions of timeless classics

• Beloved children's picture books

• Collectible cookbooks

Also nestled among the shelves:

• book-related t-shirts

• note cards, calendars and posters, including many creations by regional artists

• gift items featuring Portland author Beverly Cleary's Ramona Quimby and friends

• journals, paper weights and book-ends for all tastes and budgets

• and conveniences for library customers and staff such as pens, pads, and snacks

Figure 2-G   Friends of the Multnomah County (OR) Library "The Friends' Library Store" Brochure (Outside)

If you're setting out to explore downtown Portland, don't miss the historic Central Library, covering an entire city block at 801 S.W. 10th. First opened in 1913, the building was extensively and lovingly restored in 1997. Today this National Register of Historic Places landmark invites you to immerse yourself in an elegant blend of turn-of-the-century grandeur and unsurpassed modern library resources.

The Friends' Library Store

Among Central Library's unique offerings is the Friends' Library Store, housed just inside the building's main entrance. Operated by a non-profit community organization called The Friends of Multnomah County Library, the store offers a wide selection of quality, inexpensive used books and gifts that celebrate reading, writing and creativity.

Imagine all your best book finds over the years shelved together in one inviting place — that's the Friends' Library Store!

Support a Vital Community Institution

Your purchases at the Friends' Library Store supports neighborhood libraries and community outreach services. Recently-funded library programs include:

- Teen Lounges & Homework Centers
- *Pageturners* book discussion groups held at numerous local libraries
- Topic-specific books and teacher's guides offered to patrons in a "Bucket of Books"
- Author lectures for children and teens

Figure 2-H   Friends of the Multnomah County (OR) Library "The Friends' Library Store" Brochure (Inside)

The Ground Floor
shop | eat | drink | read
the Friends' shop at Hedberg Public Library

Drink

Small Coffee (12 oz) $1.00
Large Coffee (16 oz)....$1.25

Local Item! We offer coffee from the Stateline's own JavaMania Coffee Roastery, a small-batch coffee roaster that uses only the finest Arabica beans to create more than 70 varietals, blends and flavors.

Chai $1.25
Hot Cocoa $1.25

Tazo Tea ....50¢
Gray's Soda $1.00

Local item! Try Janesville's own Gray's Root Beer, Cream Soda and Orange Soda.

Other Sodas ....75¢
Monster Green $1.99
Calypso Lemonade $1.00
Aquafina Water $1.00

Eat

Sub Sandwiches $2.75
Muffins, Scones $1.50
Cake $2.75
Cheesecake, Pie $2.50
Pound Cake....................$1.75
Dunkin' Donuts ....75¢
Donut Fancies $1.50
Fruit Cups $1.25
Animal Crackers, Peanut Butter Crackers or Goldfish ....50¢

Granola Bars......................50¢
Potato Chips..................$1.00
Fudge $1.25
Chocolate-covered Pretzels..........................$1.25
Chocolate-covered Graham Crackers $1.25
Yogurt..................................75¢

Local item! Enjoy a locally made fudge or chocolate-dipped treats from Fudglies.

Shop

Check out **The Ground Floor** for a variety of gift items for book lovers including greeting cards, book bags, bookmarks, bookplates and other unique items.

Read

Pick up a used book to read while you enjoy your coffee or food — our inventory of paperback, hardcover and children's books is constantly changing.

Adult Hardcovers..............$1
Children's Hardcovers....75¢
Adult Softcovers ....75¢
Children's Softcovers......50¢
Paperback books..............25¢
Magazines ....75¢

Selected new books are priced as marked, many at $1.50 or $3. Books by local authors, sets and other special books are also priced as marked.

Wi-Fi Zone

Figure 2-1   The Friends of the Hedberg Public Library (Janesville, WI) "The Ground Floor" Flyer

┌───┐
│   │
│   **Chapter Three**   │
│   ‾‾‾‾‾‾‾‾‾‾‾‾‾‾‾   │
│   │
│   # Programs for Services and Outreach   │
│   │
└───┘

Chapter Three

Programs for Services and Outreach

In addition to raising money, Friends often play a role in helping to raise the profile of the community, bring new readers into the library, and honor staff and faculty through a variety of programs. Many Friends groups offer the same programs annually. These programs often grow in stature and recognition, and community or campus members begin to look forward to them. However, some Friends find that, despite their best efforts, traditional programs or even first-time events fail to find an audience—or at least one large enough to warrant repetition. Friends often struggle to come up with new ideas to help share their love of libraries and reading.

That's where the ideas in this chapter come in! Find out how to "thank" library pages with a scholarship program, as is done in Canton (MI), and learn about celebrating faculty achievement as done at Wake Forest University (Winston-Salem, NC) and the University of Cincinnati (OH). Find out how you can start a "People's University" in your community to support the library's mission of lifelong learning—the Friends of the Minneapolis (MN) Public Library will tell you how.

Programs are wonderful ways to generate publicity and excitement about the library and all it has to offer. In addition to the ideas in this chapter, be sure to look at some of the fund-raising program ideas in Chapter 1 as well. Whether raising the library's profile or raising money for the library, bringing people together to share a love of books and reading is a great way to support the library.

3-1   Scholarship Program for Library Pages

The Friends of the Canton (MI) Public Library decided about ten years ago to help their library pages pursue a degree after completing high school. Their original goal was to help students financially by providing funds to purchase textbooks.

As part of their annual budget, the Friends set aside $1,000 for scholarships. They award two $500 scholarships per year at their annual staff/Friends picnic luncheon in August. Winning students' parents are invited to attend the event for the presentation of the check and the award certificate. There are occasionally years when no one qualifies, and the money is rolled over to the following year.

Today's Date: _____ **Return Date:** August 8, 2006

APPLICATION
FRIENDS OF THE CANTON PUBLIC LIBRARY
EDUCATIONAL AWARD

NAME: _____

ADDRESS:_____
_____, MI._____

PHONE:_____

COLLEGE OR UNIVERSITY: _____
(currently attending or will be attending)

Grade point average for the past two semesters: _____
*documentation required

Attach brief essay regarding your educational goals.

Also include two letters of recommendation.

Submit the completed application to the page supervisor or Friends' coordinator by date stated at the top of the application.

Thank you and good luck!

The Friends of the Canton Public Library

Figure 3-A   Scholarship Application

How It Works

- A committee, made up of the page supervisor, a Friends' representative, and another staff member, judges the applications.
- After reading the applications, the committee reaches a consensus. There have been occasions when only one page qualified and received the entire amount of $1,000, if deemed appropriate.
- The students must meet several requirements. These are outlined in the application.
- The Friends fit the scholarship program into their mission of supporting the library and the community.

Results

The program supports library staff and makes the community more desirable by helping to educate the young people.

ᘒ ᘓ

3-2 Involve Your Friends in the Life of the Campus!

The Friends of the Libraries at the University of Memphis (TN), working under the auspices of the University's Academic Affairs division and along with the Special Events Office, were the chief sponsor of the university-wide event, Faculty Scholarship Week 2007. Faculty Scholarship Week, which occurred during Spring Convocation Week, was designed to spotlight the University of Memphis faculty's creativity and productivity. Thus, not only books and journal articles, but CDs, films, and musical scores created by faculty members were placed on display on tables in the rotunda of the Ned R. McWherter Library, the main library of the University of Memphis, during April 16–18 and then in the concourse of the campus Rose Theatre, where Convocation ceremonies were held on April 19.

How It Worked

- The Deans of the University's colleges selected works by 150 faculty members (out of a total of some 800) for display.
- Each item on display had a note placard giving basic bibliographic information plus information on any awards that the faculty member might have won.

FACULTY SCHOLARSHIP WEEK

April 15-19, 2007

In conjunction with Spring Convocation 2007, the Friends of the University Libraries are celebrating faculty scholarship, showcasing the excellent books, articles, CDs, films, art and other works produced by University of Memphis faculty. The public is cordially invited to attend all of the free (unless noted) events of the week. Parking is available in the Fogelman Center garage, 340 Innovation Drive, and in the Zach Curlin garage, 505 Zach Curlin Street.

Sponsored by the Friends of the University Libraries

For further information:

Sue Reid Williams
President, Friends of the University Libraries
276-6092
swill206@aol.com

Tom Mendina
Assistant Professor, University Libraries
678-4310
tmendina@memphis.edu

All are free events open to the public unless noted.

THE UNIVERSITY OF
MEMPHIS.

University Libraries

Events Calendar

April 15 - Sunday
Harris Concert Hall
7:30 pm – Victor Asuncion, piano and Susanna Perry-Gilmore, violin, Beethoven sonatas

April 16 - Monday
McWherter Library Rotunda
Noon – Dr. Dixie Crase, Director of University Internships, "Partners for Positive Parenting: University Interns in the Community"

April 17 - Tuesday
McWherter Library Rotunda
Noon – Dr. Cyril Chang, Director of Methodist LeBonheur Center for Healthcare Economics, "The Good, The Bad and The Ugly of American Health Care: A Conversation on Urgent Health Care Issues"

April 18 - Wednesday
McWherter Library Room 226
Noon – Dr. Beverly Bond, Assoc. Professor of History and Director, African & African American Studies, on her (and co-author, Dr. Janann Sherman's) new book, *Beale Street* (Arcadia Press)
Harris Concert Hall
7:30 p.m. – Faculty Jazz Players and Dance Troupe, "The Swing Era Begins!"

April 16-18 - Monday-Wednesday
McWherter Library Rotunda
Displays of scholarly and creative work of University faculty

April 19 - Thursday
Rose Theatre
1:30 p.m. – Faculty processional
2 p.m. – Spring Convocation and awards presentation
3:30 p.m. – Reception
3:30-4:30 p.m. – Display featuring scholarly and creative work of University faculty in Rose Theatre Lobby
University of Memphis Holiday Inn, 3700 Central Ave.
5:30 p.m. – "Great Conversations": Dinner and conversations with over 20 faculty scholars For tickets call 678-1435.
$75 per person • cas.memphis.edu/conversations

A Tennesse Board of Regents Institution. An Equal Opportunity/Affirmative Action University. • UOM15406-0607/1M PEERLESS PRINTING

Figure 3-B   Faculty Scholarship Week Flyer

- All display tables were staffed by officers and members of the Friends of Libraries to answer questions and provide information to those who stopped to view the materials.
- Staff from the Advanced Learning Center of the U of M FedEx Institute of Technology also created a display to join that of the Friends of Libraries.
- Faculty Scholarship Week featured a number of other events, such as musical concerts, noonday lectures in the McWherter Library rotunda, and a "Great Conversations" event sponsored by the College of Arts & Sciences.

Results

Many people stopped by the display tables to remark at the number and variety of the faculty's scholarly creations. The Friends also distributed Friends membership forms at the display tables. All in all, the week was a notable success for both the University of Memphis and its Friends of Libraries group.

ᴄᴏ ᴏᴠ

3-3   Honoring Faculty Scholars—Wake Forest (NC) University

On the second Friday in November, the Z. Smith Reynolds Library at Wake Forest University (Winston-Salem, NC) cohosts a reception and dinner honoring faculty authors, editors, and fine and performing artists. This began three years ago when the library joined the Associate Provost for Research in honoring faculty scholars. The first year was a reception only; in succeeding years it was followed by a five-course dinner in the library's atrium. Authors of journal articles are not included, as there are too many of them! A separate reception takes place for external grant recipients.

The Research Office has been very generous in inviting all library liaisons to attend the event so that they can develop closer relationships with faculty authors. The event is funded entirely by the Research Office. One of their librarians compiles the list of works primarily from the Institutional Research Web site, which lists faculty publications by department.

A fun side-note to the event has been the production of READ posters. The intent is to produce READ posters (which the American Library Association encourages by selling the graphics software) featuring authors of award-winning books. The first READ poster child was the University President, Nathan Hatch, who published an award-winning book at his previous institution. The series now includes posters of Reynolds Professor Maya Angelou, renowned scholar Allen Mandelbaum, and *New York Times* bestselling author John McNally, which are displayed prominently in the atrium.

How It Works

- Establish a partnership with the Research Office.
- Offer to host a celebration event honoring faculty authors.
- Compile a list of publications and performances by faculty that occurred in the last fiscal year.
- Invite all honored faculty and liaison librarians.
- Plan the dinner and program.
- Select an award-winning author to be honored with a READ poster. Secure the READ graphics software from the American Library Association (visit www.ala.org or call 800-545-2433). Arrange a publicity photo and produce the READ poster.
- Enjoy the show!

Results

Nearly 100 faculty members and librarians attend this event each year. It sets the library at the focal point of faculty scholarship on campus. The READ posters are seen by all who come into the grand atrium of the library and encourage reading, literacy, and scholarship at all levels.

Figure 3-C   Faculty Scholarship Display

3-4 Celebrating Scholarly and Creative Works at the University of Cincinnati (OH)

Each spring, University of Cincinnati's University Libraries hold the annual Authors, Editors & Composers event to celebrate scholarly and creative works published in the previous year by the university's faculty. The event includes a reception, presentation by selected faculty members, a printed bibliography, and an exhibit of the published works. While the majority of the works submitted to Authors, Editors & Composers are books and journal articles, there are also DVDs, musical scores, paintings, photographs, creative writings, and book chapters.

At the event, the dean and university librarian, along with the senior vice president and provost, give brief remarks, and three selected faculty members discuss their work. Attendees are invited to view the exhibit of published works and to enjoy light refreshments.

After the event, the exhibit is moved to the central library's fourth and fifth floors and runs until mid-June (after the university's commencement ceremony). The year 2007 marked the 16th year University Libraries held this event.

How It Works

The director of library communications organizes Authors, Editors & Composers.

- Set the date and location: In the fall, a date and location are determined for the event based on several factors, including availability of desired location(s), other competing events taking place on campus, the dean's and provost's schedules, and the campus calendar.
- Call for submissions: In January, a call is issued to faculty requesting that they submit their publications for inclusion in the event. The initial call is made via a faculty listserv, with two to three reminders. A printed postcard is mailed to all faculty members in February reminding them of the call to submit publications. The deadline for submitting publications to Authors, Editors & Composers is typically in early March. Faculty members submit information regarding their publications via a Web site form. The director of library communications works with the university's publicity office to place announcements in the university press and on the university Web site to encourage participation.
- Print a bibliography: Once the submissions are received in March, work begins on the printed bibliography. The publication information provided on the Web site form is gathered and imported into a Word document, where it is organized by college and by author. The bibliography includes

the colleges, participating faculty, and published works. It is printed and given to attendees at the event.

- Create an exhibit of published works: An e-mail is sent to participating faculty asking them to send a copy of their publication(s) for use in the exhibit that will be on display both at the event and later in the central library. As the publications arrive, tags are made for each that includes the bibliographic information. Exhibit banners are designed and created for use both at the event and in the display in the library.
- Organize the logistics: Throughout the planning process, the director of library communications works with the campus catering service, musicians, the campus schedule, the library media department, and others to arrange the elements of the event. Typically, the event follows the same format—a catered affair with light refreshments and musician(s)—so the logistics are similar from year to year. A spreadsheet listing the tasks and a timeline for their completion keeps things organized and on schedule.
- Plan the event program: As the publications are submitted, the dean, university librarian, and director of library communications choose three faculty members to present their work at the event. The director of library communications contacts the three members and then corresponds with them regarding the details and expectations. Other speakers, such as the dean, university librarian, provost, and the president of the university, are confirmed, and speaker notes are written.
- Run the event: On the day of the event, the exhibit of published works is set up, along with chairs, tables, table settings, and any necessary audiovisual equipment. At the event, library staff and volunteers greet attendees and hand out name tags and bibliographies. They also help clean up at the end.
- Set up the exhibit: The day after the event, the exhibit of published works is moved to the central library's fourth and fifth floor display cases, where it remains through mid-June (after the university's commencement). Announcements about the exhibit are put into the university and library press.
- Return the publications: After commencement, the exhibit is taken down and the publications are returned to the faculty members. They receive a thank-you note for participating and a copy of the printed bibliography.

Budget

The Friends of University Libraries funds Authors, Editors & Composers. The budget of approximately $3,000 pays for the food and music at the event, exhibit materials, the printed bibliography, and submission reminder postcards.

Results

Authors, Editors & Composers is a positive outreach tool for the University Libraries. Participation and attendance at the event continues to grow each year. In 2007, 250 faculty members and 380 creative and scholarly works were represented. Participating faculty members represented each University of Cincinnati college plus five academic units, including University Libraries and the Division of Professional Practice. Each year, approximately 125 people attend the reception. The subsequent exhibit is open to the public and is located in an area in the central library that experiences a high volume of walk-through traffic.

The event and exhibit generate publicity in the university press, including announcements in the all-staff electronic newsletter, articles in the student newspaper, features in the university magazine, and articles and press releases on the University Libraries' Web site and in its newsletter. In addition, the frequent communications with the participating faculty throughout the planning process both promote the library and build positive relationships.

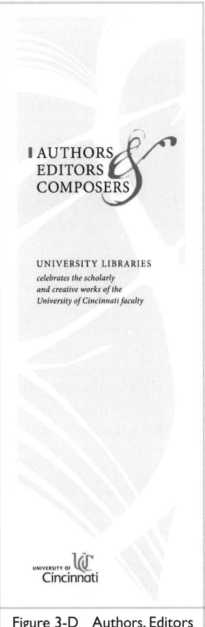

Figure 3-D   Authors, Editors & Composers Banner

3-5 A Day of Distinguished Speakers, Photography, and Music at the University of Memphis

The event was called "The Delta—Everything Southern!" More than 100 people, most of them Southern themselves, gathered in the Fogelman Executive Conference Center on the University of Memphis (TN) campus to learn about and be entertained by Southern culture. It was a perspective that even Southerners—especially Southerners, perhaps—rarely get.

The event was sponsored by Friends of the University of Memphis. The panel of presenters, moderated by a Friend of the Library member, mesmerized the audience with their personalities, knowledge, and tales of Southern life as experienced in the Mississippi Delta. Although the buffet luncheon was delicious and provided lively social interaction, extended during morning and afternoon breaks, it was the presentations that made the day memorable.

How It Worked

Howard Stovall, descendent of a family who settled on Delta land in the 1840s, provided insight into the cotton business past and present and speculated on what Delta cotton businesses would face in the future. Willie Bearden, who has documented Southern culture through his writings and films, regaled the audience with tales and photographs of blues musicians. David Evans, Professor in the University of Memphis School of Music, demonstrated Delta sounds on his guitar and in song as he explored the history of the blues and the people who contributed to the genre. Acclaimed photographer Maude Schuyler Clay showed images of Delta places such as Money and LeFlore County, Mississippi, where Emmett Till was murdered.

After lunch, the keynote speaker James Cobb, Professor of History at the University of Georgia and renowned author of several books on the South, shared the scholarship that enabled him to write *The Most Southern Place on Earth: The Mississippi Delta and the Roots of Regional Identity*. Paul Canonici, retired pastor and author, focused on the Italians who migrated to the Delta to find life unexpectedly challenging. After the presentations were completed, the audience was eager to ask questions of the presenters. A few in the audience even added information that contributed further to the insight gained from the speakers.

Results

At the end of the day, attendees could be heard expressing the pleasure gained from the event and requesting that another be held the next year. A future program under the banner "The Delta—Everything Southern!" is currently being planned. Topics include the impact of the Civil War on the Delta, the literature and writers of the

Delta, important historical personages of the Delta, the music of the Delta, and the history and importance of Dockery Farms, and more are yet to be finalized. The Delta seminar will be open to the public and will include a nice lunch and free parking along with refreshment breaks. The cost is expected to again be around $50.

ᖰᕼ ᕼᖰ

3-6 Faces of Courage

A newly created Friends group for the Dundee Township (IL) Public Library District worked with their library director to present a program on the subject of courage. The library had received grants from the American Library Association and from the National Endowment for the Humanities that included a donation of books focusing on courage. The library then decided to sponsor a series of programs involving real-life heroes and their stories of courage.

The Friends were eager to help out as their first project. The Friends immediately began planning an event that would connect the library with community members, and soon the Faces of Courage program was born.

How It Worked

The first step was to invite community members to nominate people who embodied courage, such as a firefighter who saved a family from a burning house or a tireless fund-raiser working for the local hospital. The Friends wanted to show the community that anyone can be a hero and that it is important to recognize everyone who acts like one.

The Friends used the local newspapers to send out the call for nominations. Library staff members were encouraged to talk to friends and neighbors and to explain the nomination forms to patrons while checking out books. Friends members spoke with local Lions clubs, Rotary clubs, VFW organizations, chambers of commerce, women's leagues, school districts, and other active social groups in hopes of finding many "faces of courage" from the more than 54,000 residents throughout the five communities in the library district. The Friends planned a luncheon and invited the nominees to attend a ceremony at the luncheon.

Friends members split into committees to address the different aspects of the Faces of Courage program. One group was in charge of the actual luncheon, including decorations, food, and seating. Friends went out into the community soliciting donations from local restaurants and businesses in order to support their meager funds. Another group was in charge of publicity and materials, including a brochure with pictures of the nominees. The last group was in charge of the nominees, including selection, invitations, and award certificates.

The luncheon was held in the library meeting room where tables were set up and the room festively decorated. Invitations were sent to the 20 nominees, and the local media were invited. The Friends were looking forward to seeing the outcome of their first event.

Results

Six months after the Friends were formed, they held a successful Faces of Courage luncheon. Eighteen nominees were present for the awards ceremony, as was the library director, those who nominated their heroes, and the local media. Each nominee was presented with a certificate of recognition after his or her name and courageous deeds were read.

Although they differed in so many ways, all the heroes were alike in another. These people had done courageous acts, ranging from fighting wars to maintaining a positive attitude while undergoing chemotherapy; however, none displayed anything

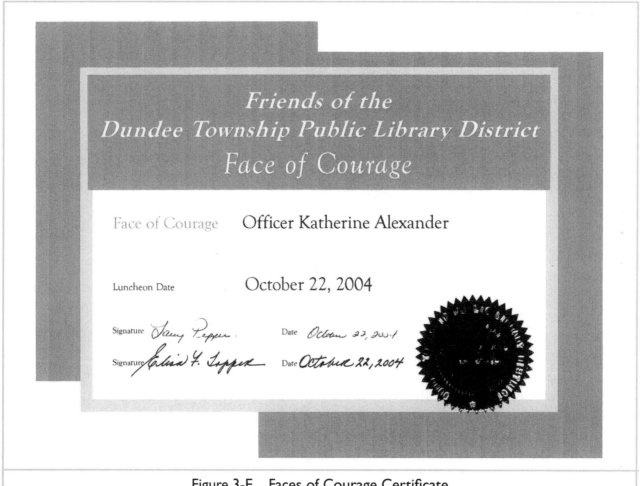

Figure 3-E   Faces of Courage Certificate

more than modesty. This humble group and the grateful crowd was the measure of success the Friends were looking for.

The program served as a bridge to connect the library, members of the community, and local organizations. The media loved the story and made sure that everyone knew who these "faces of courage" were. They also proved that few would have known had it not been for the efforts of the Dundee Library and the brand new Friends.

ᴄᴥᴅ ᴥ

3-7 Author Program for Annual Friends Meeting

The Friends of the Henderson (KY) Public Library almost always present an author program for their annual meeting. In their town of 27,000 (or the metropolitan area, which is around 200,000), usually someone has recently published a book that will be of local interest. In addition, the Kentucky Humanities Council sponsors a Chautauqua program that features writers and others who have agreed to speak around the state for a nominal fee (traveling and hotel expenses).

Last year, the Friends presented the Chautauqua speaker Sena Jeter Naslund, whose book, *Abundance: A Novel of Marie Antoinette*, had coincidentally just been released that day. The Friends considered her appearance the beginning of her national tour!

After the speaker concludes, the Friends serve cookies and punch. This gives the audience a chance to mingle and have their turn talking with the author. In addition to their annual meetings, the Friends sponsor book signings throughout the year for local authors who contact them (they do not offer an honorarium in these cases). By supporting local authors, the Friends feel they are providing a good service for the community and for the author as well.

How It Works

- Summer: Determine who to invite to be the guest speaker.
- Summer: Contact speaker to make arrangements.
- Summer: Arrange and schedule a room for the event.
- Summer: Arrange accommodations for speaker, if necessary.
- Fall: Send press release to local media. For a longer article, the newspaper usually arranges to interview the speaker. The radio often asks members of the Friends to appear on Speak Up, a morning talk show that highlights local events.
- Just prior to the event: Arrange for Friends to bring punch and cookies.

Results

So far, the Friends have never had an author charge a fee, but they always make it clear that they will present an honorarium (usually $100 and one of their Friends of the Henderson Library tote bags). At times, Barnes & Noble sends a representative to sell the speaker's books, and the Friends profit through a percentage of the sales. At other times, members of the Friends sell the book, or the author brings a friend to sell them. In addition to the author's book, the Friends also sell their tote bags, framed pictures of the library and of other historic local places, and other items that they generally have for sale at the library. Also, because this is their annual meeting, the group kicks off their membership drive that night.

A hundred people usually attend, and sometimes there are more. Because the Friends of the Henderson Public Library have presented a writer (or, at rare times, an enactor of historical matter) for many years, the public has come to look forward to their presentations. An added bonus is that the local newspaper and radio station always gives the Friends plenty of coverage.

⤳ ⤳

3-8　Talk of the Stacks at the Minneapolis (MN) Public Library

Talk of the Stacks is a reading series of The Friends of the Minneapolis Public Library, held at the Minneapolis Library, exploring contemporary culture and literature. The Friends host 12 to14 events annually. Like the library itself, Talk of the Stacks features a wide variety of literary forms—fiction, science, travel, history, poetry, mystery, biography, and so forth. It is diverse in format, mixing traditional single author readings with pairings of local and national authors and panel discussions on book topics.

The series is unified by its commitment to connecting leading authors with the Minneapolis community of readers. Talk of the Stacks participants have included Nancy Pearl, Matthew Pearl, Neil Baldwin, Charles Baxter, David Rakoff, Kate Di-Camillo, Dava Sobel, Judith Guest, Tess Gallagher, and Michael Dirda. In response to member requests, all Talk of the Stacks are recorded and made available on the group's Web site and on podcast directories such as iTunes.

How It Works

- Volunteers: The Friends put together a volunteer committee of local authors, publishers, community members, and media who help choose and solicit the talent.

- Partnerships with other organizations: The Friends meet with local publishers semiannually to learn about their upcoming books. The Friends also have strong relationships with national publishers to receive advance notice of book tours. These connections are critical to securing touring authors.
- Timeline: The Friends produce the Talk of the Stacks series all year long. They begin planning the book author events three to five months in advance; the longer the lead time, the more likely you are to get good media coverage.
- Working with the library: The program benefits from free use of the library's meeting spaces, free listings in its events catalogs and on its Web site, and distribution of posters and postcards through its internal mail.

Tip list to get Friends programming in the media at a low cost:

❑ If the presenters involved in your event have Web sites or e-mail lists, request that they promote the event.

❑ If your "friends" and "partners" have newsletters or e-mail lists, request they promote the event.

❑ Submit events to specific college department Web sites topically associated with your event, such as English, Creative Writing, Art History, Sciences, and others.

❑ Use face time at events to announce future events and get members signed up for e-mails.

❑ Look beyond traditional publications for calendars, poster distribution, and blogs.

❑ Use e-mail and Web resources. We use Constant Contact.

❑ Make sure to use internal publications that already have a print budget like newsletters, catalogs, annual reports, etc.

❑ Do not overprint—outline where and to whom you will distribute print pieces in advance of choosing your print run.

❑ Put multiple events on 1 print piece.

Figure 3-F Tips to Get Friends Programming in the Media at a Low Cost
—Friends of the Minneapolis (MN) Public Library

Budget

The Friends have a healthy budget ($20,000) to produce a color postcard for each mailing as part of their sponsorship agreement, but they have implemented the following measures to keep costs low or to bring in revenue:

- To avoid costly honorariums, the Friends utilize local authors in unique pairings or nationally renowned authors who are on a book tour.
- When requesting a national author on book tour, they put in a request to the publisher five to six months in advance.
- The Friends partner with a local hotel to provide complimentary lodging for out-of-town authors.
- The Friends have also partnered with a local bookstore to handle the book sales at the library, and they receive 10 percent of the sales. The Talk of

Figure 3-G   Talk of the Stacks Postcard (Front)

the Stacks benefits from cross-promotion and attracts more publishers and authors because of the potentially greater book sales. The partnership also reduces the volunteer and staff time required to present each reading.

- The Friends solicited a local magazine to donate a free ad each month and to mention the events online and in e-news blasts.
- The events are featured on the library's Web site and in its newsletters.
- For the past two years, a corporation has donated money to help offset staff and publicity costs.
- All donors are recognized in publicity, at the events, online, and in publications.

Results

Total attendance for readings and related events for the first year of Talk of the Stacks was 2,170. The promotional reach extended much further. The series received significant media coverage, especially from Minnesota Public Radio, which overlaps particularly well with their target demographic. Nancy Pearl and Neil Baldwin were both featured in hour-long midmorning interviews. George Rabasa and Tess Gallagher

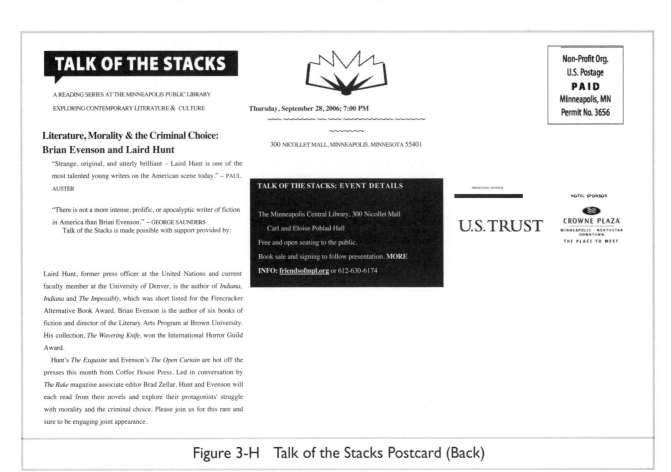

Figure 3-H   Talk of the Stacks Postcard (Back)

were profiled on the evening show *All Things Considered*. Dava Sobel was interviewed by the local NBC affiliate. Additional coverage was provided by state and local newspapers, magazines, and other radio stations. *The Rake* magazine was so impressed by the quality of programming that it has asked to become a promotional sponsor.

The program provides a great vehicle to engage the Friends' current members and to make prospective members aware of their organization. In addition, the Friends have been able to engage major donors more in depth by inviting them to pre-receptions and private lunches and dinners with the authors when they are available. The program is a great stewardship and recruitment tool.

೮ᴑ ᴑ꬇

3-9   From One Note to a Symphony: One Book, One Community

When the Friends of the Stark County District Library (Canton, OH) were given a copy of the book *The Children of Willesden Lane*, by Mona Golabek and Lee Cohen, the donor explained that the book was written as a tribute to the author's mother and that Mona Golabek herself was a world renowned concert pianist. Being deeply moved by the book's themes of survival, courage, identity, belonging, and a passion to achieve one's dreams, the Friends felt the book would be perfect for a gala event featuring it and a performance by its author. The event would be a fund-raiser for their scholarship fund, which awards grants to library employees pursuing an advanced degree in library science.

When the Friends found out that the Mayor's Literacy Commission was planning its first "One Book, One Community" project, they felt that Golabek's book would be perfect. They nominated the book and it was selected.

The Friends later learned that the Milken Foundation had funded the development of a teacher's study guide for the book and that several school districts around the country had incorporated it into their curriculums. It was clear that the city schools needed to be involved as well.

How It Worked

- Books were purchased with contributions from the Canton City Schools, the Mayor's Literacy Commission's Literacy Partners, and Mona Golabek's personal manager.
- Special requests made to individuals, Friends of the Library life members, local colleges, area Rotary clubs, foundations, local businesses, and the Jewish Federation funded two performances by Ms. Golabek.
- Special discussion sessions with preselected themes were planned. Each session consisted of a brief presentation by panel members who reflected

on the theme and shared their reactions to the book. Following the presentation, community members asked questions and shared their personal feelings about the book and its themes.

- The kickoff discussion session was held at the central library, and the library director was one of the panelists.

- Three other sessions were planned at various sites around the community.

- To kick off the school component of the project, Eric Snow, a graduate of a local high school and a Cleveland Cavaliers guard, spoke to city school students about the importance of libraries, reading, and setting goals.

- Students read the book and participated in classroom activities related to the book.

- Students and participants were invited to two concert performances by Mona Golabek.

Join the Community

Everyone is invited to take part in this program by reading the book and attending one or more of these discussion sessions, which are free and open to the public.

Monday, October 17, at 7 p.m.
Community Leaders Choose to Make a Difference
Location: Stark County District Library
715 Market Avenue N, Canton
Monday, October 31, at 1:30 p.m.
Personal Memories of Music – Love and Survival
Location: Massillon Senior Center
39 Lincoln Way West, Massillon
Monday, October 31, at 7 p.m.
Survival – Refugees Past and Present
Location: Temple Israel
333 25th Street NW, Canton
Thursday, November 10, at 7 p.m.
Bridging the Gaps That Divide Us
Location: Deliverance Christian Church
2130 31st Street NW, Canton
Thursday, November 17, at 11:45 a.m.
Hold On to Your Music and Your Dreams
Location: Canton Museum of Art
1001 Market Avenue N, Canton
Brown bag lunch

Presentations by the Author

Monday, November 21, at 9 a.m.
The Book and the Music
Umstadt Hall, McKinley High School
2323 17th Street NW, Canton
Monday, November 21, at 7 p.m.
The Book and the Music
Church of the Savior United Methodist
120 Cleveland Avenue SW, Canton

Literacy Commission Partners

AEP Ohio	Lee Thomas Construction
AFL-CIO	Lowry Lithograph
James Anderson	Marathon Petroleum Company
Aultman Hospital	Mercy Medical Center
City of Canton	Merrill Lynch
DLH Industries	Motter & Meadows Architects
Duncan Press, Inc.	The Repository
Everhard Products	Sam's Club
First Merit Bank	Stark County District Library
Friends of the	Stark Industrial, Inc.
Stark County Library	The Timken Company
Key Foundation	Unizan Bank
	Wal-Mart

Mona Golabek Project Sponsorships

Platinum
Herbert L. Fisher
Rotary Clubs of Stark County
Gold
Canton Marriott - McKinley Grand Hotel
Silver
Kent State University - Stark Campus
Leona Genshaft
Martha Lottman
Dave & Jeanne Freitag
Mr. & Mrs. Robert Vail
Canton Jewish Community Federation
Steinway Hall - Akron
Bronze
Walsh University
Black & Davis Pianos
Mrs. A.L. Riegler
Dr. Niall Slater & Thelma Slater
Mr. & Mrs. G. W. Bradshaw
Corita Childs
Susan Swallen
Jess & Carol Simon
William & Sharon Luntz
Allen & Christine Schulman

One
Book
ONE COMMUNITY

Canton, Ohio
A Community-Wide Reading
Program

The Children of
Willesden Lane

By Mona Golabek

Figure 3-1   One Book, One Community Brochure (Outside)

Results

The kickoff event for the school component of the project drew 125 students. As publicity about the school project circulated throughout the county, other school districts wanted to become involved. The project ultimately grew to include over 1,300 students representing six Stark County school districts and a Youth Arts Council group.

Attendance at community sessions continued to rise over the course of the project, and the Friends sold over 100 copies of the book as well as raised money to support their scholarship fund. The Friends reported that they were passionate about providing an enriching experience for students, a magnificent fund-raiser for their scholarship fund, and a literary bond for their community. They persevered and reached their goals.

One Book – One Community

"What would happen if everybody in the community read the same book?" One Book-One Community founding organizers asked the same question in Seattle, Washington in 1998. They found their answer, and now with more than 300 communities participating, One Book-One Community is a resounding success. Beginning in September, the Mayor's Literacy Commission will invite the Stark County community to join together in reading the same book and participating in group discussions of the themes that emerge from the book itself. Five different locations have been chosen for the events which conclude with an appearance by the author.

Community Ties

Co-sponsored by the Mayor's Literacy Commission, Friends of the Stark County District Library, Canton City Schools, the City of Canton and the Repository, the goal of the program is to encourage reading and to forge community bonds where citizens of all ages and backgrounds will become linked by reading and discussing the same book.

Read the Book

Reading the book along with friends, family, fellow students, co-workers and other community members is the first step in the program. Next, to enrich your experience, you are encouraged to attend one or more group discussions.

Books may be borrowed from the libraries or purchased at the Friends of the Stark County Library bookstore or local bookstores.

About the Book

"The Children of Willesden Lane" is a deeply moving, poignantly written book by Mona Golabek as a tribute to her mother, Lisa Jura. In 1938, fourteen-year-old Lisa Jura said goodbye to her mother at a Vienna train station. Lisa's mother spoke words that would inspire her for a lifetime: "Hold on to your music. It will be your best friend."

An aspiring pianist, Jura traveled from Vienna to England aboard the Kinderstransport, a train that took 10,000 children out of Europe to England to save them from the Nazi peril. Throughout World War II, Jura continued to nurture her dream of becoming a concert pianist as she lived in an orphanage on Willesden Lane with other displaced children.

Golabek's book has been embraced throughout the U.S. It has been chosen for various city-wide reading projects and has been incorporated in the Canton City Schools academic curriculum.

Discussion Sessions

Three primary themes emerge from the book – **music, love and survival.** The five scheduled discussion sessions will begin with brief presentations by panel members who will touch on these themes as they reflect on their reactions to the book. Audience members will then be invited to ask questions of panelists and to share their own feelings about the book.

About the Author

In addition to being the author of "The Children of Willesden Lane," Mona Golabek is a world renowned Steinway artist. In 1984, she was awarded the prestigious Avery Fisher Prize. Golabek, who has been nominated for a Grammy, has played with numerous orchestras at such venues as the Hollywood Bowl, the Kennedy Center, the Lincoln Center and London's Festival Hall. In 1998, she debuted "The Romantic Hours," a nationally syndicated classical music radio program during which she shares inspirational readings.

•**All events are free and open to the public.**

• **Please call the Mayor's Literacy Commission at 330-458-2633 to register for each event you wish to attend.**

• **You may submit your written comments about the book for possible publication in The Repository or on the Stark County District Library's web site. Send to the Commission at 715 N. Market, Canton, OH 44702.**

Figure 3-J   One Book, One Community Brochure (Inside)

3-10   The People's University at the Minneapolis (MN) Public Library

The People's University offers free classes in the library taught by local professors and cultural experts on a variety of subjects from art history to poetry to rap music to archaeology. The Friends of the Minneapolis Public Library typically organize and sponsor 10 to 15 classes annually, with each course meeting one to three times. This exciting educational program provides everyone in the community a fun and intellectually stimulating way to continue their education and to participate in a college class. For some, The People's University is a step into higher education—a safe entry point without fees, bureaucracy, or exams. For others, it is an opportunity to reconnect with higher education as an adult and participate in lifelong learning. In response to member requests, some People's University classes are recorded and made available on the group's Web site and through podcast directories such as iTunes.

How It Works

- Partnerships: The Friends partnered with different community organizations to develop each course. The partnerships expanded their publicity and audience and created a wonderful pool of expertise, talent, and educational resources. Partners in 2006 included The College of Saint Catherine Center for Women, Economic Justice and Public Policy; Mill City Museum; Minnesota Planetarium Society; Minnesota Public Radio; Springboard for the Arts; Hubert H. Humphrey Institute of Public Affairs at University of Minnesota; University of Minnesota Extension; Walker Art Center; and Witness Tree Literary Arts Education, Inc.
- Timeline: The program began as a summer program but has now expanded into a year-round series, with three-week classes in the summer and one-time-only lectures throughout the year. To accommodate better planning, advance registration for The People's University courses is required. The Friends predict they will have about 15 classes in 2008.
- Working with the Library: The program benefits from free use of the library's meeting spaces, free listings in its events catalogs and on its Web site, and distribution of posters and postcards through its internal mail.

Budget

The Friends offer honorariums to all lecturers, but by partnering with local cultural organizations (and including their name in publicity materials) the Friends are able to attract high-level presenters at a lower cost. To accommodate better planning, advance registration for The People's University courses is required. The Marquette Financial Companies (Minnesota-based financial services) provide financial sup-

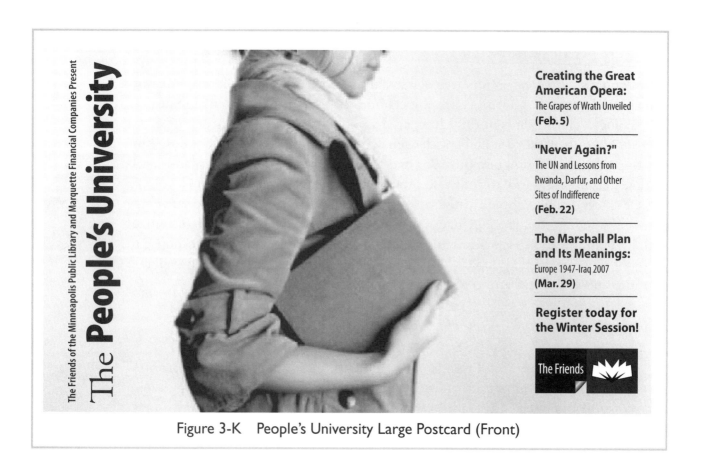

Figure 3-K   People's University Large Postcard (Front)

port. The Friends produce three brochures a year, each listing about four to seven programs for each series.

Results

In 2006, The People's University offered eight free classes (each meeting three or four times) and served 650 students with 2,900 classroom hours. Six out of eight classes were filled to capacity with waiting lists.

The Friends surveyed students at the last session of each course to measure satisfaction and to help guide them as they develop future courses. Students ranged in age from 17 to 85 years, with a nice mix of each age group. In all, 97 percent of respondents ranked the instructors and class content "good" or "excellent." Over 70 percent of the students had never taken a People's University course before, and 25 percent of them had never taken a college class before.

3-11   Sample Promotional Materials

MANSFIELD READS!
One City, One Book

The Friends of the Mansfield Public Library are proud to sponsor **Mansfield Reads!** *One City, One Book*. The first Mansfield Reads! program took place in April 2004. It was such a great success that we are doing it again. The featured book for 2005 is *Had A Good Time: Stories From American Postcards* by Pulitzer Prize winner Robert Olen Butler.

How does it work? In the month of April everyone in the community is encouraged to read the same book at the same time. The Friends and the Library sponsor many events, programs and activities in conjunction with reading the book. Public dialogue and discussion of the book is encouraged as a way to open conversation between all members of the community. Everyone gets to share a good book!

For more information visit www.mansfieldreads.org or call the library at 817-473-4391.

APRIL 2005

"Fifteen gloriously imaginative and utterly hypnotizing short stories [are] gathered here in a book destined to enrapture a broad readership. . . .Scintillating, soulful, and surprising, Butler's virtuoso stories are deeply satisfying."
— Donna Seaman, *Booklist* (Starred Review)

"I'll never stop believing it: Robert Olen Butler is the best living American writer, period."
— Jeff Guinn, Book Editor, *Fort Worth Star Telegram*

MANSFIELD READS!
One City, One Book

"All of Mansfield reads the same book at the same time."

MANSFIELD PUBLIC LIBRARY

Mansfield Reads!
One City, One Book.
Friends of the Mansfield Public Library

Figure 3-L   Mansfield (TX) Reads Brochure (Outside)

HAD A GOOD TIME

STORIES FROM AMERICAN POSTCARDS

ROBERT OLEN BUTLER
Pulitzer Prize-winning author of A Good Scent from a Strange Mountain

www.mansfieldreads.org

"Fifteen gloriously imaginative and utterly hypnotizing short stories [are] gathered here in a book destined to enrapture a broad readership."

-Donna Seaman, *Booklist*
(Starred Review)

"I'll never stop believing it: Robert Olen Butler is the best living American writer, period."

-Jeff Guinn, Book Editor,
Fort Worth Star Telegram

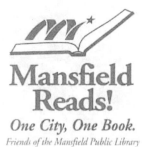

Mansfield Reads!
One City, One Book.
Friends of the Mansfield Public Library

Thanks to our 2005 sponsors:

First Edition Sponsor
Methodist Hospital

Leather Bound Sponsors
Ramtech Building Systems
Linco Contractors

Classic Sponsors
Cricket Alley
Walnut Creek Animal Clinic
All American Insurance
FastSigns, S. Arlington
ChemGuard
Supreme Lending
Bartolucci Custom Homes
Flowers, Etc.
Millennium Family Entertainment Center
Turf Masters
Mansfield Glass and Mirror

Tom Thumb
One Fine Day Caterers
Comfort Inn
Nuthouse Grill
Blue Bell Ice Cream

Barnes & Noble
Mansfield News Mirror
Fort Worth Star Telegram
JMH Printing
Rick Sales Graphics Pad
SPECIAL THANKS TO
DELLA ICENHOWER

Mansfield Reads!
One City, One Book.
Friends of the Mansfield Public Library

Figures 3-M & N   Mansfield (TX) Reads Bookmark (Enclosure)
(Front-*Left*, Back-*Right*)

MANSFIELD READS!
One City, One Book
2005 Events

March 28: KICK-OFF
Mayor Mel Neuman proclaims April as Mansfield Reads! month and announces *Had A Good Time: Stories From American Postcards* by Pulitzer Prize winner Robert Olen Butler as the featured book for the second annual community reading program.

March 29-April 30: BOOKS AVAILABLE
Get your copy of *Had A Good Time* at the Friends Bookstore at the library, Barnes and Noble on S. Cooper St. or bn.com, and the Mansfield Tom Thumb Store. The library also has many copies available for checkout.

March 29-April 30: @ YOUR LIBRARY
Visit the library to see Mansfield's own American Postcards from the collection of Della Icenhower. See displays related to the setting of *Had A Good Time* and memorabilia from Mansfield's Turn of the Century presented by the Mansfield Historical Society.

April 11-April 16: NATIONAL LIBRARY WEEK
Visit the library for ongoing activities during the National Library Week observance. Check out the works of Robert Olen Butler and other Pulitzer Prize winners.

April 16: TURN OF THE CENTURY DAY 11:00 a.m. – 3:00 p.m.
Spend the day in the midst of the turn of the century! See antique cars, watch the movie The Music Man, have some popcorn, peanuts and Cracker Jacks or check out the general store penny candy counter. Come hear Mansfield's Barbershop Quartet. At 1:00 p.m., bring the kids to see Dale Cosgrove present "The Sound of the Times", a musical program that entertains and teaches about music at the turn of the century.

April 19: AS THE PAGE TURNS - 6:30 p.m.
Join the library book club for a discussion of *Had A Good Time*. Reader's guides for book discussion groups are available at the library or www.mansfield reads.org.

April 29: AN EVENING WITH ROBERT OLEN BUTLER - 6:00 p.m.
Join the Friends of the Mansfield Public Library and Jeff Guinn of the Fort Worth Star Telegram in an evening with Robert Olen Butler. Space is limited for this invitation only event. For more information or *to request an invitation* call 817-453-2273.

April 30: WRITER'S WORKSHOP – 10:00a.m. – 12:00 noon
Robert Olen Butler will present a writer's workshop using *Had A Good Time* and his new book From Where You Dream:The Process of Writing Fiction. Space is limited. **Registration is required**. Form is available in the library, at www.mansfieldreads.org or by calling 817-453-2273.

To visit Robert Olen Butler's archived interactive writing class on the web go to www.FSU.edu then search "inside creative writing".

Visit www.mansfieldreads.org for more information

Figure 3-O   Mansfield (TX) Reads Brochure (Inside)

CELEBRATE 10 YEARS OF

The 2006 Concert Series Presents

Music @ the Library

A Series of Quality Music Performances

Presented by

The Pasco County Board of County Commissioners
The Friends of the Pasco County Library System, Inc.
The City of Zephyrhills
and Individual Contributors

Music @ the Library

*The Friends of the Pasco County Library System, Inc.
invite you to attend the other programs
in our Concert Series...*

Joseph Swartz
Concert Pianist
Sunday, January 8, 2006
@ 2:00 p.m.
Hudson Regional Library
8012 Library Road, Hudson
Telephone: (727) 861-3040

Z Street Band
Swing, Jazz & Big Band
Sunday, January 22, 2006
@ 2:00 p.m.
South Holiday Library
4649 Mile Stretch Drive, Holiday
Telephone: (727) 834-3331

Brotherhood A Cappella
Doo-Wop
Sunday, January 29, 2006
@ 2:00 p.m.
New River Library
34043 S.R. 54, Zephyrhills
Telephone: (813) 788-6375

Jammin' Jambalaya
Dixieland
Sunday, February 12, 2006
@ 2:00 p.m.
Zephyrhills City Hall
5335 Eighth Street, Zephyrhills
Telephone: (813) 780-0064

Florida Orchestra Brass Quintet
Sunday, February 19, 2006
@ 2:00 p.m.
Centennial Park Library
5740 Moog Road, Holiday
Telephone: (727) 834-3204

John & Mary K. Wilson
Sunday, February 26, 2006
@ 2:00 p.m.
New River Library
34043 S.R. 54, Zephyrhills
Telephone: (813) 788-6375

Opera Workshop from USF
*Vignettes from "The Magic Flute"
Celebrating Mozart's 250th Birthday*
Sunday, March 5, 2006
@ 2:00 p.m.
South Holiday Library
4649 Mile Stretch Drive, Holiday
Telephone: (727) 834-3331

Arioso
*String Quartet from the Florida
Orchestra "Classical Meets Jazz"*
Sunday, March 19, 2006
@ 2:00 p.m.
Hudson Regional Library
8012 Library Road, Hudson
Telephone: (727) 861-3040

Figure 3-P   Friends of the Pasco County (FL) Public Library Concert Series Brochure (Outside)

PROGRAM

Sweet Georgia Brown
Dinah
Bourbon Street Parade
Birth of the Blues
Just a Closer Walk with Thee
Jambalaya
I've Found a New Baby
Doctor Jazz
The Preacher
What a Wonderful World
Basin Street Blues
Shine
I Can't Give You Anything But Love
Mardi Gras in New Orleans
Hey, Bah Bah Ree Bop
Kansas City
Lady Be Good
Won't You Come Home, Bill Bailey
Do You Know What It Means
Hello Dolly
Radio
Blackbird
Mardi Gras Mambo
Tin Roof Blues
When The Saints Go Marchin' In

The Friends want to thank the Music Advisory Committee:
Mrs. Marsha Goldstein, Mrs. Marie Hanff, Mrs. Ruth Urbanski and Mr. Ron Turner

A special thank you to our Supporters:
Barbe Bonjour & Otis G. Pike, *Angel*
Helen Parente, Louis & Denise Vanacore, *Special Friend*

Refreshments are provided courtesy of the Zephyrhills Historical Association.
Sound and video recording is prohibited.

TICKET PRICE:
$3.00

General Seating. Doors Open 30 Minutes
Before Performance. First Come, First Served.

On Sale Day of Concert, Beginning @ 1:30 p.m.

Jammin' Jambalaya
Sunday, February 12, 2006

Jammin' Jambalaya is a 5-piece musical group lead by husband and wife team, Mark and Kathy Zauss. Together they are dedicated to keeping the music of New Orleans alive by performing a unique mix of Dixieland, Mardi Gras, and traditional American music. Jammin' Jambalaya features trumpet virtuoso Mark Zauss who is endorsed by the Conn-Selmer musical instrument corporation. Vocalist and entertainer Kathy Zauss has performed in some of America's finest showrooms, including Rosie O'Grady's Good Time Emporium, and The Mississippi Queen Steamboat. Mark and Kathy's company, Band Source Productions, Inc. is based out of Orlando, and their bands perform for over 140 events annually.

Figure 3-Q   Friends of the Pasco County (FL) Public Library Concert Series Brochure (Inside)

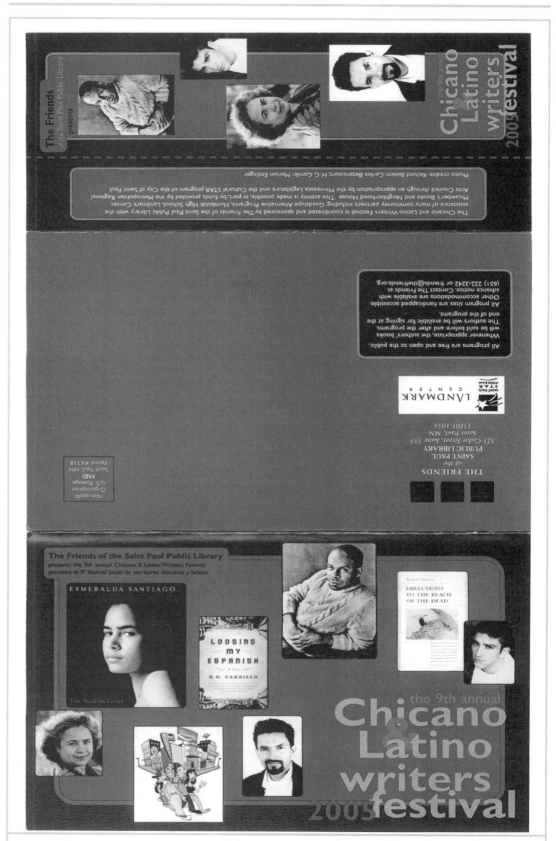

Figure 3-R   The Friends of the Saint Paul (MN) Public Library Writers
Festival Brochure (Outside)

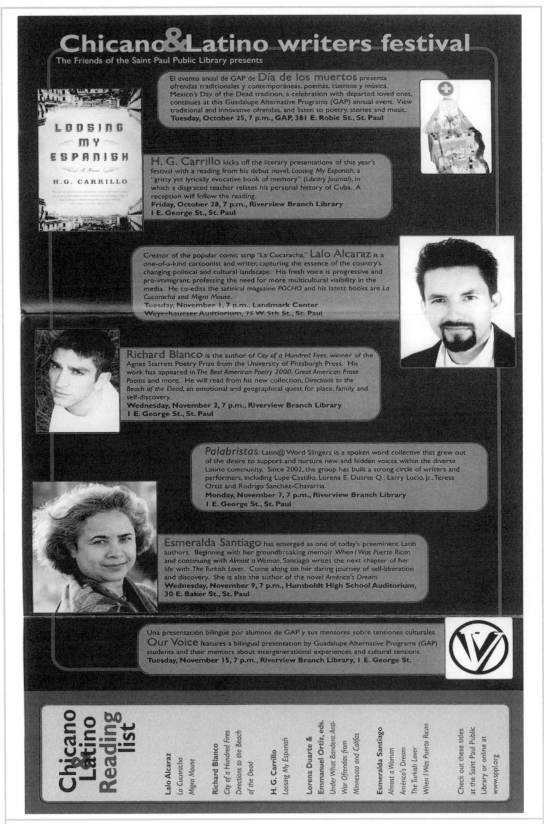

Figure 3-S   The Friends of the Saint Paul (MN) Public Library Writers Festival Brochure (Inside)

The Friends of the Saint Paul Public Library presents the 11th annual Fireside Literary Series

Come join us

by the fire

Come in from the cold and stoke your literary fire with free author readings during The Friends' annual Fireside Series. Pull up a chair by the hearth at the Hamline Midway Branch Library.

Nonprofit
Organization
U.S. Postage
PAID
Saint Paul, MN
Permit #6318

THE FRIENDS
of the
SAINT PAUL PUBLIC LIBRARY
Suite 555
325 Cedar Street
Saint Paul, MN 55101

Join Fireside Readers

Don't forget to join Fireside Readers! From January 20 through February 24, you can enter your name for a grand prize drawing of Fireside authors' books and Friends merchandise!

Stop by or call the Hamline Midway Branch Library (651/642-0293) for details on how to participate and win!

Visit Micawber's Books at 2238 Carter Avenue, Saint Paul.

Hamline Midway Branch Library

Lexington
Snelling
Minnehaha

Figure 3-T   The Friends of the St. Paul (MN) Public Library Fireside Literary Series Brochure (Outside)

120

Hamline Branch Library
1558 West Minnehaha Avenue, Saint Paul

Fireside Readings

Co-sponsored by Micawbers Books

Minnesota Authors

Susan Power

January 20, 7:00 pm

Susan Power reads from *Roofwalker*, which weaves the forces of tradition and belief in the lives of modern Native Americans through both fictional and non-fictional pieces. The end result is a powerful blend of story and history in which the spirits and the living commingle, where Sioux culture and modern life collide with power, humor and joy. Power is the author of the PEN/Hemingway Award-winning book, *The Grass Dancer*.

Valerie Miner

January 27, 7:00 pm

Valerie Miner reads from her new collection of short stories, *Abundant Light*. Miner's fourth collection of short fiction shows the evidence of a master storyteller at work as she explores the possibilities of forgiveness, acceptance and reunion. Miner is the award-winning author of eleven books, including *Range of Light*, *A Walking Fire* and the memoir. *The Low Road*.

Erin Hart

February 3, 7:00 pm

Erin Hart reads from *Lake of Sorrows*, her follow-up to the highly acclaimed *Haunted Ground*. Hart revisits the peat bogs of Ireland for her second mystery featuring pathologist Nora Gavin, as she investigates the murder of an archaeologist. She also returns to some well-liked characters, including Nora's sometime lover and investigative partner, archaeologist Cormac Maguire. *Publisher's Weekly* says that "Hart's language sings, and the gothic atmosphere lingers" in this rich novel of suspense.

Freya Manfred

February 10, 7:00 pm

Freya Manfred reads from her latest collection of poetry. *My Only Home*, a volume of meditation on life, death and observations of family, both hilarious and touching. The collection also includes illustrations by the author's twin sons. Manfred is the author of several books of poetry, including *American Roads* and *Yellow Squash Woman*. She is also the author of the poignant memoir *Frederick Manfred: A Daughter Remembers*.

Jack Weatherford

February 17, 7:00 pm

Jack Weatherford reads from his book *Genghis Khan and the Making of the Modern World*, a fascinating blend of personal and world history about Genghis Khan and the turmoil brought to the world by a nation of itinerant hunters. Weatherford also dismantles popular notions of Genghis Khan as a brutish personality—painting a portrait of a progressive free-trader, faithful Christian, regretful parent and a loving (polygamous) husband. Weatherford is also the author of *The History of Money and Indian Givers*.

David Haynes

February 24, 7:00 pm

David Haynes finishes the series with a reading from his recent novel. *The Full Matilda*. The daughter of an indispensible majordomo. Matilda Housewright grew up in the household of a powerful senator. As she begins to question who she is and who she is serving, Matilda must maneuver through a web of secrets, expectations and worn-out social mores in order to find answers. Haynes is the author of several critically acclaimed novels, including *All American Dream Dolls*, *Live at Five and Somebody Else's Mama*.

Figure 3-U   The Friends of the St. Paul (MN) Public Library Fireside Literary Series Brochure (Inside)

Chapter Four

Advocacy and Public Awareness

A member of a Friends group once said, "We can raise $20,000 through a book sale or $2,000,000 through an effective advocacy campaign, and they are both about the same amount of work!" While this may be a bit of an exaggeration, the truth is that libraries need advocates to ensure healthy budgets and the passage of bond issues and to educate the public about how important the library and all its services are.

This chapter shares the wonderful ways in which Friends are working as library "ambassadors" in Johnson County, Kansas, and how the Friends of the Wyndham Robertson Library at Hollins University in Roanoke, Virginia, are highlighting a very special collection. You'll find out how to create an advocacy campaign with a tool kit from the American Library Association, and you'll learn about passing a library-friendly Home Rule Charter Amendment from the Friends of the Fargo (ND) Public Library.

In addition to public awareness efforts for the library, you will learn about creating a high profile for Friends groups by capitalizing on National Friends of Libraries Week. The more you can highlight the group, the more members you can attract. The more members you attract, the more advocates the library has! It's a perfect circle.

Clearly, anyone who volunteers to work for or support the library is an advocate by default, but libraries and Friends groups need to be aggressive in ensuring that this default role becomes a major part of the Friends' mission. No one has more power in their voices than citizens! Many of the ideas, tips, and tool kits in this chapter will show you how to better use that power on behalf of the library.

4-1 Friends—The Library's Ambassadors

Because the Friends of the Johnson County (KS) Library volunteered to clean a local park, the Merriam Visitors Bureau is well on its way to having various historical locales and buildings in Merriam designated the Freedom's Frontier National Heritage Area. *Say What?* It happened like this: The bureau's executive director heard from Friends members who clean the Merriam Historic Plaza Park how much the library can help in researching practically anything, which "opened her eyes to the library." She submitted an inquiry to the library reference staff, the research was performed, and she was able to complete the application.

This is just one outcome of the Friends' new strategic plan that refocuses their energies on being ambassadors for the library. The Friends started as advocates, after all, emanating in 1956 from the group of founders that established the library. Advocacy had been its very first mission, and in 2006 members rededicated that focus.

The Need to Reevaluate

The Friends have a budget of more than $200,000, a membership base of 800 members, and an active board. The Friends donate more than $100,000 annually to the library to support the Summer Reading Club, adult programs, staff development, and collections. Sales of used books in its two bookstores in two library facilities and over the Internet generate a large portion of its annual budget. Hundreds of volunteers assist with sorting books, operating the stores, and tracking the sales.

In 2005, however, nearing their 50th anniversary year, the Friends realized that most of their effort during the past ten years was spent opening and running used bookstores in two libraries and conducting a whirlwind of book sales to raise money to support library programming and collections. Despite this large business operation, the Friends always considered their chief role to be advocacy, and they had compiled an impressive track record over the years in supporting library expansion to 13 facilities.

But, was "mission creep" invading the Friends? They admitted to themselves that selling books is easy, while advocacy—for many people—is harder. The logistics of coordinating bookstores and sales was sapping their energy and attention. In addition, the need to provide supplemental funding to the library was now being addressed by the new Johnson County Library Foundation, charged with raising millions of dollars to form an endowment for collections and to support programming. The Friends board felt the need to reevaluate.

The Resolution

The Friends board initiated a strategic planning process in 2005–2006 that resulted in a new vision focusing on library visibility and a strategic plan with specific activities, outcomes, and quantifiable measurements. This plan directed the Friends board to adjust its organizational structure to better balance operations with its traditional advocacy role.

The new vision and plan have had two immediate results:

1. A new structure consisting of seven standing committees to implement action plans, freeing the board itself to focus on mission and set direction
2. Vigorous community outreach to raise the library's visibility in the community

Ambassadors in the Community

After finalizing the strategic plan in early 2006, the Friends board members initiated their "connect to the community" outreach plan. With a Best Friends Forever theme for their year-long 50th anniversary celebration, they demonstrated their "cheer-

Figure 4-A   Book Bags and Reading Journal Membership Incentives—
Friends of Johnson County (KS) Library

leading" role for the library with a chant, complete with pompoms, at a luncheon for current and former Friends and library volunteers. The annual spring Bookmark Design Contest, with more than 500 entries, utilized the same theme. In October, concluding the year-long celebration, their anniversary gift to the community was a performance by cowboy poet Baxter Black, attended by more than 250 people.

Marching in the Turkey Creek Parade to promote the library's Summer Reading Club, the Friends got the crowd to join in the chant: *"2-4-6-8, who do we appreciate? The Library!"* They also held a special book sale to raise funds for the New Orleans Public Library, adopted the park surrounding the Merriam Visitors Bureau and Historic Plaza, and cosponsored a Kansas Day Celebration at the University of Kansas. In addition, they started a Speakers Bureau.

Five Friends board members have attended the American Library Association (ALA)/Friends of Libraries U.S.A. (FOLUSA) Advocacy Institute, priming them for activism. The energetic advocacy committee, whose members include nonboard and non-Friends individuals, regularly contacts the county commissioners, state legislators, and members of Congress. Wearing their golden "Library Friend" 50th Anniversary lapel pins, members attend Legislative Day in Topeka and Board of County Commissioners' meetings. They conduct e-mail blasts and talk to community leaders. They are also preparing to participate in national efforts such as FOLUSA's Virtual March on Washington (see Unit 4-11).

Results

Through the visioning and strategic planning process of 2005–2006, the Friends reminded themselves that fund-raising activities support their real mission: advocacy. The new committee structure is allowing board members to "see the forest instead of the trees" and is engaging more Friends members. The Friends have made political strides. Their initial forays as ambassadors in the community have raised the library's visibility and have already yielded many questions about the library, hopefully "opening eyes to the library."

Figure 4B   The Friends Present a Cheer—Friends of the Johnson County (KS) Library

Figure 4C   The Friends Participate in a Parade—
Friends of the Johnson County (KS) Library

4-2 Celebrating 75 Years of Library Service: Collaboration + Cooperation + Celebration = Success

Figure 4-D   75th Anniversary Bookmark

Learning that their library's 75th anniversary was coming up, the trustees of the Caldwell County (NC) Public Library decided to make the day special. They created a planning committee, which included Friends, trustees, and library staff. A local fabric printing company printed and donated 5,000 bookmarks and 100 banners to be used at all three library locations, a local reporter was recruited to ensure media coverage, and invitations to the day's events were designed and mailed to local and state officials as well as retired library staff. The public was invited to celebrate with historical remembrances, refreshments, and door prizes.

Events leading up to the special day included a search for the holder of the oldest library card, a Forgiveness Week when no overdue fines would be charged, a Timeline for the 75 years, and a Time Capsule. The committee also designed an essay contest, a drawing contest, and a scavenger hunt. During this six-month period, Friends, library staff, and trustees worked together. Those involved got to know each other better, and a real sense of community was formed. Collaboration plus cooperation equaled success.

How It Worked

- A special planning committee was established that included trustees, Friends, and library staff and a local reporter to ensure both print and television publicity.
- Brainstorming sessions resulted in plans with assigned leaders.
- Local businesses donated prizes.
- Advertisements, invitations, and bookmarks were designed and printed.
- Information about the event and activities leading up to it was mailed to Friends membership, resulting in more volunteers to help with activities.
- Friends agreed to finance the celebration and related activities.
- Local and state officials were invited to attend.

- The final celebration was held for which programs were printed. Refreshments were also provided.

Results

- Increased communication among Friends, library staff, and trustees.
- Involvement of community patrons in contests for all ages.
- Great newspaper coverage of all events.
- Participation by local merchants who donated door prizes.
- Increased Friends' membership from 125 to 175.
- Receipt of a state library Friends award.

༄ ༄

4-3   Celebrating 100 Years of the Oldest Branch of the Chicago (IL) Public Library!

Chicago Public Library (CPL) officials set the date for the Blackstone Branch Library Centennial for the afternoon of September 18, 2004. The Friends of the Blackstone Branch Library thought it fitting to celebrate the city's oldest branch library in a festive way but also in a meaningful and hands-on manner.

There were a few bumps in the road. There was no permanent branch head, so a CPL district manager was in charge of the event. The Friends group was less than one year old with a core group of six volunteer members. The budget was tiny, earmarked mostly for performers. However, with only two months lead time, the Friends quickly mobilized to brainstorm and then recruit for an exciting afternoon of workshops, live musical performances, activities, speakers, and a fund-raising program all tapping into local talent and businesses with the aim of highlighting the library's resources.

Although a CPL district manager was responsible for planning the centennial, the Friends group proposed, contacted, and implemented the activities, entertainment, and sponsors. Local talent and businesses were happy to donate their expertise and products to the event and to the library. Cooperation between CPL staff and Friends members helped to make the Blackstone Branch Centennial and Back to School Celebration well attended, well publicized, joyous, and diverse in its offerings.

How It Worked

The Blackstone Branch Library Centennial utilized space outside and inside the building. Speeches by the neighborhood historical society archivist, politicians, CPL officials and Friends officials were held outside as were free face painting, balloons, live classical and rock and roll music, coffee, cocoa, birthday cake, and other refreshments. In the library's rotunda, surrounded by an historical display, the Friends sold T-shirts with an original linoleum cut design by a local artist. Four different crafts activities were held in the children's room. Children also got free prizes from a local toy store for participating in a library treasure hunt based on teaching about library resources. In the downstairs auditorium, local author Jenny Schroedel conducted a workshop to show kids what goes into making a book. All services and products needed for the day were obtained for free except the musicians, who were paid a nominal fee.

Planning

The Friends group did the following to plan the Blackstone Library Centennial:

- Held regular meetings with CPL officials.
- Utilized e-mail to communicate with each other between meetings.
- Sent out press releases by e-mail and fax to media and followed up with phone calls.
- Utilized local weekly newspaper and the local supermarket's newspaper to keep the public informed of the upcoming event and to call for volunteers.
- Communicated with businesses and organizations in person and in writing to appeal for donations, services, and participation.
- Worked with local children's book author Jenny Schroedel to create a proposal for the make-your-own picture book workshop.
- Utilized materials from Friends of Libraries U.S.A. to partner with a local bookstore to sponsor the author event.
- Recruited musicians and the artist who created the poster and T-shirt designs.
- Garnered community support.
- Requested officials implement a City of Chicago Citation and a Presidential Proclamation commemorating the library's centennial.
- Helped the CPL distribute the printed invitations.
- Posted flyers around the neighborhood.
- Worked with the Alderman's office to close off street for the celebration.

Volunteer and Community Involvement

Friends group volunteers were intrinsic to the centennial planning. On the day of the event, volunteers staffed the Friends' fund-raiser table. Volunteers served the food. *(Text continues on p. 132.)*

CHICAGO PUBLIC LIBRARY

Blackstone Branch Library 100th Anniversary & Back to School Celebration

Blackstone Branch Library
4904 South Lake Park Avenue
Chicago Illinois 60615
(312) 747-0511

**Blackstone Branch Library
Saturday, September 18
2 p.m.**

Please join the Chicago Public Library in celebrating the centennial of the Blackstone Branch Library!

Speakers & Activities include:
- Steven Treffman, Archivist
  Hyde Park Historical Society
- Alderman Toni Preckwinkle
- Local Children's Author Jenny Schroedel
  (*Blackbird's Nest*)
- Hyde Park Youth Symphony
  Chamber Ensemble
- Children's Activities such as arts & crafts,
  face painting & storytelling
- Balloons!

Refreshments provided by Starbucks & Bonjour Bakery

Special thanks to our local community participants including:
- Baby Ph.D.
- Bonjour Bakery
- 57th Street Bookstore
- Hyde Park Historical Society
- Joyce's Hallmark
- Toys, Etc.

Monday-Thursday: 9 am-9 pm; Friday & Saturday: 9 am-5 pm; Closed Sundays

City of Chicago
RICHARD M. DALEY
Mayor

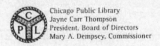

Chicago Public Library
Jayne Carr Thompson
President, Board of Directors
Mary A. Dempsey, Commissioner

READ LEARN DISCOVER CHICAGO PUBLIC LIBRARY
www.chicagopubliclibrary.org

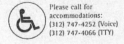

Please call for accommodations:
(312) 747-4252 (Voice)
(312) 747-4066 (TTY)

Figure 4-E   Centennial Celebration Flyer

Businesses offered their services and products for free on the day of the centennial. Library staff from all over the system came to Blackstone Library for the centennial to help out with setting up the sound system and facilitating the arts and crafts in the children's room. In order to purchase the T-shirts, the Friends accepted the help of the Hyde Park Kenwood Community Conference, which acted as a parent nonprofit organization to manage the finances.

Results

The centennial's success gave the Blackstone Library a better image in the community. The staff members wear their commemorative T-shirts with pride. The attention has given the library more visibility, and more people and businesses are willing to donate to the Friends group. Friends members were buoyed by the success of the centennial and went on to write a grant to restore the vandalized, original globe in the library's reading room. The event motivated CPL officials to consider encouraging branch library users throughout Chicago to form Friends groups.

The centennial event served more than 300 people of all ages. It raised more than $1,000 in cash and garnered more than $15,000 in in-kind donations and community support for the library.

Ⅾ Ⅿ

4-4   Raising the Library's Profile with a Centennial Celebration

The Loveland (CO) Public Library wanted to celebrate its centennial year in 2005 in a big way to set the stage for a fund-raising campaign in 2007–2008 to support a building addition and renovation. A committee comprising library staff, trustees, and Friends members began planning in 2004 to develop a 12-month-long celebration.

Specifically, the group scheduled 30 children and adult programs and commissioned a watercolor painting that was printed as a poster and on note cards, mugs, and book bags with the library's slogan "Bridging the Century 1905–2005." By e-mail and mail they solicited input from over 500 authors, Nobel Prize winners, U.S. and Colorado political figures, and celebrities and received, mounted, and framed 55 photographs and essays on what authors and/or books influenced their success. The library also held many small and several large gatherings of citizens, children, and area VIPs to present a PowerPoint history of the library, its current program scope, and its future building needs. Dedication of a "centennial cottonwood tree" surrounding a pillar in the Youth Services Room was a highlight of the large public party. *(Text continues on p. 134.)*

Bridging
the **Century**
1905–2005

The Loveland Public Library is celebrating its 100th anniversary as a city-supported library in September 2005. Loveland, Colorado is 50 miles north of Denver and enjoys a worldwide reputation for its public art collection, bronze foundries, and annual sculpture shows and sales. We would like to ask for your participation in this event by your sending an autographed photo of yourself with a written/typed response to the following questions added on the photo or printed on a separate sheet:

What book, books or author most influenced/motivated you to achieve what you have accomplished in your life? Why or how?

Your photo and response will be matted and framed by the Friends of the Loveland Public Library and placed on permanent display in the building. Because you are an acknowledged leader in your field, your response to this request will be appreciated by the 400,000 + annual visitors to the Library and will serve to introduce you to an interested public, maybe even setting someone on a new path in her or his life.

We currently have matted, framed and hung 52 letters and photos from three U.S. Presidents, numerous Nobel and Pulitzer Prize winners, as well as a very well-rounded selection of authors, artists, and film and television celebrities. Please send your autographed picture and response to the Library at the address listed below.

Thank you in advance for participating in our celebration of 100 years of reading here in Loveland. Your response to this request will be cherished for many years to come.

Sincerely,

Laura Krebill, Chair of the Board of Trustees

Ted Schmidt, Library Director

300 North Adams Avenue • Loveland, CO 80537 • ph 970-962-2665 • fax 970-962-2905

Figure 4-F   Letter Sent to VIPs Requesting Photographs and Essays

How It Worked

- Many ideas were brainstormed and vetted. Some were discarded and others kept for implementation.
- Subcommittees were developed to implement each idea that survived the vetting process above. The subcommittees were formed for the following:
  - Commission a watercolor and create a fine art poster.
  - Create a logo and market mugs, book bags, note cards, and other products.
  - Develop a Wall of Fame to include responses from U.S. presidents, senators, governors, and other celebrities to a question about what books and/or authors influenced their success.
  - Create floats for two local parades.
  - Organize public parties to celebrate the library's centennial.
  - Create a "centennial cottonwood tree" in the Youth Services area of the library.
  - Create three DVD productions on local history subjects.

Results

Telephone and mail solicitations during the centennial year generated over $5,600 in donations. Sales of the centennial poster, mugs, and book bags added $1,740.

The library director and Friends president made 31 presentations to over 1,000 people about the library's history and its current need for expansion and renovation. The library's history was published in a number of local newspaper articles in addition to 26 other articles written by staff members and the directors. Public awareness about the library—its past, present, and future—was achieved!

♋ ♋

4-5   North Carolina's Smartest Card Campaign

Across North Carolina, public library staff delivered the message: North Carolina's smartest card is at your public library! For three consecutive years in September, the State Library of North Carolina, through a Library Service and Technology Act Statewide Leadership Project, coordinated a library card sign-up campaign. Based on the Public Library Association's (PLA) national campaign, the North Carolina campaign promoted the value of public libraries by focusing on how the library card is the key to learning and enjoyment for all people. Using the PLA's national

Goldsboro Fire Department supports libraries.

It is important to get your school year off to a GREAT start! Your backpack should be filled with all of the necessary school supplies...pencils, notebooks, rulers and your library card! Yes, your library card! Stop by the Wayne County Public Library to pick up your FREE library card TODAY!

Wayne County Public Library ° 1001 East Ash Street ° Goldsboro, NC 27530
919.735.1824

Figure 4-G   Goldsboro (NC) Fire Department Smartest Card Flyer

campaign as a springboard, the State Library provided a full menu of resources to support libraries in reaching out to their communities. The State Library's program delivered statewide media relations, developed a clearinghouse for marketing ideas, and created and produced promotional materials.

In 2006, a state spokesperson was used to expand the focus of the campaign. Kevyn Adams, of the Center for the Carolina Hurricanes, served as the state spokesperson and delighted library patrons and local school children at a statewide kickoff at the Wake County Southeast Regional Library. Press materials focused on Kevyn's activities as the spokesperson.

How It Worked

- The State Library created a timeline and implementation plan for the September library card sign-up campaign.
- Staff wrote a marketing/communication plan.
- They created a budget for funds provided by the Library Service and Technology Act Statewide Leadership Project and by the State Library. Costs included graphic design, printing, and materials storage and fulfillment.
- They designed and ordered promotional materials. Materials varied each year and included plastic book bags, shoelaces, bookmarks, door hangers, window static clings, and posters. Materials were provided free to participating libraries, and amounts were based on size of library populations served.
- North Carolina public library staff were informed of the campaign, and contact information for participants was collected.
- Press materials were written, including press packets for the kickoff, a press release for each week, and editorials.
- Promotional materials were delivered to participating libraries.
- A kickoff press conference was held at each participating library.
- Press releases were sent out weekly.
- Promotional ideas collected from participating libraries were shared systematically.
- State Library staff participated in various library card sign-up events at libraries across the state.
- Participating libraries submitted evaluations.
- State Library staff completed a summary report.

Results

The North Carolina public library community embraced the *"Smartest Card. Get It. Use It."* campaign and promoted library card sign-up through a variety of activities

Figure 4-H   Mayor and Patrons, Oxford (NC) Library

that delivered a strong message about the value of a library card. Librarians actively involved local community officials. Across the state, officials endorsed the governor's library card proclamation, visited libraries and signed up for a library card, read stories at special children's programs, and shared their library stories with the media. One library even put its county officials to work at its circulation desk. Many libraries adapted the smartest card poster to feature their local officials.

Public librarians embraced the campaign and adapted it to work best for their community, targeting educators, city employees, day care centers, local businesses, seniors, school children, and Hispanic populations. Creative program ideas for the targeted audiences included special receptions for teachers to highlight the resources available to them at the library; invitations to local businesspeople to visit the library, sign up for a library card, and leave their business card at the library as a way to promote their services to the community; contests for children; partnerships with local businesses to hold special events for people with library cards; and participation in many community events.

Each year the campaign averaged 100 different news stories, which generated over 1,500,000 impressions in newspaper, television, and radio outlets. Participating libraries reported increases in library card sign ups from 6 to 57 percent.

Figure 4-1   Adams Library Smartest Card Celebration—Lisbeth Evans, Secretary of the Department of Cultural Resources; Mary Boone, State Librarian; Kevyn Adams, former Carolina Hurricanes player and library campaign spokesperson; and Pam Jaskot, State Library of North Carolina

4-6   Special Alumni Collections Raise Library Awareness

The Wyndham Robertson Library at Hollins University in Roanoke, Virginia, has a Hollins Authors Collection composed of works that contain a substantial contribution by alumni. Contributions include authorship, illustration, editing, or translation work. Books by and about alumni are actively collected with priority on the first edition. When appropriate, a second copy is purchased for the general circulating collection. Later editions, as well as materials in other formats, are collected as time and funds allow. Nonmonographic materials are stored in the university archives or in the media library, depending on the item's format.

The Hollins Authors Collection also includes monographs published by the university's faculty. The collection policy for faculty is similar to the policy for alumni. However, only those books and materials produced while teaching at Hollins, or by emeritus faculty, are collected.

How It Works

- Library staff learns about new publications through public relations and alumni relations offices. Publications such as the campus newsletter and departmental newsletters are also sources of information. In addition, faculty and alumni sometimes notify the library directly, often in the form of a donated copy.

- Materials are purchased with a small endowed fund. Second copies, if deemed appropriate for the general collection, are purchased with general collection development funds.

- Upon receipt, books are cataloged, with a local subject heading, "Hollins University—Alumni and Alumnae—Publications," added. If the Hollins author is not the main entry, the addition of the author's name is added after "Publications."

- Materials are sent to Special Collections for physical processing and shelving. Dust jackets are retained, and books are processed in a similar manner to rare books (i.e., Mylar dust jacket protector added, call number handwritten on an identification tag, and barcode attached to top of tag). Although books do not circulate and are to be used only in the Hollins Room, a "tattle tape" is necessary for security purposes. Valuable or fragile materials are stored in a locked cabinet in the Hollins Room or shelved in Special Collections.

- The public relations office is notified of any new titles to be added to the Hollins Web site (www.hollins.edu/grad/eng_writing/books/bookfrm.htm).

Results

Because this special collection is housed in a large room designed to both showcase alumni and faculty publications and to hold meetings, receptions, and other events, it highlights the special role the library plays in the literary accomplishments of its former students and current faculty. The large collection, as well as the room's beautiful décor, makes an impressive introduction to the literary culture of Hollins for visitors and prospective students. The room's collections also generate good will among faculty and alumni.

Wyndham Robertson Library
Hollins University
Special Collections

A collection overview

Beth S. Harris
Special Collections Management Librarian
(540) 362-6237 □ bharris@hollins.edu
http://www.hollins.edu/academics/library/services/spe_col.htm

Hollins Authors Collection

Published works by and about Alumnae, Alumni, Faculty members, and Writers-in-Residence. Books are shelved in the Hollins Room while other formats, such as journal articles, are in archival storage.

A *small* sampling of Hollins Authors:
Alumnae and Alumni
- Elizabeth Meriwether Gilmer ("Dorothy Dix"), attended 1878-1879.
- Margaret Wise Brown (Class of 1932)
- Elizabeth Forsythe Hailey (Class of 1960)
- Lee Smith (Class of 1967)
- Annie Dillard (Class of 1967, MA 1968)
- Henry Taylor (MA 1966)
Faculty
- Louis D. Rubin, Jr.
- R. H. W. Dillard
- William Jay Smith
- Jeanne Larsen
Writers-in-Residence
- William Golding
- Flannery O'Connor
- Shelby Foote
- Brendan Galvin

For a complete listing go to:http://www.hollins.edu/grad/eng_writing/books/bookfrm.htm.

Manuscripts

Modern literary manuscripts and papers including Margaret Wise Brown, Henry Taylor, P. L. Travers, Shannon Ravenel, Lee Smith, Julia Randall, Margaret Gibson, Brendin Galvin, Denise Giardina,

Figure 4-J Hollins University (Roanoke, VA) Special Collections Brochure (Outside)

Special Collections

Special Collections encompasses four unique collections: the Rare Book Collection, University Archives, the Hollins Authors Collection, and Manuscripts.

Rare Book Collection

This collection includes books and other materials which are of special value or interest due to age, rarity, literary, artistic, or historical qualities. Fragile materials or unusual formats which make an item unsuitable for the general circulating collection are also shelved here. While encompassing a wide range of subjects, the collection is particularly strong in English literature, juvenile literature, private press and book arts, and includes a large collection of incunabula (books printed before 1501).

Examples from the Rare Book Collection:

- Babylonian clay tablets, 2100-2035 B.C.E.
- Medieval and Renaissance era manuscripts, some of which are illuminated in brilliant colors.
- Robert Frost: first editions, autographed, or inscribed copies.
- Benjamin Franklin: works by, about, and printed by this famous American.

A history of the rare book collection
A generous gift of manuscripts, incunabula and books related to printing and the study of incunabula was presented to Hollins in memory of Lucy Winton McVitty, (trustee 1926-1941), by her husband, Samuel Herbert McVitty, of Salem, Virginia, in 1943. The collection has continued to grow through generous donations and purchases.

University Archives

The University Archives is an institutional archives and includes records and documents produced by Hollins and those associated with it, such as Faculty, Trustees, and Alumnae and Alumni. Records date from the 18th century to the present and include minutes, financial records, theses, catalogs, handbooks, photographs, scrapbooks, blueprints, and many other types of materials.

Examples of archival materials...

- The papers of Charles Lewis Cocke, founder of Hollins University.
- Nineteenth century student letters and diaries.
- Basketball team sweater, circa 1900.
- Student photo albums and scrapbooks.
- Faculty papers

The beginnings of the archival collection had its roots with Joseph A. Turner Jr. (1895-1937), business manager of Hollins. An avid historian and charter member of the Southwest Virginia Historical Society, he began the first systematic collecting of artifacts and documents to preserve Hollins History. For example, he was instrumental in acquiring the mill stones from the Hollins Mill in Lynchburg, Va. For the front quadrangle. In addition, many of this historical notes are found within the archives. An effort to begin a formal archives began in the late 1970s, at the encouragement of Frances J. Niederer, Art professor and author of *Hollins College: an Illustrated History*. The first archivist was hired in 1981.

Figure 4-K   Hollins University (Roanoke, VA) Special Collections Brochure (Inside)

4-7   Home Rule Charter Amendment Supports Fargo (ND) Public Library

After seven years and three separate studies showing a need for improved and expanded library facilities to support a growing community, the Board of Directors of the Fargo (ND) Public Library decided to go directly to the citizens for a vote. To do so, the board had to convince three members of the city commission to initiate a ballot measure for a half-cent sales tax over an 18-month period dedicated to library expansion.

Two of the commissioners were already supportive, but two were solidly against. That left one member of the city commission to be convinced to support the ballot measure. Many people were encouraged to lobby for this crucial vote. They were successful, and the proposal would go on the ballot—with only five weeks to wage

---

Library Initiative

The **Home Rule Charter Amendment,** listed below as it will appear on the November 2 ballot, must pass by 60% of the voters in order to be enacted:

Home Rule Charter Amendment
"Shall Article 3(R) be added to the Home Rule Charter of the City of Fargo authorizing the collection of one-half of one percent (1/2%) municipal sales/use tax beginning January 1, 2005, and continuing until June 30, 2006 (18 months), to be utilized by the City of Fargo for the construction, improvement, maintenance and operation of the Public Library and library expansion pursuant to an adopted library facility plan, all as provided in the Notice of Proposed Home Rule Charter Amendment as published in **THE FORUM** on the 3rd day of September, 2004?"

SHALL SUCH AMENDMENT BE APPROVED?

(   ) YES

(   ) NO

Funds raised will be used to
  • expand/construct, furnish and expand the collection of a 45,000 square foot downtown library
  • to construct and furnish and expand the collection of a 15,000 square foot southpoint branch library
  • to renovate and open a 2,500 square foot northside storefront library.

To read the complete text of the Amendment, visit
http://www.ci.fargo.nd.us/auditors/homerulecharteramend.htm

Figure 4-L   Home Rule Charter Amendment as Included on the Ballot

FRIENDS OF THE FARGO PUBLIC LIBRARY

September 22, 2004

Dear Friends:

I'm writing as the President of the Friends of the Library to let you know about an exciting opportunity that faces us as citizens of Fargo.

On the November 2nd ballot, **the very last measure** will be an **Amendment to the Home Rule Charter** which proposes to enact a 1/2 of one % sales tax for 18 months for the purpose of expanding library facilities.

If the measure passes by a 60% majority of the voters, the 18 month tax will generate 12 million dollars to be used to expand, acquire and provide facilities, materials, and technology to meet the MINIMUM needs of Fargo citizens including:

- 45,000 sq ft downtown   instead of   31,000 sq feet
- 15,000 sq ft at Southpointe   instead of   3,300
- 2,500 sq ft in North Fargo   instead of   a book drop
- 270,000 books/items   instead of   160,800
- 324 seats   instead of   106
- 11 study rooms   instead of   0
- 100 computer/Internet stations   instead of   36
- 206 parking spaces   instead of   48

For details I invite you to review the enclosed brochure and also to visit the website sponsored by *Citizens for Better Libraries* which will be updated regularly at www.newfargolibrary.com

You can help the library to grow by:
- **voting yes** on the Amendment to the Home Rule Charter on November 2nd
- **inviting the *Citizens for Better Libraries* to speak** at your club or organization
- **making a donation to the *Citizens for Better Libraries*, 1104 2nd Ave S. Fargo, ND 58103** to support their educational efforts.
- **downloading copies** of bookmarks, brochures, postcards and other items off the website at **www.newfargolibrary.com** and duplicating them for your friends, family, coworkers, church members, etc.

Thank you for your support in this important effort to expand and enhance library services in our community.

Sincerely,

Bev Quamme

Bev Quamme
Friends President

Figure 4-M   Letter to Friends Membership

a campaign! An additional hurdle was that, by law, the ballot would have to pass by 60 percent.

How It Worked

- A campaign committee was formed, with a former library board member and current Friends member as its chair.
- The Friends of the Library agreed to finance the campaign.
- The Friends sent a direct mailing to their 411 member households asking for monetary and/or other support, such as writing letters to the editor or going door to door with campaign materials.
- The special campaign committee Citizens for Better Libraries held a meeting where plans were made to:
  - Get the word out before the vote.
  - Raise money for ads and brochures.
  - Develop a Web site.
  - Create pamphlets and fliers.
  - Find volunteers to distribute campaign materials.
  - Find speakers for making the case at service clubs and community groups.
  - Work with local media for local radio talk show appearances.

Results

With no appreciable grassroots opposition (the mayor, one commissioner, and the local newspaper did voice opposition), the proposal passed with 62 percent of the vote! Approximately $12 million was raised by the measure for new library construction.

Fargo has grown...
our library has not.

A new library is
long overdue.

VOTE YES on Nov. 2
to approve the **Home Rule Charter
Amendment** for a 1/2% sales tax for
18 months to support Fargo Libraries.

www.newfargolibrary.com

Paid for by Citizens for Better Libraries, Virginia Dambach, chair

Fargo has grown...
our library has not.

A new library is
long overdue.

VOTE YES on Nov. 2 *!*

www.newfargolibrary.com

Paid for by Citizens for Better Libraries, Virginia Dambach, chair

Figure 4-N   Campaign Brochure (Outside)

Fargo has grown...
our library has not.

When it opened in 1964, the **Fargo Public Library** was designed to serve Fargo citizens until the year 2000. It has served its purpose well. But **we have outgrown its space.** We deserve better library facilities to meet today's needs. The proposed **Home Rule Charter Amendment** would enact a 1/2% sales tax for 18 months to fund new library facilities.

The current Fargo Public Library was designed to serve a city of 54,000. But in 2000, Fargo's population was 90,599, and it's expected to reach 108,000 by the year 2020.

Fargo is an "All American City." We're proud of our city and its amenities. Our city is consistently ranked by national sources as having outstanding "quality of life" and as a great place to live, work, raise children or start a business.

Yet, by every standard measure, the **Fargo Public Library is rated "far below average."** We have fewer books, less space, fewer computer terminals, fewer seats, and less parking per capita than other cities our size. We're **long overdue** for better library facilities.

In 2003, an average of more than 1,000 people visited the library EACH DAY and borrowed a total of 819,759 items from the collection of 170,000 books, tapes, videos and other materials. The Fargo Public Library and its below-average resources are being used by more people, more often. It's true, even in the Internet age, the **demand is growing** and continues to grow.

To meet the **MINIMUM needs** of Fargo citizens, the Fargo Public Library needs:

needs:	instead of:
45,000 sq ft downtown	31,000 sq ft
15,000 sq ft at Southpointe	3,300 sq ft
2,500 sq ft at north Fargo	a book drop
270,000 books/items	160,800
324 seats	106
11 study rooms	0
100 computer/Internet stations	36
206 parking spaces	48

After passage of the proposed **Home Rule Charter Amendment**, Fargo's sales tax rate would still be only 6.5% (Grand Forks, Valley City, Jamestown, Minot, and Dickinson all have higher sales tax rates). The 1/2% tax to support libraries will simply replace the 1/2% sales tax that expired in 2002. For this 18-month investment, the citizens of Fargo will get:

a 45,000 sq ft **Downtown** library
a 15,000 sq ft **Southpoint** branch library
a 2,500 sq ft **Northside** storefront library
110,000 **new books** for adults and youth
64 new **computer/Internet stations**
206 **parking spaces**

We're long overdue.

Vote YES on the **Home Rule Charter Amendment** for a 1/2% sales tax for 18 months to support Fargo Libraries.

Figure 4-O   Campaign Brochure (Inside)

4-8   Advocacy Mondays

Like too many libraries, the Minneapolis Public Library System experienced budget cuts resulting in reduced service hours. All libraries are now closed on Mondays. Hundreds of would-be patrons continue to come to the libraries on Mondays, reasonably expecting them to be open. In response, The Friends of the Minneapolis Library set up an Advocacy Mondays table in the Central Library's atrium every Monday. The atrium is open despite the library itself being closed.

On the table, patrons learn why the library is closed and how they can help. Patrons can pick up a Keep Libraries Open button, take a flyer about the budget crisis and the Friends, and sign up for e-mail updates on the situation.

How It Works

- The Advocacy Mondays table requires little time and money. Expenses are limited to making photocopies and purchasing Keep Libraries Open buttons. Staff and volunteer time is limited to setting up the table, producing the flyers, and entering the collected e-mail addresses into their e-mail system.
- The library gave the Friends permission to set up the table.
- Those listing their e-mail address at the table are sent a personal e-mail shortly thereafter, thanking them for signing up, further introducing them to the Friends, and describing the e-newsletters to follow.
- It is important to follow up with all subsequent correspondence.

Results

After 16 Mondays with the table available, over 300 individuals have signed up for the e-newsletter. Slightly more have taken the flyer with information on the budget crisis, The Friends of the Minneapolis Public Library, and how they can help. Hundreds more have taken Keep Libraries Open buttons, which are commonly seen in the surrounding neighborhood on Mondays. At least two individuals have since become members. About three dozen have contacted the Friends for more information or to report that they asked elected officials to support public libraries.

Why are Minneapolis Public Libraries closed on Mondays?

It's a good question. Because of a budget crisis, Minneapolis Public Libraries have been closed on Sundays and Mondays since January 2007. Budget problems began in 2003, when Minnesota local government aid was drastically cut. The situation became critical with rising costs and the re-opening of libraries that were closed for remodeling. The Library Board held public forums to hear from Minneapolitans on the hard decisions ahead. It was decided to temporarily shutter three libraries (Roosevelt, Southeast, and Webber Park) and modify hours at remaining libraries.

2007 Minneapolis Public Library Hours		
	Wednesdays, Fridays, and Saturdays	Tuesdays and Thursdays
Central Library	10 am – 6 pm	10 am – 8 pm
Community Libraries	10 am – 6 pm	12 pm – 8 pm

What solutions are being considered? The state legislature recently approved the unification of the Hennepin County Public Library and the Minneapolis Public Library. Both systems would be strengthened by consolidating their complementary assets. Details of the prospective consolidation are being worked out at this time.

Get involved. Minneapolis has great libraries with great services, but with some of the worst service hours in the country. Minneapolis deserves libraries that are all open at least six full days a week. Let your elected officials know how much libraries mean to you. **Your libraries need you now.**

KEEP LIBRARIES OPEN

Learn more and stay up to date. The Friends of the Minneapolis Public Library want to keep you informed, answer your questions, and help you stand up for libraries. *Visit our website to learn about The Friends, read more on the budget crisis, and sign up for updates by e-mail, or call 612-630-6159.*

www.friendsofmpl.org

The Friends of the Minneapolis Public Library

Prepared on May 21, 2007 by The Friends of the Minneapolis Public Library, 300 Nicollet Mall, N-290, Minneapolis, MN 55401

Figure 4-P   Flyer Distributed on Advocacy Mondays

4-9   I Love Libraries—Celebrating Libraries Virtually

ILoveLibraries.org is a Web site designed for people who use and love libraries. The site is designed to keep citizens informed about everything libraries have to offer as well as how to develop new ways to involve individuals in their continued health and vitality.

ILoveLibraries.org is an initiative of the American Library Association (ALA), the oldest and largest library association in the world, with members in academic, public, school, government, and special libraries. The ALA is a more than 64,000-member-strong organization that seeks to provide leadership for the development, promotion, and improvement of library and information services and the profession of librarianship in order to enhance learning and ensure access to information for all.

Visit ILoveLibraries.org today and download Web buttons to add to your library and Friends group Web sites. Encourage your Friends, staff, and library patrons to visit and share their story.

> As you know, one of the most wonderful places there is, is your own favorite library. Your library serves you—and your community—by helping you find and obtain the information you need, helping young people with their homework assignments, providing meeting space for local events, teaching seniors computer skills, and more. Your library—all libraries—truly are the cornerstones of democracy. Now and again, libraries need your help, your advocacy, to continue to provide the services your community relies on. Visit ILoveLibraries.org where you will find many ways to help by taking action, either at the local, state, or federal level.
>
> Millions of people all over the world love their libraries! From libraries that became winter refuge for children through engaging story hours to librarians who turned their libraries into health resource centers for their aging patron populations, you'll find stories from everyday people who have something wonderful to say about their experiences with libraries.
>
> From www.ilovelibraries.org

ప్రం ుు

4-10   Celebrating National Friends of Libraries Week

Friends of Libraries groups now have their very own national week of celebration! The first National Friends of Libraries Week was held October 22–28, 2006. It was such a success that Friends of Libraries U.S.A. (FOLUSA) sponsored the second celebration October 21–27, 2007. The now annual celebration offers a twofold opportunity to celebrate Friends. Use the time to creatively promote your group in the community, to raise awareness, and to promote membership. This is also an excellent opportunity for your library and board of trustees to recognize the Friends for their help and support of the library.

Promotion Ideas for Friends Groups

- Download the sample proclamation available at www.folusa.org, tailor it to your community or campus, and ask the mayor, school principal, or president of the college to sign.
  - Place copies of the proclamation in visible places in the library.
  - Reprint the proclamation in the Friends' and/or library's newsletter.
  - Post a copy of the proclamation on the Friends' and/or library's Web site.
- Download the template bookmarks at www.folusa.org (available in PDF format) to copy and distribute in your library and throughout the community. With quotes about libraries, reading, and literacy, these bookmarks are an easy to way to promote National Friends of Libraries Week and your group.
- Plan a membership drive to coordinate with National Friends of Libraries Week.
  - Place a special display in the library's lobby (main and branches) that includes copies of your membership brochure. Make it creative and fun and tell the story of the Friends through pictures and props.
  - Schedule volunteers to staff the table or display during busy times at the library. Be sure to recruit outgoing volunteers who are willing and able to "sell" the Friends. Hand out membership brochures, and consider offering a membership "special" with a reduced rate, such as 15 months for the price of 12, or a special drawing for those who join during a specified time.
- Contact the newspaper about a feature article about your Friends group and all the great work you have done on behalf of your library. Download the sample press release at www.folusa.org and add information about your group. Highlight your programs, money donated to the library, number of volunteer hours, and so forth—anything that helps to paint the picture of how your group supports the library.

Promotion Ideas for State Friends Groups or Library Associations

- Get the word out! Let all libraries and Friends groups in your state know about National Friends of Libraries Week. Direct them to the FOLUSA Web site for resources and celebration ideas.

- Add a link to your Web site and include National Friends of Libraries Week when promoting library and literacy-related celebrations.
- Coordinate a state proclamation in honor of National Friends of Libraries Week. See the FOLUSA Web site for a sample from New York, including information on how the effort was coordinated.

Promotion Ideas for Libraries

- Assist the Friends in getting the proclamation signed by your city or campus official.
- Offer a prominent location in the library where the Friends can place a display and/or a membership table during National Friends of Libraries Week.
- Promote the week in the library's newsletter.
- Use the event to evaluate how the library currently helps promote the Friends. Look for additional opportunities to promote the Friends on an ongoing basis, including membership, programs, and fund-raisers. Consider a bulletin board in a prominent location, brochure holders at the circulation desk, bookmarks distributed by the circulation staff, and other simple ways to promote the Friends to all patrons.
- Tell your city or campus officials how important the Friends are to the ongoing success of the library. Use this opportunity to convey to officials how the Friends raise money, promote the library, and volunteer in many ways.
  - If you submit a monthly article or information to the mayor, city council, or college officials, be sure to talk about the contributions of the Friends. Make it personal and quantify the support whenever possible (amount of money donated, number of volunteer hours, number of programs supported, and number of people who attended, etc.).
  - Submit an article to a citywide or campuswide publication. Tell the personal story of a longtime volunteer with the Friends, the impact of Friends support on programs, services, and/or collections, or how the Friends supported the library in another way.
- Create a large Thank You card to post near the Friends' display or membership table (if they decide to do this). Ask staff to personalize the card and/or sign their names.
- Ask staff to write "love letters" to Friends that can be posted throughout the library showing their support. Include quotes in the library's newsletter and on the library's Web site. Personal recognition makes volunteers feel appreciated!

Results

Share your story with other Friends and libraries around the country. Be sure to mail or e-mail a story (and include photographs or other graphics) to FOLUSA to be added to its Web site and possibly included in its newsletter. Contact information can be found at www.folusa.org.

⁊ ⁊

4-11 One Voice Can Make a Difference—Join the Annual Virtual March on Washington

Each year the American Library Association coordinates National Library Legislative Day. On this day, hundreds of librarians (and a handful of Friends and trustees) make their way to Washington, DC, to visit their senators and representatives to discuss library issues. As important as it is for librarians to go to Washington, it is equally important for those who cannot go to make their voices heard—even if "virtually."

Okay, so the trip to Washington isn't in your budget. No problem! Friends of Libraries U.S.A. sponsors a virtual trip to Washington to expand the reach and impact of National Library Legislative Day. There is strength in numbers, and libraries need your help. Get started now planning for the Virtual March on Washington.

How It Works

- Visit www.folusa.org and click on "Advocacy" and then "Virtual March" for a flyer you can print and distribute in your community.
- Additional resources available online include downloadable bookmarks, statistics about library usage, and information about how the library is important to the community. This information can be used in articles, letters, press releases, and more.
- Note the date of the march in your next newsletter, add it to your Web site, and don't forget to include it in flyers and bookmarks distributed in the library and throughout the community.
- Contact English and Social Studies teachers at your local middle and high schools. Don't forget the media center specialists too! Suggest that students write a letter or send an e-mail during the Virtual March as an assignment.
- Consider sponsoring an essay contest about why the library is important to your community. Send selected or all entries to your elected officials. Personal stories do make a true impact on elected officials.

- Contact organizations with whom the library or Friends partner and share the information about the Virtual March. Library funding affects everyone, even if they don't use the library. Encourage these organizations to spread the word to their staff and members.

- Contact businesses in your community and/or work through the local chamber of commerce. Ask businesses to contact their elected officials during the Virtual March to communicate the role the library plays in their lives (see www.folusa.org for some information about how libraries provide services and support the business community).

- Download the sample press release at www.folusa.org, tailor it to your community, and distribute it a minimum of four weeks in advance of the Virtual March. Follow up and ask the newspaper, radio station, and other media outlets to help you spread the word.

- Remind all Friends, trustees, and library staff to write, call, or send an e-mail during the Virtual March. Our strength lies in numbers, and one voice can make a difference!

⁓❦ ❦⁓

4-12 The Advocacy Action Plan

The Advocacy Action Plan Workbook, which follows, was developed by the American Library Association (ALA) Office for Advocacy, the ALA Advocacy Institute Task Force, the ALA Public Awareness Committee, and Friends of Libraries U.S.A. (FOLUSA). Much is derived from *Making Our Voices Heard: Citizens Speak Out for Libraries*, a publication of FOLUSA.

While the workbook will help you develop a plan for advocacy in your community, please consider attending an Advocacy Institute in person for hands-on enrichment, typically held at the ALA Midwinter Meeting and the ALA Annual Conference. You can find out about upcoming Advocacy Institute programs online at www.ala.org or www.folusa.org.

The Advocacy Action Plan Workbook

ALA Advocacy Institute

American Library Association
50 E. Huron St.
Chicago, IL 60611

Contents

Preface

January 2007

We are pleased to present this action-planning guide, developed in collaboration with the ALA Advocacy Institute Task Force of the Library Advocacy Now! Subcommittee of the ALA Public Awareness Committee.

Grassroots advocacy is the key to the success of our libraries. In an increasingly complex world, with strong competition for funding, the library community must stand up and speak out for America's libraries.

Our voices can be made stronger if we stand up and speak out in a unified voice. Critical to the Advocacy Institute is the idea that library staff, trustees and Friends must work together to make our voices heard. Once we convince community leaders and to citizens at large about the importance and necessity of libraries, they can begin to speak out for libraries at the state and national levels.

Therefore, thank you for your interest in library advocacy. Together, we can do it. ¡Si, si puede!

Sincerely yours,

Sally Reed
Chair, Advocacy Institute Task Force

Carol A. Brey-Casiano
Chair, Library Advocacy Now! Subcommittee
2004–2005 ALA President

Judith Gibbons
Chair, Public Awareness Committee

The Advocacy Action Plan Workbook

Permission is granted to libraries, other groups and individuals to reproduce this toolkit for nonprofit use.

Much of the content and concept for this workbook comes from *Making Our Voices Heard: Citizens Speak Out for Libraries* published by Friends of Libraries U.S.A., 2004. For more information on this publication, please call 1-800-936-5872.

The Advocacy Institute project was the recipient of the 2004 World Book Goal Award. The Regional Advocacy Institute project is made possible by a grant from the Ford Foundation. To learn more, visit www.ala.org/advocacyinstitute.

American Library Association
50 E. Huron St.
Chicago, IL 60611
Telephone: 1-800-545-2433, ext. 2431
Fax: (312) 280-5274
E-mail: advocacy@ala.org

3

Before You Begin

This guide is designed to help you create an action plan for library advocacy. It will help you focus on what you need to do, how you intend to get it done, and how to ensure that the timing is maximized for the best results. The types of activities and task forces listed below are only suggestions. Depending on the type of campaign you design and what you believe will work best in your community, you might create other types of task forces with other types of activities.

Do not worry that you'll need more volunteers than you think you can get. First of all, the Coordinating Committee will include those already involved—the library administration, the library trustees, and the Friends' executive committee. The task forces will require recruitment but not all the task forces need a lot of volunteers. In some cases just two or three "worker bees" will be plenty. On the other hand, the more people you engage to be active in this campaign, the better your chances of success!

If you are presenting this program to a group, plan for a half-day or longer meeting to accommodate the full presentation and discussion. Consider reviewing each file in advance to estimate the time needed to present to your Friends group.

Section 1: Setting Your Goals

What library issues are important to you? What are your goals? What brings you here today? Key issues mentioned in ALA's Advocacy Survey include:

- Passing local library referenda
- Building a new library or new library addition
- Maintaining or increasing funding
- Lobbying/Passing state or national legislation
- Library development and fundraising

ACTION STEP #1: Determine your key issues.

List three key issues here:

_____

_____

_____

_____

_____

_____

_____

_____

_____

_____

_____

_____

5

Prioritize your goals. Can you zero in on your most important goal? What is it?

ACTION STEP #2: Determine your goal.

_____

_____

_____

_____

_____

_____

_____

_____

_____

_____

_____

_____

_____

_____

_____

6

Section 2: Strategies for Developing Your Message

ACTION STEP #3: Name your key audience.

1. _____

2. _____

3. _____

4. _____

5. _____

1. Determine who your audience is.

   A. What groups or individuals are currently most supportive of your library? What key decision-makers would you like to have on your side? What other groups would you like to reach with your message?

   B. Why are your issues this important to them?

   C. List three supporting points:

_____

_____

_____

_____

_____

_____

_____

_____

_____

7

2. Determine your key messages.

What is the most important thing you want others to know? That is your key message, one that you will repeat over and over again. This message should be something you can say in conversation, in interviews or presentations to groups. It should be easy to say and remember—no more than 15 words. It may be simple as:

"Millions of people pass through the library each year, but without adequate support, these resources may not be there when you need them."
Or, *"There is no such thing as good education without good libraries."*

Your key message should be used consistently in news releases, letters-to-the editor and other communications. It may also be distilled into a pithy campaign slogan.

In developing your message, think first about your audience. What do you want them to think? Feel? Do? Feelings are what motivate people to act. That feeling may be compassion, concern, anger or joy. One of your goals in delivering your message should be to spark a feeling, whether it's pride, frustration or outrage.

ACTION STEP #4: What are your key messages?

1. _____

_____

_____

2. _____

_____

_____

3. _____

_____

_____

8

3. Develop your talking points.

What stories or examples support your key message? You will need at least three talking points, stories or examples that support your key message. Using descriptive, local examples is an effective way to get the attention of decision-makers. These may change based on the needs and interests of your audience. Examples include the following:

"A 2002 ALA study confirmed that when the economy is down, library use is up. Unfortunately, at the same time, tight city and state budgets are closing library doors and reducing access when it's needed most."

"Libraries and librarians provide free and equal access to information for people of all ages and backgrounds—in schools, on college and university campuses and in communities large and small."

"Libraries return substantially more benefits to its users for each $1 of annual local taxes."

Tips for Telling an Effective Story*

Effective stories:

✓ are simple, brief and personal;
✓ have a beginning, middle and end;
✓ have a "punch line";
✓ do not use real names unless you have been given permission;
✓ have a message;
✓ are appropriate;
✓ are specific;
✓ are personal;
✓ show the library/librarian clearly solving a problem or filling a need; and
✓ illustrate to a potential funder what giving you the funds will mean in real-life terms.

*Tips for Telling an Effective Story used courtesy of Patricia Glass Schuman.

9

Bridge, Hook and Flag

These are three techniques for controlling the conversation or interview so that you are sure to get the main point or points that you want remembered across to your legislator or legislative staff member.

Bridge. This technique will allow you to move from an area in the conversation that you don't want to discuss or that has the potential to sidetrack the issue, and get the conversation back to your message. If the legislator says, for example, "Why shouldn't we be supporting policy that will help software companies? Isn't a good economy good for libraries?" Rather than getting into a discussion about the economy and whether or not new legislation will help the economy overall, you can use this as a platform for your point by saying: "I think the real question is . . ." and go back to your main point. For example, "I think the real question is "doesn't everyone benefit from good consumer laws?" Then, answer that question!

Hook. This is a technique that can lead your listener to follow-up on your first point allowing you to get a second point in. For example, you can say, "There are two very important considerations that must be taken into account before you support this proposed policy. The first is . . ." then expand on that point. It is likely that the legislator or staff person will then ask you (or allow you) to follow up with the second point. This keeps the conversational ball in your court longer and gives you the opportunity to make both (or all points)

Flag. This technique is the easiest and most people use it unconsciously all the time. Flagging alerts your listeners to what you consider most important. It's a good way to emphasize the key point or points you want the audience to remember. Flagging is simply giving your audience a verbal clue about what is important: "The most important thing to remember is . . ." or "If you remember nothing else, please remember these two points . . ."

10

Section 3: Strategies to Get the Message Out

There are a wide variety of avenues to use in getting your message out, including the following:

Library Newsletter: Your newsletter gives you the "power of the press." Once you have come up with a message or slogan that is powerful for the library, use it often and remember to explain what's behind the message.

Web site: Be sure to have a list of ways that supporters can help present on the very front page of your site. These can include:
- Volunteer to help with the campaign (and give them a number to call).
- Write a letter to the editor (give the newspaper's address along with "talking points" to help them make the case.
- Vote yes for our library and ask all your neighbors and friends to do the same.
- Call your council members and let them know you support the Friends of the Library campaign. Be sure to list council members' phone numbers and/or addresses.

General Promotion Materials: Book marks, book bags, program flyers, membership renewals, direct mailings for membership drives—all of these materials are opportunities to get your message out. Try these other avenues as well:
- Leave pro-library bookmarks at doctors' offices and other places where people go and wait.
- Ask the local grocery store to put your message on their bags for a given length of time.
- Ask your utility company if you can include a bookmark (with your message and information about the library) in a citywide mailing.
- Send a selected list of new business resources at the library to members of the Chamber of Commerce and be sure to include how the library benefits all business in your city.

Letters to the Editor: Everyone reads letters to the editor! So why not be sure that a pro-library letter slips in every now and then? A good way to "hook" library promotion into a letter to the editor is to respond to a big issue that the press is covering showing how libraries can make a difference.

Op-Ed pieces: It can be harder to get your local paper to print an op-ed piece. Here is what will help you get some excellent press coverage via this more in-depth citizen editorial:
- Have a well known citizen write it.
- Tie into a major issue facing the city and show how the library helps (see "Letters to the Editor" above).

11

• Call the editor and talk to him or her about writing an op-ed piece and find out what topic is likely to be printed and how you can increase your chances.

Radio: Develop radio spots for airing on local channels. Visit your local radio station and ask them if they would create some Public Service Announcements (PSAs) for the library as a contribution. If not, ask if they would do so at a discounted price.

Visit with the radio station and tell them about what the library has to offer and why it matters to everyone in the community. Ask the station to develop three or four spots using your message or slogan as a tag line. Finally, be sure the station is willing to air the spots.

Television coverage: Getting coverage of library events is very difficult unless the event is highly unusual. The key is to try to hook the station into covering something that will have significant visual appeal and/or special interest appeal. Talk to the station manager about what kinds of community programs are most likely to get some air time.

Another television avenue—and one that is easier—is to get time on a local noon show or on public access television. This will give you an opportunity to really get your message across whereas coverage of an event is likely to last no more than 10 seconds. Call the station manager to see about being a guest on a local show.

Presentations: Nothing is more effective than personal contact. That's the upside. The downside is that you can't reach as many people at once with your message. You'll need to create and train an entire cadre of Friends and volunteers to get the message out in person.

Civic organizations such as the Lions, Rotary, Kiwanis, etc. always welcome guest speakers. Many of your Friends will belong to their own clubs and organizations as well. Make a list of all the opportunities there are in your community to get some "face time" and begin scheduling speaking engagements to get your message out.

Remember to "know your audience." Make sure when you talk about the importance of the library and its services, you are tailoring your comments to what is of interest to your audience. If you are talking to physicians, for example, talk about the link between health and literacy and all that the library does to support literacy—beginning at birth. If you are talking to the gardening club, talk about the importance of lovely, well maintained libraries as an important part of civic beauty.

Consider the following when deciding which strategies to use:

WHO is your audience?

WHAT is the best way to convey the information to the target audience—radio, TV, direct mail, other? What kind of image do you want to project? Will it be an effective part of your total communication effort?

WHEN is the deadline? Will your message be distributed in time to be effective?

HOW much will it cost? Is this the most effective use of available funds?

WHY is this the best strategy for this audience?

Strategies Checklist

How will you deliver your message? What public relations tools (brochures, fact sheets, etc.) will you need to help build your case?

ACTION STEP #5: Strategies

Postcard Campaigns

Work with radio station to develop Public Service Announcements (PSAs)

Develop ad(s) for local paper and determine best time to run the ad(s)

Mobilize a "Letter to the Editor Campaign"

Find local television and radio stations that will interview campaign volunteers on talk shows

Write an op-ed piece

Other ways (List here) _____

_____

Other ways (List here) _____

_____

13

Section 4: Team Building

ACTION STEP #6: Name Your Network

Library Friends

_____

_____

_____

Faculty Members

Community or Campus Leaders

Trustees

_____

_____

_____

Library Staff

_____

_____

_____

Other

_____

_____

_____

14

ACTION STEP #7: Staying Connected

Write down three things you'll do when you get home to strengthen relationships with the members of your network named above.

1. _____

_____

_____

_____

2. _____

_____

_____

_____

3. _____

_____

_____

_____

Tactics for Success: Creating a Coordinating Committee

The purpose of the Coordinating Committee is to ensure that your advocacy efforts become a reality. The Coordinating Committee can keep track of the many facets of your project, assign deadlines to specific tasks, or delegate specific tasks to others. This group can create an overarching timeline for your entire project and help ensure that your deadlines are met. When creating a Coordinating Committee, think about these questions:

- Who will serve as Chair?
- Who might serve on the committee?
- Who will contact and recruit members?
- When should the committee begin meeting?

In projects large in scope or long-term, you may want to create task forces or subcommittees to help complete specific tasks. If this is the case, ask yourself these questions in planning your subcommittees:

- Will you need other task forces to help achieve your goal?
- How many volunteers per task force are necessary?
- Who might be recruited?
- When should their work begin and be completed?

16

Types of Task Forces

There are many types of task forces, covering specific projects. Some of these are listed here:

Oversight Task Force: Essentially, the Coordinating Committee becomes the Oversight Task Force to keep the campaign going smoothly. This task force develops talking points for the campaign (with the help of library administration), sets up task forces, and calls regular meetings of the task force chairs to ensure steady progress.

Publications and Design Task Force: Creates a design for the campaign so all materials developed will have a consistent look and be readily identified with your campaign. The task force will also develop the materials you'll need for distribution and will coordinate distribution. *For downloadable artwork, visit www. ala.org/@yourlibrary*

Media Task Force: will use local media to get the word out about the campaign. To ensure a consistent message, use the talking points already developed. When developing print advertisements, use the same "look" that the Publications and Design Task Force is using. *For more information see ALA Communications Handbook, www.ala.org/ala/pio/availablepiomat/online_comm_handbook.pdf*

Presentations Task Force: will determine the various venues in your town/city that will give campaign volunteers an opportunity to share information about the campaign. This task force will also recruit and schedule a group of volunteers who are willing to go out and speak to identified civic organizations while using the talking points developed by the Media Task Force.

Finance Task Force: works with the Oversight Task Force and other task force chairs to determine what kind of funding will be needed to accomplish the campaign goals and to identify possible funding resources. Keeps track of the campaign budget.

Evaluation Task Force: works with the Oversight Task Force to monitor the campaign as it moves along and makes recommendations for modifications. This task force will also ensure that acknowledgements are sent out to volunteers, including those who provide professional services, financing or in-kind support. This group will schedule the final meeting following the outcome of the campaign to celebrate or to assess the strengths and weaknesses of the campaign, especially if the campaign needs to be continued for another year.

Section 5: Putting It All Together

What are your goals?

Who is your audience?

What are your key messages?

Who comprises your team?

What committees and task forces will have to be created?

What strategies will you implement?

1. Create a timeline:

Activity	Volunteers Involved	Start Date	End Date

18

Section 6: Checklist for Library Advocates

Following are ways you can support your library. As a member of the library staff, as a Friend, as a library trustee, faculty or administrator, every day is an opportunity to confirm and communicate how important your library is to the entire community, school, or campus. Use these tips to start you on your own advocacy plan.

✓ Talk, talk, talk!

Look around you. There are people everywhere who could use their library, and who don't know about the valuable resources just waiting for them. At the grocery store, student union, the bank, PTA or staff meetings, the post office, in dorms, on a walk with your dog—talk to people and tell them why you love and value the library. Help them see what they could learn there, and how they can help bolster support for this cornerstone of their community, campus or school. It doesn't take much more than a friendly conversation for you to be a hero for your library!

✓ Keep informed.

Stay up to date on state and national activity. Visit the Advocacy Resource Center at www.ala.org/issues&advocacy to view the latest resources, publications and information on library advocacy, as well as sign up for advocacy discussion lists. Contact your state association for information on important issues affecting your state. (You can link to your state chapter through the Advocacy Resource Center.)

✓ Get to know your representatives (and their staffs).

You've elected them; but how can you get them to help your cause? Get to know them—and their staffs—first. Visit your representatives' Web sites to learn their issues and priorities. Invite them to your libraries and let them see, firsthand, how valuable your library is to the community and to academic excellence. Let them know you want them to support all types of libraries, and library-friendly policies and give them specific ways they can get involved. You can schedule an appointment by calling your legislator's office, or even better, invite your representatives to visit the library for a special event you've planned. Let them see how their constituents are using the valuable services provided by the library, and you'll gain an important ally.

✓ Work on your library's print or online newsletter.

Many libraries now have a regular newsletter for patrons, students and faculty. Volunteer to write an advocacy column for the newsletter, highlighting ways that patrons and advocates can help the library, whether that is through a letter-writing campaign, volunteering at events, calling their legislators, or other means. Collecting all the valuable information in one place helps interested parties pick and choose among the many ways to help.

✓ **Make—and/or distribute—handouts.**

Important information about the library, its services, and needs can be distributed in writing, for people to read later or pass on to others. If you have desktop publishing skills, or know someone who does, work to build written materials that can be passed along to others. These can include the library's hours and services, a "wish list" of things the library needs, information about an upcoming event, or any other pertinent library information. These ideas should be posted on your library's bulletin board for all to see. ALA provides a wealth of materials to help you get started through @ your library®, the Campaign for America's Libraries. Visit www.ala.org/@yourlibrary and click on PR Tools & Resources.

✓ **Plan a library event.**

Any event during the year is an opportunity to showcase your library. Create an event or promotion that will get your Friends, trustees or other volunteers involved. You can host the event at the library or a local mall, county fair, park, or any campus venue and invite the media to attend. Visit www.ala.org/pio and click on "initiatives" for information on initiatives celebrated nationwide, including Banned Books Weeks, Library Card Sign-up Month and National Library Week. Always invite elected officials to your events!

✓ **You have your own built-in army of advocates. Use it!**

Many who work in libraries forget that they have a built-in army: the library staff. From library director to custodian, no one knows—and appreciates—the inner workings of your library like they do. Teach them the basics on library advocacy— share the resources ALA has to offer and keep them abreast of current events.

✓ **Lobby.**

Attend state library legislative days—and the ALA National Legislative Day, if possible. Bring Friends, trustees and other supporters. To learn about federal issues, visit the ALA Advocacy Resource Center at www.ala.org/issues&advocacy. Click on "Take Action" to contact your legislator. To learn about state issues, visit the Web site of your state library association.

✓ **Offer Internet tours.**

For those without a computer at home, the library is the number one point of Internet access. Your library can be the window to the Internet for many people in your community. Offer to show patrons how to use it, and walk them through your library's Internet policies. You can even invite local politicians and community leaders to a community-wide Internet orientation event, and show them how the library offers everyone equal access to technology.

20

✓ Get press.

Speaking publicly about the specific value in your library. Are you good at public speaking? Call your local or campus radio talk show or TV news show. Like to write? Write a letter to the editor or an op/ed piece for your local paper, or ask students and faculty to write editorials for the campus paper. However you get in touch with the local or campus press, make sure you've developed your key messages and anticipated tough questions ahead of time, and be ready with statistics and information you can rattle off on the spot. To build your skills visit: www.ala.org/issues&advocacy and click on "Tools & Publications."

✓ Be your library's ambassador to the public or academic community.

Go out into your community and do public appearances to advocate for your library. Visit your local Lions, Elks, or Rotary Club, student and faculty meetings, parent meetings at neighborhood schools, union meetings, and neighborhood watch groups—wherever people gather. Offer to speak about the things your library offers, and how many people are served there. Paint a picture of your school and community without this wonderful resource—and then enlist the help of these powerful groups in supporting the people and buildings behind it!

✓ Build your network.

You are a powerful agent for change on your own, but involving more people makes your message even stronger. Developing a network of library advocates in your community or on campus is a great way to add voices to the chorus of support. When you find people who are willing and able to help, keep track of their contact information and availability. Start a phone tree or an e-mail list to keep in touch with everyone so that when an issue arises, you'll know just who to contact to get the word out.

✓ Add your idea here.

They say that necessity is the mother of invention. As you move forward in your advocacy endeavors, please let ALA know about your successes and new ideas. Send an e-mail to advocacy@ala.org to share your experiences or tips. Your input—fresh ideas and energy—will keep library advocacy moving forward!

Notes

Chapter Five

Building Membership in Friends

Raising the support your library needs works best when you have a strong, large, reliable cadre of self-selected library lovers—in other words, Friends! For almost a century, Friends groups have been helping libraries purchase furniture and equipment, supporting programs, donating to special collections, and working to get bond issues passed and budgets increased. It's hard to imagine a highly successful library without a highly successful Friends group.

Friends groups can't function without members, and recruiting members—both active and contributing—is a constant concern for Friends. Whether you are working on behalf of an academic or public library, you will find many ideas in this chapter for starting a group and keeping it active. You'll find ideas for membership drives and membership incentives. You'll learn about surveying your members to determine their satisfaction with the organization so you can be sure your group is being responsive to its membership—very important for retention!

In a perfect world, all library users would contribute to the Friends—you might want to list that as Goal #1 in your planning process! In addition to attracting a large number of contributing members, you also want to be sure that you provide opportunities for them to be active members as well. How do you do that? You just have to ask! Let your Friends and community see how much fun you are having and what a difference you are making for the library, and then pick up the phone and start inviting them in.

5-1   No More Used Book Sales!

Recently, the Friends of the Georgetown (TX) Public Library opened a used book-store in the library and ended their annual book sales. They were concerned about losing membership, because many people previously joined in order to attend "pre-view night" at the members-only book sale. They adopted an idea described on the Friends of Libraries U.S.A.'s listserv called *Book Bucks*.

How It Works

The Friends' lowest price membership is $10, but *all* new and renewing members receive a green business card–sized coupon printed on card stock with $5 signs around the perimeter. These are Book Bucks, and members can use them in the bookstore to purchase up to $5.00 worth of books. The volunteers running the store write their initials over the dollar signs to show which ones have been used. The cards are good for a year.

Results

The response to the Book Bucks was very positive. It motivated members to renew, even though there is no longer a book sale. Current membership is just over 300, but few Book Bucks are actually redeemed. The Friends intend to continue to use Book Bucks to attract and keep members. Because the books in the store are donated, and the Friends don't have to pay for any premium gifts, it's a no-cost incentive!

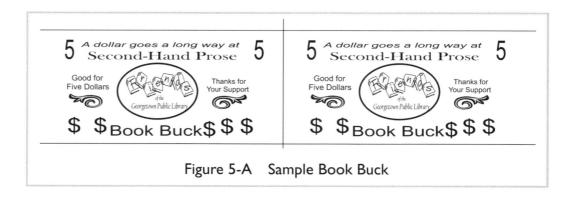

Figure 5-A   Sample Book Buck

5-2   Honoring Friends Benefactors

The Friends of the Tippecanoe County Public Library (Lafayette, IN), have a very special and easy way to honor and encourage membership at a higher level. They recognize their gift with a bookplate in a new library book.

How It Works

- When members join at the Benefactor level ($75 and up), the Friends print up a nice bookplate and put it in a new library book honoring them or their designee.
- The member can't choose the actual book but does get to request a general category (e.g., children's book, literature, history, science, cookbooks).
- The Friends then send the Benefactor member a letter with a scan of the bookplate and the title of the book that honors them.
- Make sure to work out the details carefully with the library staff, especially those who process new books, so that that the program will work easily.

Results

This has been a popular program, and the Friends report that some members have 10 or 12 "honor books" in the collection. The Friends have been doing this for over 12 years, and it costs almost nothing.

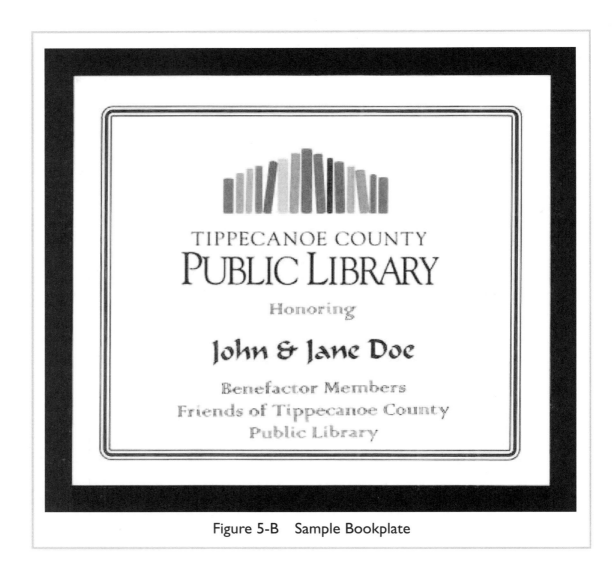

Figure 5-B   Sample Bookplate

5-3 Getting and Keeping Members

There are basically two types of Friends members—"contributing members," who faithfully write a check every year because they want to support the library, and "active members," who serve on the executive board and/or volunteer for committee assignments and other Friends' projects. Both types of members are important contributors because their money helps the library and active members because they help with the work and leadership of the group.

How It Works

- Define your mission and why people should join. Then be sure you make the case for support at every opportunity—during your membership drive, the Friends' book sale, and all Friends' events and programs.
- Set your dues so that membership is available in a number of levels, from a minimum (for seniors and students) to increasingly higher patron levels.
- Design an attractive brochure that gives members an idea of the group's purpose and offers ways for them to become involved. List the types of committees and volunteer opportunities you have, and be sure to call anyone who indicates interest. These new "active members" can become future executive board members, keeping your group dynamic and fresh.
- Be sure that all programs you sponsor include an opportunity for the audience to become members of the Friends. These programs should entertain, educate, and stimulate the audience. Provide hospitality at every function so that members and nonmembers are made to feel welcome.
- Have membership brochures available at the check-out desks of libraries, book sales, and all Friends' functions. Keep the community aware by notifying the media about the Friends' events.
- Membership benefits can include special ticket prices for events sponsored by the Friends and a preview night "for members only" at the book sale. Publish a newsletter for members a minimum of twice a year; quarterly is better, and monthly is best.
- Be prompt in sending out renewal notices. Let members know how their dues help the library and what the Friends have accomplished during the year.
- Solicit local businesses to join. Have a special membership category for them, and list their names so they receive recognition.

Additional Resources

The previous information is from Friends of Libraries U.S.A.'s (FOLUSA) Fact Sheet #18: Getting and Keeping Members. Visit www.folusa.org for additional fact sheets on a variety of topics related to Friends and foundations. For ideas on reenergizing your Friends group, refer to Chapter 4, "Creating, Growing, and Re-Energizing Friends Groups," in *101+ Great Ideas for Libraries and Friends* by Sally Gardner Reed, Beth Nawalinski, and Alexander Peterson, published by Neal-Schuman Publishers, and also available as a tool kit for FOLUSA members online at www.folusa.org.

cô⊙ ⊙w

5-4   Membership Drives That Work

The Friends of the Joseph T. Simpson Public Library (Mechanicsburg, PA) conduct several annual membership drives. Their active and aggressive approach has worked well for them, and their membership continues to grow.

How It Works

- In January, the Friends send a "Dear Friend of the Library" letter to current members asking them to renew their membership. The letter mentions the Friends' membership size, amount of money raised through membership dues, and how the library uses these funds. It also includes a list of the dates for Friends of the Library events in the current year. The letter includes a remittance envelope for mailing and has the membership application printed on the inside flaps of the envelope.
- In April, the Friends send an "Are We Still Friends?" letter to those members who have not renewed their membership from the renewal letter initially sent in January. Another remittance envelope is included to make it easy and convenient for people to send in their renewal payments.
- Each year the Friends send a "Dear Neighbor" letter to people whom the Friends of the Library Board and the Library Board of Trustees have identified as possible members, and they handwrite and sign a personal note on the "Dear Neighbor" letter asking them to join.

Results

In the past three years, the Friends of the Joseph T. Simpson Public Library have doubled their membership from 400 to 800 Friends!

Friends of the Joseph T. Simpson Public Library
16 North Walnut Street
Mechanicsburg, PA 17055-3362
(717) 766-0171

January 2007

Dear Friend of the Library:

We are presently conducting our annual Membership Drive for January through December 2007. A new year means that the time is here for you to **renew** your membership in the Friends of the Joseph T. Simpson Public Library! This past year has been a successful year! We continued to meet our annual goal of increasing our membership and recruited 115 new members in 2006! Through the support of Friends like you, membership dues brought in nearly $21,000 last year.

Along with our fundraising events, the dues enable us to meet our annual financial commitment of $30,000 to the library's operating budget. In addition to this, we fund a variety of other programs and services, such as the Summer Reading Program for children and teens, book purchases, and the library's wireless "wi-fi" network, valued at more than $10,000 per year.

The contributions and talents of our many Friends volunteers allow us to sponsor several fundraising events, including the Holly Trail House Tour and our very popular book sales. When you **renew** your membership, take a moment to review the volunteer opportunities available and let us know if you can give us a few hours of your time.

We value your continued membership so that we can carry out our mission of providing resources which help keep the library running smoothly and enables us to add new services for our community of readers.

Sincerely,

Karen Cochran

Karen Cochran, President
Friends of the Joseph T. Simpson Public Library

2007 Friends of the Joseph T. Simpson Public Library Dates to Remember:

February 9-11	Book Sale at BOOKS BY THE GROSS
March 10	Honeymoon Suite at the Little Theatre of Mechanicsburg
April 3	'Dine Out' at Isaac's Restaurant & Deli at Silver Spring Commons and Rossmoyne Business Center
April 26	Annual Dinner at the Church of God Community Center
June 21	Jubilee Day® Book Sale at BOOKS BY THE GROSS
October 26-28	Book Sale at BOOKS BY THE GROSS
November 25	Holly Trail House Tour

Figure 5-C "Dear Friend of the Library" Sample Letter

ARE WE STILL FRIENDS?

We've Missed You!!

The Friends of the Joseph T. Simpson Public Library have missed you and are hoping you will renew your membership. In case you misplaced the envelope we sent you in January, we have enclosed another one for your convenience.

We would not have been able to provide all of the assistance and financial support we have given to our library if it weren't for your generous and continued support.

Thank you.

The Membership Committee of the Friends of the Joseph T. Simpson Public Library

Love reading. Love libraries.

Figure 5-D   "Are We Still Friends?" Sample Letter

16 North Walnut Street
Mechanicsburg, PA 17055-3362
(717) 766-0171 - www.ccpa.net/simpson

2007

Dear Neighbor:

The Friends of the Joseph T. Simpson Public Library are a vibrant and active organization devoted to the support of the Simpson Public Library in Mechanicsburg. We would love to have you become a member, and this letter will give you several good reasons to do so.

This past year was a very successful one for the Friends of the Library as we increased our membership by 115 new members in 2006. We now have 750 members total! Income from Friends membership dues raised more than $21,000 last year.

Along with our fundraising events, the dues enable us to meet our annual financial commitment of $30,000 to the library's operating budget. We also fund a variety of programs and services, such as the Summer Reading Program for children and teens, book purchases, and the library's wireless "wi-fi" network, all valued at more than $10,000 per year.

We are presently conducting our annual Membership Drive for 2007. We hope that you will consider becoming a member, and perhaps a volunteer for the Friends of the Library. As a member, you will be eligible to attend Preview Night at our popular book sales with the option of buying up to 25 books before the general public is given access. You will also receive *The Browser* which is a bi-monthly newsletter containing advance notices of our many activities. As a volunteer, you can assist the library with many of our special events that support both the library and our community, such as the Holly Trail House Tour and the book sales.

Please consider joining the Friends of the Joseph T. Simpson Public Library. We'd love to have you as a member of our organization dedicated to supporting the Simpson Public Library.

Sincerely,
Karen Cochran
Karen Cochran, President
Friends of the Joseph T. Simpson Public Library

Figure 5-E   "Dear Neighbor" Sample Letter

5-5   Keeping in Touch with Members

You've cashed the check and entered the membership into your database. Now what? Keeping in touch with your members is key to developing long-term relationships, maximizing member retention, and turning "checkbook" members into "active members." Following are a few ideas to help.

Membership Acknowledgments

The Friends of the Lawrence (KS) Public Library mail a postcard to all new and renewing members. Every member gets a postcard-size receipt/thank you. The group has three bulk mailings of these per year, after the membership drive and after each of its two book sales. Between these bulk mailings, the postcards are hand addressed. The postcard is printed four per page on a minimum 70# weight paper with the return address on the reverse side. The Friends have received much positive feedback from members who commented that they appreciated having a receipt for their records. It has also reduced the number of questions library staff is having to field with regard to the Friends and its book sales. This is especially a boon, as the group strongly believes that it serves the library and not the other way around.

Keeping Members Informed

The Friends of Bryant Library (Roslyn, NY) have a catchy slogan they use to communicate with members. Appearing on several different communication pieces, "Friends Don't Let Friends Miss Out!" is both eye catching and attention grabbing. The two-sided piece shown in Figures 5-G and 5-H was used to announce an upcoming fund-raiser at a local bookstore. The group also took the opportunity to reacquaint members with the Friends and all they provide. These handouts were also mailed to nonmembers with a membership envelope encouraging them to join the Friends in addition to supporting the fund-raiser.

Electronic Newsletters

The Friends of Minneapolis (MN) Public Library publish a regular e-newsletter to keep members informed about upcoming programs and fund-raisers, advocacy issues, and membership benefits. Using an online e-newsletter program, the group has an eye-catching and professional electronic communication piece. Using e-mail also enables the Friends to quickly get the word out about last-minute changes to events as well as advocacy issues that need to be addressed quickly.

Figure 5-F   Member Postcard from the Friends of the Lawrence (KS) Public Library

Calling on Members

If you look around the room at every event and program and see the same people volunteering, it's time to bring in some additional help. Update your membership form to include check-off boxes for various areas of Friends' work that utilizes volunteers (e.g., book sales, mailings, programs). Be sure to ask for an e-mail address on your membership form—this is the easiest and cheapest way to reach members. Compile these names into your database in an easy-to-access format. When a need for volunteers arises, send a quick e-mail to those who checked off interest in volunteering in that area. If the response to your e-mail is low, pick up the phone and make a quick call. Be sure to spell out in the e-mail and explain on the phone exactly what type of help you need and include pertinent information (date, time, location). For example, "We need five volunteers to sit at a membership table in the library lobby on Saturday, May 1st, from 1:00 to 2:00 p.m. Volunteers will hand out brochures about the Friends and register patrons for our prize drawing."

FRIENDS DON'T LET FRIENDS

MISS OUT!

Friends build bridges with people who love their community and want to keep it intellectually and culturally vital. Your friendship and support are priceless. Your membership contributions help us provide:

- Programs for all--the Building Bridges Series, Annual Poetry Workshop, Einstein Toy Invention Convention, summer/school vacation shows and activities
- The William Cullen Bryant Lecture
- State-of-the-Art Equipment to enhance your Library experience
- Special Friends events for the entire community
- The Friends Bookstore/Fundraising

Please take a few moments to fill out your membership envelope and mail in your tax-deductible check. Make a difference! JOIN THE FRIENDS TODAY!

Barnes & Noble
Bookfair Voucher Supporting
Friends of Bryant Library

May 6 - 12, 2007
Barnes & Noble
1542 Northern Blvd., Manhasset

Simply present this voucher at the cash register at the time of purchase. A percentage of the net sale will be donated to the Friends of Bryant Library.

_____
Buyer's Name

OFFICE USE ONLY_____

Register #   Transaction #

Amount of sale before tax less purchase of Gift Cards, Membership Cards, and Cafe consumables:

_____

THE FOLLOWING TRANSACTIONS ARE NOT INCLUDED IN BOOKFAIR TOTALS: THE PURCHASE OF GIFT CARDS, MEMBERSHIP CARDS, AND CAFE CONSUMABLES. NON-PROFIT AND BUSINESS ACCOUNT DISCOUNTS MAY NOT BE APPLIED TO BOOKFAIR PURCHASES.

Figures 5-G & 5-H   Postcard from Friends of Bryant Library (Roslyn, NY) (Front-*Top*) and (Back-*Bottom*)

FRIENDS DON'T LET FRIENDS

_____

_____

_____ FROM

FRIENDS OF BRYANT LIBRARY

2 PAPER MILL ROAD, ROSLYN, NY 11576

Figure 5-1   Membership Envelope from Friends of Bryant Library (Roslyn, NY) (Outside)

Enclosed are my tax-deductible membership dues payable to Friends of Bryant Library

MEMBERSHIP LEVELS

Lifetime Member	1,000.
Benefactor	500.
Sponsor	100.
Contributor	50.
Patron & Family	25.

CORPORATE LEVELS

Contributor	1,000.
Patron	500.
Sponsor	250.

Name _____

Street _____

City & State _____

Zip _____

Phone _____

Thanks for being a friend!

FRIENDS DON'T LET FRIENDS

MISS OUT ON PROVIDING:

- Building Bridges Series for Families; Annual Poetry Workshop; Einstein Invention Convention; Year-round Shows and Activites.
- Prestigious William Cullen Bryant Lecture
- State-of-the-Art Library User Equipment
- Special Events for all Ages and Interests
- Friends' Bookstore Fund-Raising Project

Friends help keep our community culturally and intellectually vital. Please mail in your tax-deductible membership and JOIN US!

Figure 5-J   Membership Envelope from Friends of Bryant Library (Roslyn, NY) (Inside)

5-6   Getting Corporate Members

Many Friends groups are beginning to realize just how valuable corporate and local business sponsors can be. Not only do they contribute more than the average member, but also, once they "buy in" to the good work your Friends are doing, they are far more likely to support special projects, donate materials and services when needed, and even advocate for your library when called upon to do so. The following is a list of corporate incentives designed by the Friends of the Library in Waterloo (IA).

Friends of the Library
2007 Corporate Membership Incentive Packages

Corporate Membership Incentive Levels:
* Corporate Friend
* Corporate Sponsorship
* Major Corporate Sponsorship

Each level has its own donation requirement and associated benefits of that sponsorship. The donated amount is in direct proportion to the longevity of the program and the publicity that it generates. The levels are as follows:

I. Corporate Friend
* Donation: $100–$300
  Corporate Friends receive:
  1. Engraved name on plaque in the library
  2. Bi-monthly issue of "Off the Shelf" FOL newsletter
  3. Certificate to display in your place of business

II. Corporate Sponsor
Donation:
  * Poetry Slam: $500
  * Battle of the Bands: $500
  * Author or Performer Appearance: $500
  * Book Collection: $500

Corporate Sponsors receive:
  1. Engraved name on plaque in the library
  2. Mention in all promotion, including press releases, newspaper ads, fliers, and newsletter
  3. Bi-monthly issue of "Off the Shelf" FOL newsletter
  4. Certificate to display in your place of business

Friends of the Library

Waterloo Public Library
415 Commercial
Waterloo, Iowa 50701

Phone: 319 291-4497 ext. 5513
http://www.wplwloo.lib.ia.us

Business Name

Street

City, State, Zip

The Friends of the Waterloo Public Library are inviting area businesses to enter into partnership as Corporate Sponsors and Friends in support of the Waterloo Public Library (WPL) and its programs for 2007.

Since 1976, the Friends have raised over half a million dollars to enhance the programs and services offered by WPL. Our Friends members have volunteered thousands of hours in the past year, and performed fundraising, but we need your help too.

Recent Friends purchases include:

- Print and non-print materials
- Computers, software, and digital camera
- Shelving and display units
-

The Friends also support projects such as the Friends Shop and the semi-annual Used Book and Magazine sales. They provide hundreds of volunteer hours each year in support of these and other programs such as:

- Third Age Project (Home delivery of books)
- Traveling Tales (Reading in area pre-schools)
- Crafts for Children
- Special Library Events
- Volunteer Recognition and Staff Appreciation
- Cedar Valley Reads and other Literacy Initiatives
- Summer Library Program
- Retired Living Book Delivery

As a Corporate Sponsor or Friend, you have the opportunity to directly support the public library and its programs. You will be recognized in "Off the Shelf" the Friends of the Library newsletter, as well as receive a certificate suitable for framing, recognizing your contribution.

We hope you will give serious consideration to our request. The enclosed Membership Incentives may help you determine your giving level. Your support is greatly appreciated!

Sincerely,

Karol Erdmann, Board President
Friends of the Waterloo Public Library

WATERLOO
PJ3LiC
LIBRARY

Figure 5-K   Corporate Partnership Letter from Friends of the Waterloo (IA) Public Library

III. Major Corporate Sponsor
Donation:
- Summer Library Program: $1,000 and up
- Author Visits and Workshops: $1,000 and up

Major Corporate Sponsors receive:
1. Engraved name on plaque in the library
2. Mention in all promotion for the event, including press releases, newspaper ads, fliers, and FOL newsletter
3. Bi-monthly issue of "Off the Shelf" FOL newsletter
4. Certificate to display in your place of business

∽ ∾

5-7 Raising University Friends

The Friends of University of Arizona Libraries is a very active academic group. They recently revised the bylaws and developed a structure to accomplish their many goals—chief among them, raising the level of support from the academic and local communities. Their new committees are Donor Identification Committee, Donor Cultivation Committee, Program Committee, and Book Sale Committee.

Figure 5-L   Alexandrian Circle Logo

How It Works

In 2006, the Donor Identification Committee worked to recruit new Friends members. The chairperson and individual board directors sent personalized letters to their friends as well as to community business leaders, faculty, staff, and college deans.

In addition, the Friends board set up a new participation class, the Alexandrian Circle. The Circle is for those members who donate $1,000 or more, and the benefits are terrific. Not only do members get invitations to special functions and events and personal meetings with authors and other guests, but they also get remote access to *Academic Search Premier Friends Edition*, an electronic database that allows Alexandrian Circle members to search full-text articles in nearly 1,000 publications. Recently, the board added *Business Sources Alumni Edition* to help expand this level of membership. Another integral part of maintaining and recruiting new members is the *Friends'* program series in partnership with other departments of the University of Arizona.

Results

During the membership campaign, the Friends recruited 206 new members, and 160 members upgraded their level of contribution! In addition, within the first year of the creation of the Alexandrian Circle, 79 members joined. Seventeen out of 20 board directors belong to this elite group.

ഷ ഇ

5-8   Determining Benefits for Alumni and Donors

The development office of Washington University in St. Louis was interested in what other academic Friends and development offices offered as electronic database access for donors and alumni. Below is their survey of their counterparts.

Online Database Access Survey

1. How long has your university been offering online database access to your alumni and/or donors?
    - ❑ Less than 1 year
    - ❑ 1–2 years
    - ❑ 3–4 years
    - ❑ More than 4 years
2. Reason why your university offers online database access to your alumni/donors? (Check all that apply)
    - ❑ Alumni interest/good relations
    - ❑ To obtain donors to institution
    - ❑ Offer as benefit of gift club
    - ❑ Other (specify) _____

3. What department monitors the server from which alumni/donor enter or authenticate?
    ❑ Library　　　❑ Alumni office　　❑ Information systems dept.
    ❑ Vendor　　　❑ Other department (specify) _____

4. Who pays for the online database access for your alumni/donors (A&D)?
    ❑ Library　　　　　❑ Alumni office　　❑ Divide cost Library/A&D
    ❑ User is charged　❑ Donor funded　　❑ Other (specify) _____

5. Which vendor(s) do you contract with for online database access for alumni/donors?
    ❑ ABI Informed　　　　❑ EBSCO　　　　　❑ ProQuest
    ❑ Expanded Academic　❑ Other (specify) _____

6. Alumni population of your university:
    ❑ Less than 25,000　　　　❑ 25,000–50,000
    ❑ 51,000–75,000　　　　　❑ 75,000–100,000
    ❑ Over 100,000

7. Which databases are most requested by your alumni/donors (specify)?
    _____
    _____
    _____

8. Suggestions for institutions looking into offering this service?
    _____
    _____
    _____

Results

Almost all of the respondents have been offering online database services for one year or less, with one for just under four years. The main reason for offering the service is to respond to alumni requests, but the libraries and development offices realize that this also generates good will and could be useful for further fund-raising. This service is managed either by the library or by the alumni office and is either free (with the library, foundation, or donors paying the costs) or paid for by the alumni at a reduced rate. One library offers the access free to graduating seniors for the first two years after graduation.

5-9 Surveying Friends Members

The Friends of the Minneapolis Public Library use biennial membership surveys to better meet their goal of being continually responsive to their members. Through the survey, they get feedback on all aspects of Friends' activities. They share the results with all library staff and board members and incorporate them into strategic planning. The Friends also include highlights in their newsletter.

In 2007, for the first time the Friends used an Internet-based survey. As an incentive to participate, all survey respondents were entered to win a $50.00 gift certificate from a locally owned bookstore. Members received e-mails and postcards inviting them to participate and referring them to the Web site to take the survey. Members preferring to complete the survey on paper could contact the Friends' office to receive one by mail.

The survey consisted of 19 short questions and could be easily completed in less than ten minutes. Most questions involved checking boxes with an option to write comments. The Friends used Constant Contact, an Internet-based electronic newsletter and survey company.

How It Works

- Set a budget and a timeline, and identify board and staff members to guide the survey project.
- Identify what should be learned through the survey.
- Choose a survey delivery method (e.g., by mail, online, annual meeting).
- Decide on an incentive (e.g., raffle entry), and choose survey promotion methods (through events, mail, e-mail, library displays). Let members know how important their input is.
- Draft survey questions. Make the survey as easy to complete as possible. Avoid redundant questions, questions that assume advanced knowledge of the respondent, inconsistent language, and inconsistent formatting.
- Circulate draft questions to additional staff and board members for feedback.
- Finalize and launch promotional efforts and the survey.
- Collect and analyze responses. Prepare a report to the board. Keep the results on hand for frequent future reference.
- Don't forget to send the raffle winner's prize.

Results

The Friends heard from 578 members—a response rate of approximately 11 percent. Thirty individuals chose to complete the survey by mail. Many respondents were

The Friends of the Minneapolis Public Library
300 NICOLLET MALL, MINNEAPOLIS, MN 55401

Non-Profit Org.
U.S. Postage
PAID
Minneapolis, MN
Permit # 3656

Your Friends Need to Hear from You!

Your Friends Need to Hear from You!

The more we hear from you, the better we are able to serve our Friends members and support the libraries you love. Please take a minute to log onto www.friendsofmpl.org and fill out our membership survey today. **Complete the survey and enter to win a $50 Magers & Quinn Booksellers gift certificate.**

If you wish to fill out the survey but prefer not to do it online, please call 612-630-6175.

The Friends of the Minneapolis Public Library are entering discussions with the Library Foundation of Hennepin County about a potential merger of our organizations to support the new consolidated library system. Your opinion matters!

Please complete the survey by Friday, July 6th.

Figures 5-M and 5-N   Postcard Mailed to Members (Front-*Top*) and (Back-*Bottom*)

members not otherwise in regular contact with the organization. It was an invaluable learning opportunity.

The Friends used an online service to host the survey and to process the results. Despite the survey being online, the response rate was similar to that of previous years. The $30.00 expense was easily offset by savings in staff time, postage, and printing. By using bulk mail to send the postcard invitations, expense was limited to $0.10 per postcard.

578 Friends Members Speak Up

Thank you! 578 people took the time to fill out our membership survey which will help The Friends in our planning in coming years. Survey results confirmed our belief that advocating for more public funding for our library system is the MOST important Friends activity, followed closely by raising funds for system-wide collections. Here are some other useful points that we learned about you:

49% have contacted an elected official about **LIBRARY FUNDING** last year

48% use the library at **LEAST** once per week

6% are **NOT IN SUPPORT** of the consolidation between **Hennepin County** and the **Minneapolis Public Library System**

93% say the Friends are effective or **VERY EFFECTIVE** in supporting our libraries.

These numbers and your comments will guide our strategic planning and programming as we position ourselves to be a strong and responsive member-driven organization. Thank you again for taking the time to give us your thoughts on how we are doing.

Figure 5-O   Survey Results from Newsletter

The Friends of the Minneapolis Public Library Survey

✳ Required Question(s)

1. How important are the following Friends activities to you:

	Not a Priority	Somewhat of a priority	Important	Very Important
Advocating for more public funding for our library system.	○	○	○	○
Coordinating volunteers, e.g., internet tutors, reading mentors & home delivery	○	○	○	○
Operating The Friends Book Store	○	○	○	○
Raising funds for literacy programs, e.g., summer reading, homework help, etc.	○	○	○	○
Raising funds for new book purchases and collections system-wide	○	○	○	○
Sponsoring cultural events such as Talk of the Stacks and People's University	○	○	○	○

2. Amongst the local institutions and organizations I support, I consider the Minneapolis Public Library to be:

○ The most important.

○ Among the top five.

○ Important, but not a top priority.

3. In supporting our libraries, I believe The Friends are:

○ Very effective

○ Effective

○ Not effective

Comment:

150 character(s) left.

4. I feel _____ about Minneapolis Public Library issues and the role The Friends play in supporting the library.

○ Well informed

○ Informed

○ Unclear

5. Regarding the consolidation of the Minneapolis Public Library system with Hennepin County Library system, I:

○ Support the consolidation.

○ Do not support the consolidation.

○ Am not sure.

Figure 5-P   Friends of the Minneapolis (MN) Public Library Membership Survey

6. I use/my family uses the library:

○ At least once a week.

○ At least once a month.

○ Once a month or less.

○ About once a year.

○ I can't remember the last time I/we used a library.

7. I have been a member of the Friends of the Minneapolis Public Library for:

○ Less than 2 years

○ 2-5 years

○ 6-10 years

○ 11-19 years

○ 20 or more years

○ I am not currently a member

8. Rate how important the following Friends membership benefits are to you:

	Not a Priority	Somewhat of a priority	Important	Very Important
10% off at 19 local independent bookstores, including The Friends bookstores	○	○	○	○
Subscription to The Friends newsletter, Speaking Volumes	○	○	○	○
Invitations to members-only book sales and events	○	○	○	○
Advance registration for space-limited programs	○	○	○	○
Recognition in The Friends Annual Report	○	○	○	○

9. How often do you read the following:

	Never	Occasionally	Always
Speaking Volumes, the bi-monthly joint newsletter of The Friends and the Library	○	○	○
Check It Out, the twice monthly e-newsletters from The Friends	○	○	○
Event postcards, including free lectures, classes, or special events	○	○	○
Friends Website	○	○	○

Comment:

150 character(s) left.

10. In the past 2 years, I attended: (Check all that apply.)

☐ Grand Opening of the new Central Library

☐ Friends Annual Meeting

☐ Friends Holiday Toast

Figure 5-P   Friends of the Minneapolis (MN) Public Library Membership Survey *(continued)*

☐ The People's University classes

☐ Talk of the Stacks author series

☐ Film Chronicles or Movietime for Kids

☐ A Friends Book Sale

11. In the past year, have you contacted elected officials about library funding?

○ Yes

○ No

Comment:

150 character(s) left.

12. Check each of the following organizations in which you are a member or to which you make financial contributions:

☐ Animal Humane Society

☐ The Children's Theater Company

☐ Guthrie Theater

☐ Hennepin County Library Foundation

☐ The Loft Literary Center

☐ Minneapolis Institute of Arts

☐ Minnesota Historical Society

☐ Minnesota Public Radio

☐ Science Museum of Minnesota

☐ Twin Cities Public Television

☐ Walker Art Center

☐ Other

13. Which of the following newspapers and periodicals do you read on a regular basis? This information helps us identify and recruit other potential Friends members. (Check all that apply.)

☐ Atlantic Monthly

☐ The Bridge

☐ City Pages

☐ Downtown Journal

☐ Mpls/St. Paul Magazine

☐ Minnesota Monthly

☐ New York Times

☐ The New Yorker

☐ Northeaster / North News

☐ The Rake

☐ St. Paul Pioneer Press

Figure 5-P   Friends of the Minneapolis (MN) Public Library Membership Survey *(continued)*

☐ Smithsonian

☐ Southwest Journal

☐ Southside Pride

☐ Star Tribune

☐ Minnesota Women's Press

☐ Other

14. Are you: (Optional)
○ Female
○ Male

15. In which of the following age groups do you belong? (Optional)
○ 24 and under
○ 25 - 34
○ 35 - 44
○ 45 - 54
○ 55- 64
○ 65- 74
○ 75+

16. To assist in development of Friends programs, please let us know if you: (Check all that apply.)
☐ Have children or grandchildren (nearby) under the age of 5.
☐ Have children or grandchildren (nearby) between the ages 6 and 16.
☐ Work in downtown Minneapolis.
☐ Would attend events downtown during day time hours.
☐ Do not feel comfortable traveling to downtown Minneapolis for events.
☐ Feel comfortable traveling to downtown Minneapolis for events day or night.

Comment:

150 character(s) left.

17. Additional notes or comments for The Friends:

500 character(s) left.

Figure 5-P   Friends of the Minneapolis (MN) Public Library Membership Survey *(continued)*

18. **Please add my e-mail to receive future communications from The Friends about the merger, special events, or membership information. All e-mails will be registered to win a $50 gift certificate for Magers & Quinn Booksellers. Name and e-mail will be stored separately from your survey answers.**

50 character(s) left.

19. **Name: (Optional)**

50 character(s) left.

Figure 5-P   Friends of the Minneapolis (MN) Public Library Membership Survey *(continued)*

5-10   Surveying Friends and Trustees

The Joseph T. Simpson Public Library (Mechanicsburg, PA) wanted to include membership opinion in its planning process. Below are two surveys, one given to the Friends members and one to the trustees. These surveys were made available in print and online. The results were used in the development of a strategic plan (see Unit 6-9).

**Joseph T. Simpson Public Library Friends Board Survey
June 2007**

1. In your opinion, what is the main purpose or objective of a Friends Group for a public library?

2. In your opinion, do any of the following descriptions describe the Friends of the Library Board meetings?
    Check those that apply.
    ❑ Meaningful and productive discussion.
    ❑ Tend to rehash topics longer than is necessary.
    ❑ Everyone contributes during the meetings.
    ❑ A few people monopolize Board discussions.
    ❑ Some people don't participate during the meetings.
    ❑ Well-planned and properly covered agenda.
    ❑ Poorly organized Board meetings.
    ❑ Information provided is usually sufficient to make sound decisions.
    ❑ Information provided is sometimes insufficient to make a sound decision.
    ❑ Library Director provides good supportive information about the library.

❑ Library Director needs to provide more information.
❑ Good attendance at Board meetings—most people are usually there.
❑ Poor attendance at Board meetings—some people miss fairly frequently.
❑ Difficulty agreeing on course of action because Board is split into opposing factions.
❑ General agreement on basic objectives and plans for the Friends.
Comments:

3. In what areas would you like to have the Friends Board place greater emphasis?
    ❑ Library Advocacy
    ❑ Programming
    ❑ Book Sale
    ❑ Fundraising
    ❑ Membership Recruitment
    ❑ Community Outreach and Awareness
    ❑ Public Relations and Marketing
    ❑ Board Development (Recruitment, Retention, and Training for Board Members)
    ❑ Other (please list)

4. In what areas would you like to have the Friends Board improve its functioning?
    ❑ Library Advocacy
    ❑ Programming
    ❑ Book Sale
    ❑ Fundraising
    ❑ Membership Recruitment
    ❑ Community Outreach
    ❑ Public Relations and Marketing
    ❑ Board Development (Recruitment, Retention, and Training for Board Members)
    ❑ Other (please list)

5. What are the most important issues facing the Friends of the Joseph T. Simpson Public Library?

6. How well informed do you feel as to library activities, usage, concerns, and problems?
   ❑ Very Satisfied
   ❑ Satisfied
   ❑ Not Satisfied
   ❑ Very Dissatisfied
   Comments:

7. How would you describe the communication between the Friends Board of Directors and the Library Director?
   ❑ Excellent
   ❑ Good
   ❑ Fair
   ❑ Poor
   ❑ Don't Know
   Comments:

8. How would you describe the communication between the Friends Board of Directors and the Library Board of Trustees?
   ❑ Excellent
   ❑ Good
   ❑ Fair
   ❑ Poor
   ❑ Don't Know
   ❑ Comments:

9. How would you describe the communication among the members of the Friends Board of Directors?
   ❑ Excellent
   ❑ Good
   ❑ Fair
   ❑ Poor
   ❑ Don't Know
   Comments:

10. In your opinion and in the context of the community which the Friends of the Library represent, is the diversity of board members adequate? (age, male/female ratio, municipality of residence, etc.)
    ❑ Yes
    ❑ No
    ❑ Not Sure
    Comments:

11. What do you like about serving on the Friends Board?

12. Is there anything you dislike about serving on the Friends Board? If yes, please list.

13. List three strengths of the Friends of the Joseph T. Simpson Public Library.

14. List three weaknesses of the Friends of the Joseph T. Simpson Public Library.

15. How do you see the Friends of the Library changing in the next five years?

Friends of the Joseph T. Simpson Public Library
Long Range Planning Survey for Library Trustees
June 2007

1. In your opinion, what is the main purpose or objective of a Friends Group for a public library?

2. In what areas would you like to have the Friends Board place greater emphasis?
    ❑ Library Advocacy
    ❑ Programming
    ❑ Book Sale
    ❑ Fund-raising
    ❑ Membership Recruitment
    ❑ Community Outreach and Awareness
    ❑ Public Relations and Marketing

❑ Board Development (Recruitment, Retention, and Training for Board Members)
❑   Other (please list)

3.   What are the most important issues facing the Friends of the Joseph T. Simpson Public Library?

4.   How would you describe the communication between the Friends Board of Directors and the Library Board of Trustees?
  ❑ Excellent
  ❑ Good
  ❑ Fair
  ❑ Poor
  ❑ Don't Know
  Comments:

5.   List three strengths of the Friends of the Joseph T. Simpson Public Library.

6.   List three weaknesses of the Friends of the Joseph T. Simpson Public Library.

7.   How do you see the Friends of the Library changing in the next five years?

For further information on designing an effective survey, see www.surveymonkey.com/DisplayDetail.asp?SID=360076&RID=29903060.

❧ ❧

5-11   Membership Samples

Following are a variety of membership-related materials from Friends groups around the country. From membership brochures to postcards and more, these materials are sure to spark some ideas for your group. Friends of Libraries U.S.A. welcomes samples of your materials as well. Please e-mail or mail your samples; contact information is given online at www.folusa.org.

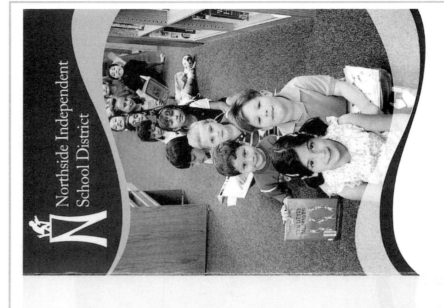

Friends of NISD Libraries
Department of Library and Textbook Services
6632 Bandera Road, Bldg. D
San Antonio, Texas 78238
office: (210) 397-8190
fax: (210) 706-8974
email: fonl@nisd.net
library.nisd.net/friends

Founding Board of Directors
Joyce Hultgren, Chair, Alumna
Lisa Charlton, Vice Chair, Parent
Norma Murphy, Secretary, Elementary Librarian
Dr. Benito Resendez, Treasurer, NISD Principal
Jana Knezek, Director, Library and Textbook Services
Patricia Blattman, Community Member
Sovreyne Dougherty, High School Student
Kathy Lindley, Secondary Librarian
Dr. Martha Mead, Community Member
Rep. Jose Menendez, Community Member
Ed Rawlinson, Community Member

Librarian Founding Committee
Janice Cayton, Library Specialist
Carrie Damon, Rayburn MS
Melinda Dawson, Library Specialist
Camille Fiorillo, Palo Alto College
Faye Hagerty, Howsman ES
Janis Lappeus, Stinson MS
Kathy Lindley, Pat Neff MS
Judith Penington, Pease MS
Steffanie Persyn, Brauchle ES
Frances Ramos-Contreras, Hatchett ES
Jana Knezek, Director, Library and Textbook Services

Northside Independent School District
5900 Evers Road
San Antonio, TX 78238

Friends of Northside ISD Libraries

December 2006

Figure 5-Q   Friends of Northside Independent School District Libraries (TX)
Membership Brochure (Outside)

Friends of NISD Libraries Membership Form
Please clip and send with payment to Friends of NISD Libraries, Library Services,
6632 Bandera Road, Bldg D, San Antonio, Texas 78238
Or turn in to your campus librarian

Name_____ Address _____
City_____ State _____ Zip _____
Home phone _____ Cell phone _____ e-mail _____
    NISD Student-free   Individual - $5   Family - $10   Contributing - $50   Patron - $100   Lifetime - $250

Amount enclosed: $ _____

I am interested in helping with:
☐ Public Relations   ☐ Special Events   ☐ Advocacy   ☐ Membership   ☐ Other

Friends of NISD Libraries is a Designated Fund of Northside Education Foundation 501(c) 3 #74-2591569 (Tax ID Number)

Services Provided by Northside Libraries

- Curriculum integration
- Books
- eBooks
- Videos
- Subscription full-text online databases
- Local and national newspapers
- Popular and scholarly magazine subscriptions
- Spanish resources
- Foreign language resources
- Internet access and other technologies
- Interlibrary loan
- Extended hours at some campuses
- Professional resources for educators
- Resources for parents
- Author visits
- Storytellers
- Book fairs

Mission

The Friends of NISD Libraries promotes and supports the vital role of the school library in the educational experience.

Goals and Objectives

- Educate the community (parents, students, employees, residents) about library services that impact reading, critical thinking, and lifelong learning essential to a democratic society
  - a. Sponsor district-wide literacy events
  - b. Host an informational and educational website
- Support activities of the NISD libraries
  - a. Publicize campus library literacy events
  - b. Facilitate the establishment of campus Friends groups
  - c. Establish an information bank for activities and opportunities for campus Friends groups
- Advocate for school libraries at all levels (campus, city, state, nation)
  - a. Establish an eMail distribution list of persons willing to correspond on behalf of school libraries
  - b. Establish a list of persons willing to speak on behalf of school librarians

Why do Northside ISD Libraries need Friends?

- To help promote reading, literacy and lifelong learning
- To help advocate for school libraries
- To help raise funds for special initiatives

Who can be a Friend?

- Parents
- Administrators
- Students
- Grandparents
- Teachers
- Community members
- Employees
- Anyone!

Northside school libraries annually...

- Circulate over 2,000,000 books and other resources
- Serve over 73,000 classes
- Are used by over 1,200,000 students, teachers, parents, and employees

Figure 5-R   Friends of Northside Independent School District Libraries (TX) Membership Brochure (Inside)

Figure 5-S   Friends of South Pasadena (CA) Public Library, Inc., Membership Brochure (Outside)

More than a Century of Friendship

Since our library's genesis as a "free public reading room" in the 1890s, it has enjoyed the support of public-spirited community leaders. In 1950, that support crystallized with the formation of the Friends of the South Pasadena Public Library, Inc. Today, more than 700 member Friends help to maintain our library's role as a cornerstone of community life.

The Friends Bookstore

Our Bookstore, located on the library's second floor and accessible by elevator, offers donated books for sale at bargain prices. Special sales are frequently featured on the main floor, along with a monthly silent auction.

A high point of the year is the annual Holiday Gift Book Sale, with a members-only preview and reception on the eve of the event. The Bookstore is staffed by more than 60 dedicated volunteers and a Steering Committee. In its first 25 years, the all-volunteer operation has netted approximately $750,000 in support of the library.

Endowment Funds

Two Endowment Funds, administered by the Friends Board of Directors, allow for the purchase of materials which would otherwise not be obtainable within the library's budget. Interest from the Funds, contributions to which are often made as memorials or tributes, is used to supplement the library's collections. Since 1984, the Book Endowment Fund has provided special reference works and other high-quality volumes.

The Technology Endowment Fund, established in 2007, supports the purchase of digital resources for library patrons.

Becoming a Member

Friends receive invitations to special programs and events, such as the members-only preview of the Holiday Gift Book Sale. A quarterly newsletter, Between Friends, keeps members up to date. The annual meeting of the Friends of South Pasadena Public Library, Inc. is held in January.

Senior/Student	$ 10
Individual	$ 25
Family	$ 40
Bronze	$ 50
Silver	$ 75
Gold	$ 100
Platinum	$ 500
Friend for Life	$ 1000

Membership dues are tax-deductible donations

Membership envelopes are available from the Reference Desk or the Friends Bookstore 1100 Oxley Street, South Pasadena, CA 91030.

Figure 5-T   Friends of South Pasadena (CA) Public Library, Inc., Membership Brochure (Inside)

Future Friend of the Library

The Friends of the Library for Huntington City-Township Public Library benefits the Library on a continuing basis:

- Delivers books to shut-ins/nursing homes
- Assists with Children's Room activities
- Provides activity packets for hospitalized children
- Helps fund & promote young adult activities
- Provides "perks" for Junior Volunteers
- Helps fund Summer Reading Programs for all ages
- Operates magazine recycling/resale booth
- Operates the Annual Used Book Sale in June and the Holiday Book Boutique in December
- Provides funding for special programs at both the Main Library and the Markle Branch
- Helps address other specific needs not in the Library's budget
- Purchases various items for the Library, including a popcorn machine for Library activities, new tables for the public meeting room, and an awning for the entrance of the Markle Branch

The Friends of the Library are open to new members and new ideas - join today!

Figure 5-U Friends of the Library for Huntington City–Township (IN) Public Library Membership Brochure (Outside: Back-*Left*; Front-*Right*)

If you believe in a public library where information, education, and recreation are available to all people...

If you value books and reading in your own life and want to associate with others who do, also...

If you derive personal satisfaction from supporting the library, and through it, the community as a whole...

Then Join Friends of the Library for Huntington City-Township Public Library!

Together we can develop a blueprint for success and build a solid future for our Library and our community.

200 West Market Street
Huntington, Indiana
46750

Voice: 260-356-0824
Fax: 260-356-3073

Hours:'
Mon—Thurs   9am—8pm
Fri & Sat   9am—5pm

Main Library

Markle Branch

Hours:
Mon—Fri   1pm—7pm
Wed   10am—Noon &
           1pm—7pm
Sat   9am—Noon

197 East Morse Street
Markle, Indiana 46770

----- Annual Family Membership $5.00   ---- Annual Benefactor Membership $25.00

Name

Mailing Address

City/State/Zip

Phone Number

*Please make checks payable to "Friends of the Library".
This form may be turned in at either Library location:
Main Library - 200 West Market Street, Huntington, Indiana 46750

Mission Statement

The Friends of the Library for Huntington City-Township Public Library is a group of people who believe in the Library and the importance of its services.

Friends demonstrate their belief by giving their time and money to support Library activities, to secure Library materials and services, and to promote the Library as an active, dynamic education and information center in the community.

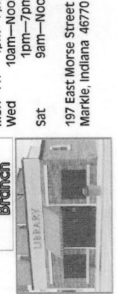

Figure 5-V   Friends of the Library for Huntington City–Township (IN)
Public Library Membership Brochure (Inside)

213

BOOKTIQUE

Hours
Tuesday through Saturday
11:00 a.m. - 3:00 p.m.

503-699-9109

Used books at

bargain prices

Location
3975 Mercantile Medical Plaza Building
Lake Oswego
at the intersection of
Boones Ferry Road and Kruse Way

Voices

in support of the

Public Library

Figure 5-W   Friends of the Lake Oswego (OR) Public Library Membership Brochure (Outside)

214

The Friends of the Lake Oswego Public Library is an all volunteer, non-profit association who have been helping the Library since 1953.

Members:
- Promote the library's role in the community.
- Enhance the Library's collections and programs.
- Financially support the Library in its goals and objectives where public funds are not available.

The Friends' members believe many voices raise the awareness of the importance of a public Library for all people.

For more information about The Friends, call 503-635-6950.

Please join

The Friends

The Friends operate the Booktique, a used bookstore, as an ongoing fund raiser. Proceeds benefit the Library and some of the funds are dedicated to the future needs of the Library.

Let your voice

be heard

The majority of the used books are donations from the public, the rest are books the Library has withdrawn from its collections. Donations can be taken directly to the Booktique during its open hours. All donations are tax deductible.

Volunteers are needed for the Booktique. You can volunteer by calling the store and speaking with the Manager. Your active participation as a Booktique volunteer or Board member is encouraged.

Join us and let your voice be heard.

The Library needs

your friendship

MEMBERSHIP APPLICATION

Join The Friends ~ Show Your Support

NAME: _____   DATE: _____

ADDRESS: _____   PHONE: _____

Please indicate: ❏ New Member   ❏ Renewal   ❏ Current Library Volunteer
❏ I wish to help the Booktique
❏ Yes, I am interested in knowing about library events: (email) _____

Yearly Dues—please check one:
❏ Individual $5.00
❏ Family $7.50
❏ Patron $25.00
❏ Sponsor $100.00
Membership is 12 months from acceptance date

Make Checks Payable to:
Friends of the Lake Oswego Public Library
706 Fourth Street
Lake Oswego, OR 97034

Checks can be mailed or left at the Circulation Desk

Figures 5-X & 5-Y   Friends of the Lake Oswego (OR) Public Library Membership Brochure
(Inside-*Top*) (Enclosure-*Bottom*)

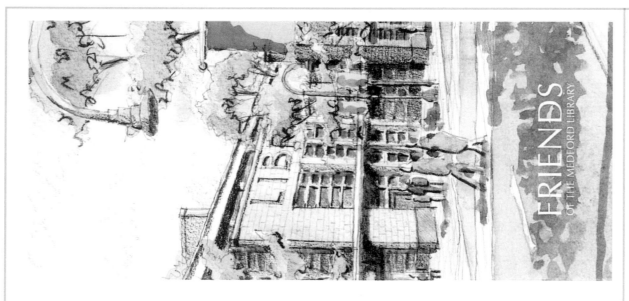

Purpose of the Friends

The purpose of the Friends is to encourage and support development and use of the Central Library in Jackson County.

The Friends provide money and support for many extra or special items when money is not available in the regular library budget.

Book Shop proceeds also support the library volunteers, children's and teen programs and Summer Reading.

The Friends is a public non-profit corporation. All contributions are tax deductible.

The Friends of the Medford Library Board of Directors meets on the second Monday of each month at 12:30 p.m. September through June. The public is welcome.

Come Join Us!

FRIENDS OF THE MEDFORD LIBRARY

205 South Central
Suite 107
Medford, OR 97501

Figure 5-Z Friends of the Medford (OR) Library Membership Brochure (Outside)

Friends Book Shop

- All books are donations
- Managed and staffed by Friends volunteers
- Located at the Central Library
- Any questions? Call 779-3246

Where Does the Money Go?

- Children's Summer Reading program
- Enhancement items not in library budget
- Teen Summer Reading and workshops
- Outreach to Childcare providers
- Books to encourage reading in Juvenile Detention facility
- Jackson County Reads
- Third Wednesday at the Library children's programs

Friends of the Medford Library Member Benefits

- Book shop discount — buy two books, receive third book free
- Volunteer opportunities
- Complimentary luncheon at Annual Meeting
- Friends of the Medford Library newsletter
- Advance notice of special library programs

For more information call 541-779-3246

Please mail to: Friends of the Medford Library, 205 South Central, Suite 107, Medford, OR 97501

Additional contribution _____

☐ Please call me, I'd like to volunteer

☐ Individual $10.00   ☐ Family $15.00   ☐ Business $25.00   ☐ Individual life member $250.00

☐ New member   ☐ Renewal

Name _____ Phone _____ E-mail _____

Address _____ City _____ ZIP _____

M E M B E R S H I P   F O R M

Figure 5-AA   Friends of the Medford (OR) Library Membership Brochure (Inside)

Support

Our Library
Our Community

Friends of the
Pasco County Library System

PASCO COUNTY
LIBRARY SYSTEM

Hudson Regional Library
8012 Library Road
Hudson, Florida 34667
Telephone: (727) 861-3020

Regency Park Branch Library
9701 Little Road
New Port Richey, Florida 34654
Telephone: (727) 861-3049

Centennial Park Branch Library
5740 Moog Road
Holiday, Florida 34690
Telephone: (727) 834-3204

South Holiday Branch Library
4649 Mile Stretch Drive
Holiday, Florida 34690
Telephone: (727) 834-3331

Hugh Embry Branch Library
14215 Fourth Street
Dade City, Florida 33523
Telephone: (352) 567-3576

New River Branch Library
34043 State Road 54
Zephyrhills, Florida 33543
Telephone: (813) 788-6375

Land O' Lakes Branch Library
2818 Collier Parkway
Land O' Lakes, Florida 34639
Telephone: (813) 929-1214

Visit the Library Website: *pascolibraries.org*

For more information on the
Friends of the Library,
Please call (727) 861-3020
or email *friends@pascolibraries.org*

Friends of the
Pasco County Library System

2006

Friends
MEMBERSHIP

NAME

LOCAL ADDRESS

CITY/STATE/ZIP

EMAIL ADDRESS

THE LIBRARY I WANT TO SUPPORT

Membership Level:
☐ Individual $ 10.00
☐ Family $ 15.00
☐ Book Donor $ 25.00
☐ Other $ _____
☐ Partner $1000.00+

Please Make Checks Payable To:
Friends of the Pasco County Library System, Inc.
Your contribution is tax-deductible.

Mail To:
Friends of the Pasco County Library System, Inc.
P.O. Box 6118
Hudson, FL 34674-6118

Volunteer Opportunities:
You may check more than one category of interest.

☐ Book Sales   ☐ Teen Programs
☐ Special Events   ☐ Membership Drive
☐ Children's   ☐ Financial Support
   Programs   Only

Cut Here

Figure 5-BB   Friends of the Pasco County (FL) Library System Membership Brochure (Outside)

Join today!

How to Support the Friends of the Library

A Friends membership is $10 for individuals and $15 for families. With your membership, you will receive a membership card and the Friends newsletter.

We suggest you consider supporting as a book donor with a $25 contribution. In addition to your Friends benefits, a book will be donated to the library in your name.

Several leading Pasco County businesses, organizations, and individuals support our *Be A Friend, Be A Partner* program with their contributions of $1,000 or more. We thank these library partners for helping to strengthen and expand the library's collection, special services, special programming and technology. ■

What the Friends of the Library do for our community...

- *Library Advocacy*

- *Cultural Programs - Music Series, Films and Lecture Series*

- *Honor with Books (Memorials/Tributes)*

- *Children's/Teen Programming*

- *Adult/Teen Volunteer Opportunities*

The Friends of the Pasco County Library System, Inc., is a 501 (c) (3), not-for-profit organization. Your contribution is tax deductible.

Welcome

Strong support of our public library is essential for continued county, state and federal funding. Our library advocacy efforts are strengthened by your support.

A Friends membership is your best way to show that the public library is important to you, your family and your community.

Friends memberships, book sales and fundraising activities make all of this possible.

If you have attended one of our cultural, art or music programs, if your child or grandchild participated in a storytime or summer reading program, then you have already benefited from Friends support. ■

Figure 5-CC   Friends of the Pasco County (FL) Library System Membership Brochure (Inside)

Join the

FRIENDS

of

FERGUSON LIBRARY

FRIENDS
of Ferguson Library

THE FERGUSON LIBRARY
Stamford's Public Library
One Public Library Plaza
Stamford, Connecticut 06904
203-964-1000 x 275
www.fergusonlibrary.org
www.friendsoffergusonlibrary.org

Ten Good Reasons to Join the FRIENDS

1. Support children's, adult, and young adult reading programs.

2. Assist the library with the purchase of the latest books, videos, and DVDs.

3. Sponsor the Books for Babies Program.

4. Help fund literacy programs.

5. Help sponsor a wide variety of valuable library programming.

6. Receive advance notice of special events.

7. Meet others who love books as much as you do.

8. Receive discounts on Used Book Shop purchases, Starbucks (Main Branch), and more.

9. Be a part of this library's vision for the future.

10. Know that your contribution will touch the lives of people in our community.

Please mail this application to:

Friends of Ferguson Library
One Public Library Plaza
Stamford, Connecticut 06904

Memberships are annual by calendar year. Memberships received after September 1st of each year will be applied to the membership year beginning the following January 1st.

The Friends of Ferguson Library is a not-for-profit organization. Your gift is tax deductible to the extent provided by federal law.

Figure 5-DD   Friends of Ferguson Library (Stamford, CT) Membership Brochure (Outside)

Membership Application

Please make checks payable to "Friends of Ferguson Library"

☐ New Member   ☐ Renewal

☐ Senior Individual ($20)
☐ Senior Couple ($25)
☐ Individual ($25)
☐ Family ($35)
☐ Patron ($50)
☐ Sponsor ($100)
☐ Good Friend ($250+)

# of Membership stickers _____

☐ I have included a matching gift form from my employer.

☐ I do not want to be a Member, but enclose a donation for $ _____

Yes, I would like to Volunteer for:

☐ Used Book Shops—Sales
☐ Used Book Shops—Sorting Books
☐ Mailings
☐ Other (Please Specify) _____

Name: _____

Address: _____

City/State/Zip: _____

Telephone: _____

E-mail: _____

Membership Benefits

Basic Membership ($20/$25/$35)

- Friends of Ferguson Coffee Mug (new)
- 10% Discount at the Friends Used Book Shops
- 10% Discount at Starbucks (Main Branch location only)
- Special Membership Sticker to place on Library Card
- Special discounts and notices throughout the year

Patron ($50)

- All basic membership benefits, plus:
- Friends of Ferguson tote bag (new)

Sponsor ($100)

- All Patron membership benefits, plus:
- A book donated to the Library in your honor

Good Friend ($250+)

- All Sponsor membership benefits, plus:
- Name listed on an honorary plaque at the Main Branch

Who are the Friends of Ferguson Library?

The Friends of Ferguson Library is a not-for-profit organization established in 1979. Our purpose is to encourage and promote community participation and support for the activities and programs of the Ferguson Library and to assist in the Library's growth and development.

Through membership, donations, used book sales and volunteerism, the Friends of Ferguson Library help support library activities for all ages, including the children's and adult summer reading programs, Literacy Labs, and Library Art Exhibits. Our continued support provides for materials, equipment, and books that would not otherwise be funded.

The Friends also organize many wonderful events throughout the year, including special book sales and the Book & Author Luncheon.

Membership in the Friends of Ferguson Library is open to all interested people, organizations, and businesses.

How Can I Help?

By becoming a member, donating, or volunteering your time and talents. Kindly fill out and return the form provided.

Figure 5-EE   Friends of Ferguson Library (Stamford, CT) Membership Brochure (Inside)

A Recipe for a Vibrant
Webster Groves Public Library

BOOKS, BOOKMARKS, BOOKPLATES, BOOKENDS,
CDS, DVDS, CASSETTES, VIDEOS, COMPUTERS,
COMFORTABLE CHAIRS, RESOURCE LIBRARIANS...
WHAT'S MISSING FROM THESE INGREDIENTS?

FRIENDS OF THE LIBRARY BOARD

President ....Deborah Ladd
Vice-President ....Nancy Hiatt
Secretary ....Cricket Vandover
Treasurer ....Mary Garavaglia
Membership .....Christine Krueger, Deborah Ladd
Newsletter ....Karen James
Publicity...............Jan Fishman, Cindy Easterling
Book Fair ....Nancy Hiatt, Bob Race
Members at Large ....Mary Gordon,
                    Jane Romines, Barrett Schroeder

Friends of the Webster Groves Public Library
301 East Lockwood
Webster Groves, MO 63119-3102

FOR MORE INFORMATION

> call 314.961.3784
> email dladd@wgpl.lib.mo.us
> access the Friends webpage through the
  library website, http://wgpl.lib.mo.us

You are!

BE A FRIEND...
Join the Friends of the
Webster Groves Public Library

Figure 5-FF   Friends of the Webster Groves (MO) Public Library Membership Brochure (Outside)

Why Do We Need You?

> To help Webster Groves enhance and expand its independent library so that it can continue to meet and adequately serve the needs of the community.

> To help us get others excited about the library, its resources, services and needs.

> To provide financial support for library services and facilities through membership dues and special events

> To encourage volunteer participation in this vital community resource

OUR ACCOMPLISHMENTS

In the last 31 years, the Friends has helped the library by contributing over $250,000 to purchase equipment, furniture and books; fund programs; match grants; and renovate facilities.

Our gifts to the library in 2005 total more than $15,000 and include new lounge chairs, tables and ottomans for a reading area, the children's summer reading program, large print books, a CD cabinet, a refrigerator, and outdoor plantings. Thanks to several volunteers, we raised over $10,000 from our Spring Book Fair and the Book Sales Cart.

FUTURE OPPORTUNITIES FOR FRIENDS' FINANCIAL SUPPORT

> Books and supplies for children's reading programs

> Large print books

> Audio books on CD (Library patrons tell us they prefer CDs to cassettes.)

> Movies and educational DVDs (This is the technology newer than videos, and demand for this format has grown significantly.)

> Public advocacy support campaigns

> Landscape improvements

> Continued support of facilities, program and equipment needs as requested by library administration

---

ANOTHER "PRIZE WINNING" COMBINATION: You and the Friends of the Webster Groves Public Library!

SPECIAL GIFTS

In October 2005, Karen Tedesco made a generous gift of $5,000 to fund children's library enhancements, including a collection of children's cookbooks and a number of updated science books. A Webster Groves resident who successfully competes in national cooking contests, Karen's talents gave her the financial capacity to make this gift, but her heart directed it, "I wanted to help energize the children's room to excite a whole new generation of Webster Groves readers."

If you have a particular interest you would like to sponsor for our library, or would like to receive our most current Wish List, please contact Friends board member Christine Krueger at 314.961.7302. Or, add your own Special Gift of $25 or more to your membership dues payment, and we will put your name in a bookplate in a new library book.

BENEFITS OF MEMBERSHIP

All members receive:

> Special Friends-only wallet and key chain library card set (Never again will you be left standing in the check out line without your card!)

> Free entry to the opening night of the annual Spring Book Fair

> An invitation to a special friends event

Additional benefits to members at higher membership levels (on a cumulative basis):

$25 FRIEND ($15 SENIORS) ....Our thanks and the three benefits listed above

$50 AUTHOR ....Friends canvas tote bag

$100 EDITOR ....$10 gift certificate to the Webster Groves Book Shop

$250 PUBLISHER..........$25 gift certificate to the annual Friends Book Fair

---

□ **Yes,** I want to be a Friend of the Webster Groves Public Library:
- □ Friend $25 (Seniors $15)
- □ Author $50
- □ Editor $100
- □ Publisher $250

□ I would also like to make a Special Gift of $_____ (the names of donors contributing $25 or more will be acknowledged on a Friends bookplate in a new library book)

□ My employer will match my gift and I've enclosed the form.

□ Enclosed is my check (payable to Friends of WGPL) for $_____

NAME _____

ADDRESS _____

CITY _____ STATE _____ ZIP _____

PHONE _____

EMAIL ADDRESS _____

□ Members may be acknowledged in future printed materials, unless you check here to remain anonymous.

Please contact me about volunteer opportunities:
- □ Book Fair
- □ Membership
- □ Marketing and Promotion of the Library
- □ Special Events
- □ One-time or ongoing service needs in the Library

Please return this portion of the brochure and your check to:
Friends of the Webster Groves Public Library
301 East Lockwood
Webster Groves, MO 63119-3102

The Friends of the Webster Groves Public Library is a non-profit 501(c)(3) organization. Contributions are tax deductible to the extent allowed by law.

Figure 5-GG   Friends of the Webster Groves (MO) Public Library Membership Brochure (Inside)

Supporting Our Libraries

Sharing A Passion for Books

THE FRIENDS OF THE MULTNOMAH COUNTY LIBRARY

BECOME A FRIEND

MULTNOMAH COUNTY LIBRARY

FRIENDS OF THE LIBRARY

JOIN US

522 SW 5th Avenue, Suite 1103
Portland, OR 97204-2128

Friends-Sponsored Programs

One of the most exciting and fulfilling ways the Friends offer support is through grants to the Library for special programs, staff support, outreach services and library collections.

Over the years, the Friends have made significant gifts that help ensure the stability of programs like **Pageturners** (the library's book groups) and the **Bucket of Books** program that creates a useful resource for teachers to incorporate library materials in their classrooms. The Friends have also sponsored the **Teen Author Lecture**, a **Teen Lounge** where teens can hone their skills at producing "zines" and other cutting-edge literary ventures, a **Staff Enrichment Fund**, **Books2U** a program that encourages children to read and become library users through "booktalks" in the classroom and many other beloved programs.

We also contribute significantly to the stability of the library by sending representatives to county meetings and mobilizing public activism for ballot measures that affect the library.

How We Do All This

With your help, the Friends support these programs through membership dues and revenues from the Friends' Library Store and our hugely successful used book sales in the fall and spring.

Figure 5-HH The Friends of the Multnomah County (OR) Library Membership Brochure (Outside)

Who are the Friends of the Multnomah County Library?

Started in 1972, the Friends of the Multnomah County Library is a non-profit, community organization dedicated to supporting the Multnomah County Library.

Our members are volunteers and advocates for a strong library system in our community. We believe that the best and most-used library system of its size in the country deserves an engaged organization that represents the community's interests on library issues.

Friends of the Library has an active board of directors, over 1,100 members throughout the county and we're growing our numbers each year. We are proud that our group has been honored by Friends of the Library USA as an outstanding Friends organization affiliated with a major metropolitan library.

What Do the Friends Do?

- We provide funding for special library programs and enrichment of neighborhood libraries and outreach services.

- We hold popular used-book sales in the spring and fall to raise money for library programs.
- We promote public involvement in our library.
- We provide advocacy information regarding library issues.
- We mobilize support for library ballot measures.

Why Become A Friend?

The Multnomah County Library is now at the forefront of the nation. Thanks to community support, our library has beautiful new buildings, enhanced collections, advanced technology, and an expert staff. Multnomah County Library has one of the highest circulation rates in the country. Your Friends' annual membership and involvement help to sustain this record of excellence.

As A Friend, You Will Receive

- The sense of fulfillment that comes with supporting an important and vital community institution.
- Admittance into members-only events such as our annual meeting and the pre-sale night of Oregon's largest used-book sale held every autumn.
- *Footnotes*, our quarterly newsletter keeps you updated on Friends' activities and volunteer opportunities.

As a member of the Friends, we help your voice to be heard on library issues just as you help our voice become louder as our membership grows.

I Want to be a FRIEND of the Multnomah County Library!

Name

Address

City

State/Zip

Phone

Email

Most used library branch

MEMBERSHIP LEVEL:

- ☐ Individual $30
- ☐ Family $45
- ☐ Senior *(age 65+)* $20
- ☐ Senior Family *(age 65+)* $40
- ☐ Supporter $75
- ☐ Sustaining .... Minimum $10 monthly on a credit or debit card

- ☐ Patron $100
- ☐ Sponsor $250
- ☐ Benefactor $500
- ☐ Additional donation .... $
- ☐ Workplace Match (attach form)
- ☐ Check enclosed
- ☐ Bill my ☐ VISA   or   ☐ MasterCard

Credit Card No:

Expiration date:

Mail form and payment to
FRIENDS OF THE LIBRARY
522 SW 5th Avenue, Suite 1103
Portland, OR 97204-2128
503.224.9176 or **www.friends-library.org**

The Friends is a 501 (c) 3 non-profit organization; your donation is tax-deductible

Figure 5-11 The Friends of the Multnomah County (OR) Library Membership Brochure (Inside)

Friends of Hedberg Public Library

Love the library? Become a friend!

What we do for the library

An elected board of trustees governs the Friends. Various committees, with the support from the library's staff, carry out the group's work. Other enhancements to the library made possible by the Friends include:

- Strollers for patron use
- Shopping carts and baskets
- Prizes for the summer reading programs for children and teens
- Visits by authors and entertainers
- Large type books for adults
- Children's programs
- Books on CD
- Computer classes in Spanish
- Computer materials
- New book carts
- A reception to recognize the efforts of library volunteers

2005 projects included:

Contributing to the Downtown Riverfront Park Project

Opening the used book, gift & coffee shop, The Ground Floor

Busing 6th-grade classes to the library for tours and training

Publishing *Library Matters* newsletter

Friends of Hedberg Public Library
316 S. Main St.
Janesville, WI 53545
(608) 758-6600
www.hedbergpubliclibrary.org

Figure 5-JJ   Friends of Hedberg Public Library (Janesville, WI) Membership Brochure (Outside)—Editor Carrie Mermanson; Designer John Burns

The Friends of Hedberg Public Library

We welcome new members who support the organization's mission of helping the library provide an extra level of services not possible through the normal operating budget. Friends also advocate for the library in the community.

Who we are

We're people just like you who appreciate the library and the many ways it serves us and members of our community. The Friends of Hedberg Public Library is a non-profit (501c 3) organization with more than 300 members that raises money through membership dues, fundraisers and The Ground Floor, a used book and gift shop located on the lower level. Proceeds have supported projects to enhance the library's collection, expand the community's awareness of library programs and services, and support demonstration projects to meet new needs. The Friends Board of Trustees meets the third Thursday of each month and the meeting is open to all members. The annual meeting of the membership is the third Thursday in January. Various committees, such as fundraising, membership and others, meet as needed.

As a member of the Friends of HPL, you can choose to simply support the work of the organization through your membership dues or get involved in a variety of activities and projects.

▲ The Ground Floor

shop | eat | drink | read
the Friends' shop at Hedberg Public Library

What Friends membership does for you

In addition to helping the library, other reasons to join the Friends include:

◆ Be among the first to find out about library issues and events with a free subscription to *Library Matters* newsletter

◆ Receive an invitation to the Friends of HPL annual meeting

◆ Meet other people who value the library as an important community resource

◆ Find out about volunteer opportunities so you can make a difference

◆ Save 10 percent on gift items from The Ground Floor

◆ Get a coupon good for a free reserve on a library item

◆ Receive a free Friends coffee mug by joining at the $15 level or above

Dues and other donations are tax-deductible to the extent of the law.

Join today!

Annual membership in the Friends of Hedberg Public Library at any of the various levels helps support the work of the Friends. Lifetime memberships are also available.

Other ways to support the Friends:

• Your grocery reciepts from Sentry and Pick'n Save help support the Friends. Ask at their service desks for more information.
• Shop at The Ground Floor.
• Donate used books at The Ground Floor.

Yes, I support the Friends of HPL!

Name _____

Address _____

City _____ State ____ ZIP ____

Phone _____

E-mail address _____

Membership categories:
(circle one)

Annual Dues
Basic $10
Donor $15*
Supporter $25*
Patron $50*
Corporate $100*
Life Membership $250*

I would like to give an additional gift to the Friends in the amount of . ... $ ____

Total amount enclosed .... $ ____

*Sign up at this level and receive a coupon for a free Friends coffee mug. (While supplies last.)

All memberships expire December 31, 2006.
Many volunteer opportunities exist at Hedberg Public Library. Please check the areas you'd like to learn more about. The volunteer coordinator will contact you with more information.

☐ Working at The Ground Floor
☐ Sorting donated books
☐ Being a Book Spotters (shelf reading)
☐ Helping with the kids' summer program
☐ Delivering library materials to homebound
☐ Serving on the Friends Board of Trustees
☐ Helping at fundraisers
☐ Handing out surveys
☐ Helping with mailings
☐ Assisting with special projects as needed

Mail with dues to:
Friends of HPL, 316 South Main St. Janesville, WI 53545

Figure 5-KK Friends of Hedberg Public Library (Janesville, WI) Membership Brochure (Inside)—Editor Carrie Mermanson; Designer John Burns

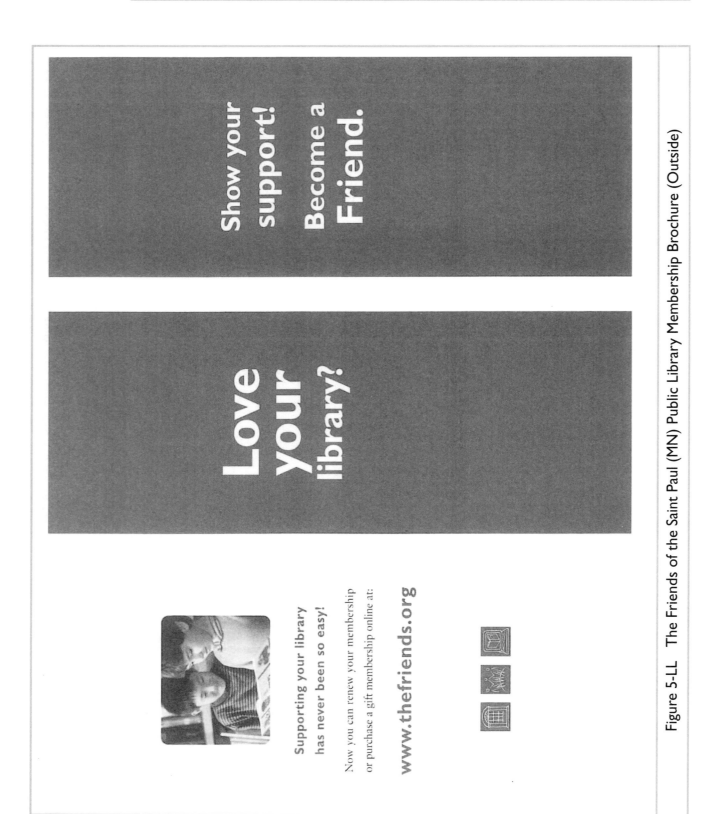

Figure 5-LL   The Friends of the Saint Paul (MN) Public Library Membership Brochure (Outside)

Your membership in The Friends of the Saint Paul Public Library helps to strengthen your library and ensure the continued improvement of library services.

Members of The Friends support a wide variety of library initiatives, including:

• Purchase of thousands of new books for the library's collection

• Innovative children's reading programs

• Award-winning literary and cultural events

• Advocacy for strong public support of the Library

Membership in The Friends brings many rewards, including the knowledge that your gift makes a real difference to the Saint Paul Public Library.

Thank you for your support!

About The Friends

The Friends of the Saint Paul Public Library was founded in 1945. The Friends supports the library through private fund-raising, advocacy, and community activities. Today, over 2,000 people support the Saint Paul Public Library through their membership in The Friends.

The Friends is a 501(c)(3) non-profit organization. Your contribution is tax-deductible to the full extent allowed by state and federal laws.

ANNUAL MEMBERSHIP LEVELS

Basic $25–49
• Subscriptions to our newsletter & calendar

Contributor $50–99
All the Basic membership benefits plus:
• $10 gift certificate to The Bibelot Shops
• Listing in our annual report (optional)

Advocate $100–249
Basic and Contributor benefits plus:
• Your choice of one of the gift items (A-D) listed below

Sponsor $250–499
Basic and Contributor benefits plus:
• Your choice of two gift items (A-D)

Patron $500–999
Basic and Contributor benefits plus:
• Your choice of three gift items (A-D)

Benefactor $1,000 and above
Basic and Contributor benefits plus all four gift items (A-D) and an invitation to the annual Donor Society author luncheon.

GIFT ITEMS

At the Advocate membership level and above, choose from the following special gift items:

A **LIBRARY NOTECARDS** A pack of six beautiful sketches of library branches in Saint Paul.

B **BOOK BAG** Medium weight book bag—handy for trips to the library, bookstore or supermarket.

C **UMBRELLA** An attractive blue-and-white striped umbrella to shield you from the rain and show your support.

D **TWELVE BRANCHES: STORIES FROM ST. PAUL** The book from The Friends with story ideas contributed by community members.

Please allow 4 to 6 weeks for your gift to arrive.

✂ Please detach and return this form.

THANK YOU!

I WOULD LIKE TO CONTRIBUTE $_____

Name(s)

Address

City _____ State _____ ZIP

Day Phone _____ Evening Phone

E-mail Address

City Councilmember's name (if a resident of Saint Paul)

PAYMENT METHOD:
☐ My check is enclosed
☐ Please charge my ☐ Visa ☐ Mastercard ☐ Amex
☐ Please charge my credit card 12 monthly contributions of $_____, starting with _____ (month and year)

Credit Card Number _____ Expiration Date

Authorization Signature

GIFT SELECTION:
☐ Advocate $100–249 . . . . .
☐ Sponsor $250–499 . . . . .
☐ Patron $500–999 . . . . .
☐ Benefactor $1000 + ...

Please list the item(s), A-D, you would like to receive:
___ , ___
A , B , C , D

☐ Please do not send me a gift. I want my full contribution to support the library. (*Gifts will reduce the tax deductibility of your donation.*)
☐ I would like my contribution to be anonymous.
☐ My employer's matching gift form is enclosed.
☐ Please contact me about including The Friends in my estate planning.
☐ On occasion, other local non-profit groups wish to send information to our members. Check here if you do **not** want to receive this information.

Please return this form to:
The Friends of the Saint Paul Public Library
325 Cedar Street, Suite 555, St. Paul, MN 55101-1055

Figure 5-MM   The Friends of the Saint Paul (MN) Public Library Membership Brochure (Inside)

Chapter Six

Organizational Effectiveness

Friends groups engage in a wide variety of programs and services, and the best groups have one thing in common—they have a solid structure. They have a mission statement that guides their decision making and a set of bylaws that informs their practice. They are able to recruit new and active members because they have clear committee charges; there is no question about what new volunteers are being asked to do. Great Friends groups engage in the planning process from time to time and reevaluate what they are doing and how they are doing it.

We admit that developing job descriptions for volunteers or revisiting your bylaws may not be as much fun as, say, creating a celebration for your library's anniversary, but it is certainly as, and maybe even more, important! Think of your groups' policies, procedures, bylaws, and committee design as the foundation upon which your house is built. Without strong foundations, houses collapse. Sadly, many Friends groups do too.

This chapter provides sample bylaws that you can compare with your own or use as a template if you are starting a group. You'll find a sample memorandum of understanding that sets mutual expectations for a Friends group and the library for working together. A table is also provided to help foster long-term respect and appreciation for the roles of the librarian, the trustees, the foundation, and the Friends and keep everyone from crossing the lines—where, often, trouble begins!

Creating a strong and functional Friends organization is a gift to the future, because you are laying that foundation for future boards and members. It doesn't have to be hard, and, with the help of the tips and ideas in this chapter, it can even be fun.

6-1   Getting and Keeping Motivated Volunteers

Both a volunteer herself and someone who works with volunteers, Susan Vittitow, Publications Specialist/Center for the Book Coordinator for the Wyoming State Library, offers this bit of savvy advice for keeping volunteers motivated and effective.

How It Works

- Never ask people if they will "help." They will say yes and then not know what to do and therefore will do nothing. Ask them to do a specific task—stuff this set of envelopes, develop the brochure, bake three dozen cookies, and so forth.
- Write up job descriptions of your major positions, including what tasks they are responsible for. Among other reasons for doing this, it will make them feel more secure about doing it because they have some instructions.
- If specific jobs are fairly complex, create instructional binders explaining the jobs so that volunteers know how to perform them. Not knowing what to do is not fun for most adults.
- Thank them profusely, again and again. It rewards the ones who are working hard and motivates the ones who are slacking.
- Publicly honor the worker bees every chance you get. It shows that service to the organization is something to be valued and treasured.
- If you recruit by saying, "It's really not much work," you'll get people who really don't do much work! Be upbeat but realistic when you describe tasks.
- Always communicate the difference their efforts make. Don't stop with how much money you've raised—tell them how many books you put in the children's room or how many people are using the computer terminal the Friends provided. Show them they make a real difference in the lives of other people.
- Never apologize for asking for help. If they're peripheral members, there's a good chance they would like to become more involved. You are asking them to do something specific—but something they're likely capable of—to support a cause they love: the library.
- It may sound counterintuitive, but the tired core members may have to learn to say "no." As long as someone is handling it, people may not step forward. If the core leadership stays too long and gets too tired, they can get a martyr complex, which also makes the leadership positions very, very unappealing to the observer. For everyone, there is always a time to step down and let the organization sink or swim by the force of new (or not!) volunteers.

6-2   Beyond the Board Meeting—Voting Remotely

Whether high or low tech, boards sometimes have to make decisions between meetings. Here is the policy for doing so from the Friends of the J.V. Fletcher Library (Westford, MA).

How It Works

- Between board or executive committee meetings, the board can vote on actions to be taken using mail, telephone, e-mail, or other electronic means. Actions voted in this manner should be important and time sensitive.

- Any board member can ask the president that a vote be taken between meetings. The request should be in the form of a motion and sent to the president either electronically or on paper. The president will determine if it is necessary and in the organization's best interest to act on the requested motion before the next board or executive committee meeting.

- The president or her designee will distribute the motion, using the method she thinks most effective, to all board members along with instructions on how to reply and the deadline for voting. In the case of telephone votes, the president or her designee will call every board member and convey the same information.

- If possible, the deadline for voting should allow time for board members to discuss the motion. It is important that all board members have the opportunity to be included in the discussion. The motion cannot be amended.

- Whenever possible, individual board members' votes should be transmitted to all board members.

- Immediately after the deadline, the president or her designee will tally the votes and inform the board of the results. The motion will pass on approval by a majority of the board.

- At the next board meeting, the president will read the motion and the results of the vote so that it will be recorded in the minutes of the meeting. No further discussion or action is needed because the motion has already been approved.

6-3   Friends' Standing Committees—Description of Charge

Knowing what you are responsible for is key to being a successful committee chair and member. Following are examples from both public and academic Friends groups.

Friends of the Johnson County (KS) Public Library

- Executive Committee: Composed of current Friends officers. Meets as needed. Determines budget request to the Friends board. President serves as chair.
- Advocacy Committee: Meets monthly or as needed to develop plans to promote the library and interact with legislators, county commissioners, and so forth, to support library budget and funding requests. Communicates plan to membership and encourages participation.
- Annual Book Sale Committee: Plans and executes the annual book sale.
- Membership Committee: Meets monthly or as needed to develop plans to promote and increase membership in the Friends of the Library and promote library activities.
- Operations Oversight Committee: Meets monthly or as needed to oversee two Friends bookstores and book sale activities. Serves as an advisory committee for the bookstore management.
- Organizational Development Committee: Meets as needed. Develops a slate of officers and board members to be voted on at the annual meeting. Reviews bylaws and, if needed, formulates changes to be brought to the board and voted on by the membership.
- Social Committee: Plans annual meeting, including speaker, refreshments, decorations, and invitations. Plans other Friends' special events as needed.

Friends of the Old Dominion University (VA) Library

The following standing committees are established:
- Development
  - Plan at least one annual event for next year intended to bring in revenue (and be relevant and interesting as well).
  - Plan the annual author dinner in plenty of time for listing in calendars, getting on president's and deans' calendars, and targeting marketing.
  - Develop a plan for identifying and soliciting potential donors.
  - Develop ways of recognizing donors.
  - Plan fund-raising events.
  - Promote sales of merchandise (T-shirts, mugs, etc.).

- Membership (in cooperation with the staff liaison)
  - Develop and monitor program for regular membership renewals, including solicitation for increasing membership levels.
  - Obtain the e-mail addresses of all members to allow for more frequent, less costly communication.
  - Make the current membership list easily available to executive committee and committee chairs.
  - Develop benefits for increased levels of membership.
  - Increase communication with members (in conjunction with the Publicity/Marketing Committee).
  - Involve members more in the library, through service activities or workshops, to foster a feeling of ownership (and interest in supporting).
  - Review and if necessary improve the membership application form.
- Program
  - Make recommendation for fall program (fall forum or other idea) during the summer to give maximum time for marketing.
  - Develop at least two other attractive programs, possibly one each semester, perhaps using the skills of board members.
  - Plan events preceding at least two of the president's lecture series events and line up speakers and locations.
  - In all programming, look for topical issues that will attract a crowd.
  - Seek out opportunities for cooperative/joint program both off campus and on campus with Town N Gown, alumni, historical or other societies, bookstores, and other organizations and businesses.
  - Seek for ways to partner with available programs such as the Book Guys or the Virginia Commission on the Humanities.
- Publicity/Marketing
  - Publish four newsletters a year, and evaluate ways to make the newsletter a more appealing and more effective tool to get members more active and to market the programs.
  - Seek out opportunities for stories about the Friends or the library that might be of interest to the media (e.g., regarding special collections, government documents, special programs).
  - Market all programs of the Friends in a targeted way; beyond the university's publicity office, find creative ways of marketing events.
  - In cooperation with library staff, evaluate and if necessary suggest changes in the Friends' Web site, perhaps adding links to other relevant sites.
- Service
  - Plan and execute the annual reception for honoring library staff.

- Continue programs for members to volunteer to perform special services for the library (e.g., with the special collections).
- Recruit and coordinate volunteers to help with the Library Staff Organization's fall book sale.
- Work with other committees to ensure that all Friends' programs are efficiently planned and well executed.

Ad hoc committees are established as needed (e.g., Nominating Committee).

∽❧ ❧∽

6-4 Sample Memorandum of Agreement Between the Library and the Friends

Sometimes nothing can do more harm than a misunderstanding between various library entities about their respective roles and responsibilities in support of the library. Below is a Memorandum of Agreement by libraries, Friends groups, trustees, and foundations in the Chestatee region, Dawson County, and Lumpkin County (GA).

MEMORANDUM OF AGREEMENT

This Memorandum of Agreement (MOA) is among and between the following entities:

Chestatee Regional Library Board of Trustees
Dawson County Library Board of Trustees
Lumpkin County Library Board of Trustees
Chestatee Regional Library Alliance, Inc.
Friends of the Dawson County Library, Inc.
Friends of the Lumpkin County Library
Lumpkin County Library Nonprofit Foundation, Inc.
Dawson County Library Foundation, Inc.

The purpose of this MOA is to acknowledge that all entities are separate and distinct and all entities share the common goal of supporting and enriching the library services provided within the Chestatee Regional Library System. No entity may speak or act on behalf of any other; however, all pledge a spirit of cooperation in the pursuit of the best interests of the Regional Library System as a whole, and all hold the desire that public confidence be maintained to the highest levels. All are valuable resources toward the common goals.

The Chestatee Regional Library Alliance qualifies as a tax-exempt organization under Section 501(c)(3) of the U.S. Treasury Code of Regulations. The four subordinate organizations to the Alliance, i.e., the Dawson County Friends, Lumpkin County Friends, Dawson County Library Foundation, and Lumpkin County Library

Foundation, also qualify under the umbrella of the Alliance. This will ensure that cash and in-kind donations to these organizations are tax deductible.

The Library Director and the staff are agents of the Regional Board. If the Alliance, the county Friends of the Library, or the Foundations need the assistance of any library staff for an event or project, the group must have the approval of the Library Director or her/his designee. The Library Director will provide from time to time the Friends and the Foundations with a prioritized list of proposed items or projects to meet the needs of the library.

All entities agree that open communication with each other and the public is of great importance. In recognition of the importance of the "sunshine laws," which apply to the Library Boards of Trustees, the Alliance, the Friends of the Library and the Foundations agree to publicize in advance general and board meetings, to distribute all meeting minutes and financial reports to the Regional Library Staff in a timely manner so that minutes and financial reports are available for public inspection. The entities agree to maintain all records in a businesslike manner.

Each entity will adopt and abide by a constitution and/or bylaws to govern the structure and operation of its organization and which will include, but not be limited to, the following: the time and procedure for the election of officers; a rotation schedule and election procedure for Board members; encouragement of active recruitment, orientation for new members, and training for new Board members; the implementation of good cash controls in the accounting procedures which will include a periodic review of the original records by other than the Treasurer and/or bookkeeper.

Projects and programs of the Alliance, the Friends of the Library, and the Library Foundations should be determined in consultation with the Regional Board, the appropriate county Library Board, and the Library Director. These may be a joint venture between or among any of the entities or may be the event or project of only one entity. The purpose and means by which projects and programs are carried out should be a common decision. It is, therefore, advisable that a representative of each entity attends pertinent meetings of the other entities in order to foster and maintain good communications and cooperation. It is also advisable that a library staff person attend all entity meetings.

The Regional Board and the County Boards acknowledge that they do not supervise the activities of the other entities; however, they reserve the right not to participate in and/or to disavow any projects or events believed not to serve the best interests of the Library.

Each entity understands that members are allowed inside the library building proper only when the library is open to the public or the library staff is present.

All entity funds shall be maintained separately and not co-mingled nor integrated. The Regional Board may accept gifts from the entities, whereupon those funds become solely the funds of the designated library to be expended for the specific purpose for which they were made. In the event the Regional Board becomes the custodian of entity funds, those funds shall be kept as separate funds for audit and bookkeeping purposes.

Nothing in this Memorandum of Agreement shall be construed or interpreted to conflict with any provision in the Articles of Incorporation, Constitution or Bylaws of any entity. Any perceived conflict shall be resolved by interpreting such provision so as not to conflict with it.

Any entity may propose changes, additions, and/or deletions to this Memorandum of Agreement at any time. Such changes, additions, and/or deletions will be presented to the Library Director for inclusion on the agenda at the next Chestatee Regional Library Board of Trustees meeting. If the Regional Board approves the proposed amendment to the MOA, said proposed amendment will be submitted to the other entities for their approval.

This Memorandum of Agreement is agreed to on the dates signed by the authorized officials below and will be effective as of the last date signed.

SIGNATURE PAGE

Chestatee Regional Library Board of

Trustees

Friends of the Dawson County Library, Inc.

_____
Authorized Signature and Title

Date
_____

_____
Authorized Signature and Title

Date
_____

Dawson County Library Board of Trustees

Friends of the Lumpkin County Library

_____
Authorized Signature and Title

Date
_____

_____
Authorized Signature and Title

Date
_____

Lumpkin County Library Board of Trustees

Lumpkin County Library Nonprofit Foundation, Inc.

_____
Authorized Signature and Title

Date

_____

_____
Authorized Signature and Title

Date

_____

Chestatee Regional Library Alliance, Inc.

_____
Authorized Signature and Title

Date

_____

Dawson County Library Foundation, Inc.

_____
Authorized Signature and Title

Date

_____

6-5 Bylaws—Friends of the Dublin (CA) Library

Friends of the Dublin Library
Bylaws and Standing Rules
As Approved on May 9, 2001

STANDING RULES:

1. As defined in Article II (Purposes) of the Bylaws of this organization and in support of the Library, the members of the Board of Directors shall by a vote of the majority distribute an amount of money, to be determined by the Board of Directors, to the benefit of the Dublin Library Trust Fund at least once a year, if possible, for use of the Branch Manager at her/his discretion to benefit the Library.

2. In addition to the disbursement above, additional amounts to be determined by a majority of the Board of Directors shall be allotted each year for special needs such as Children's programs, Senior Outreach, or others at the request of the Library staff.

3. Upon a majority vote of the Board of Directors, a maximum of $100.00 per year may be spent toward any political campaign that benefits the Alameda County Library System or other Library related issue.

4. The finances of this organization shall be deposited in a bank selected by the Board. Checks must be signed by two authorized members of the Board.

5. A list of members of the association shall be created annually for the purpose of eliminating any member two years beyond the expiration date of the last renewal.

BYLAWS:

ARTICLE I
The name of this association shall be Friends of the Dublin Library.

ARTICLE II
Purposes
It is recognized that the administration of the Dublin Library is vested in the Alameda County Board of Supervisors which is responsive to the recommendations of the Alameda County Library Advisory Commission.

The purposes of the Friends of the Dublin Library shall be to maintain an association of persons interested in books and libraries; to focus public attention on library services, facilities, and needs; and to stimulate gifts of materials, desirable collections, endowments, and bequests. All finances from the sale of books or other sources are to be used solely to benefit the Dublin Library.

ARTICLE III
Membership
Membership in this organization shall be open to all individuals in sympathy with its purposes and to representatives of organizations and clubs when such representation is desired, in which case dues shall be paid by that organization.

ARTICLE IV
Officers and Committees
Section 1: The officers shall be president, vice-president, secretary, treasurer, and members-at-large as appointed by the president with the approval of the other members of the Board. The term shall be for one year beginning on January 1 and ending on December 31. With the exception of the secretary and treasurer, no person shall serve for more than two consecutive one year terms unless otherwise indicated by a motion of the Board.
Section 2: The standing committees shall be as flexible as the needs of the group so indicate. The president shall appoint Standing Committee chairmen with the approval of the board.
Section 3: The officers, members-at-large, and standing committee chairmen shall be known as the Board of Directors and shall serve as the governing body of this association. The board shall meet at the call of the president.
Section 4: A majority of the members of the board shall constitute a quorum for the transaction of business.
Section 5: Such other special committees as may be necessary from time to time shall be appointed by the president, with the approval of the board.
Section 6: The president is an ex-officio member of all committees, with the exception of the Nominating Committee.
Section 7: A Nominating Committee of three members of the board and one alternate shall be appointed by the Board at the second to last meeting of the year. A slate of officers shall be presented by the Nominating Committee at the last meeting of the year. Nominations from the floor will be entertained and no one shall be nominated without his/her consent.
Section 8: The officers shall be elected at the last meeting of the year to take office January 1 of the following year.
Section 9: Vacancies arising on the board shall be filled by appointment made by the president with the approval of the board.

ARTICLE V
Meetings
Section 1: At the last meeting of the year the association will hold election of officers, receive various reports, and enact any other business necessary for the close of the year.
Section 2: Regular meetings of the Board of Directors and any interested members

shall be held each month, with the exception of the month of July, on regular day and time as set by the board.

Section 3: A special meeting may be held as directed by the president or any member of the Board of Directors, provided that the members of the board are notified with the business to be transacted stated.

ARTICLE VI
Dues

Section 1: The annual dues shall be determined by the Board of Directors.

Section 2: The fiscal year of this association shall begin on January 1 of each year and end on December 31 of the same year.

ARTICLE VII
Funds

Section 1: Adequate books of accounts shall be maintained by the treasurer, who shall be responsible therefor.

Section 2: No funds over $200.00 shall be disbursed without the authority of the Executive Board.

Section 3: The Board of Directors shall appoint an auditor, not an officer, to audit the treasurer's books. The books will be closed on December 31 at which time they will be audited, and the auditor will make a report at the second meeting in the new year.

ARTICLE VIII
Amendments

These bylaws may be amended at any regular meeting of this association by two-thirds of the board members present, provided that notice of the proposed amendment(s) shall have been given two weeks before the said meeting.

ARTICLE IX
Parliamentary Authority

All meetings shall be conducted according to Robert's Rules of Order Newly Revised.

ARTICLE X
Dissolution and Termination of Association

Section 1: In the event of dissolution of the organization, all assets of the Friends of the Dublin Library will be liquidated and the money turned over to the Dublin Library.

Section 2: No part of the net earnings of this association shall ever inure to or for the benefit of or be distributable to its members, trustees, officers, or to any private persons, except that the association shall be empowered to pay reasonable compensation of services rendered and to make payments and distributions in furtherance of the exempt purposes for which it was formed.

Section 3: Notwithstanding any other provisions of these articles, the association shall not carry on any other activities not permitted to be carried on by a corporation exempt from Federal Income Tax under Section 501(c)(3) of the Internal Revenue Code of 1954.

⤜◉ ◉⤏

6-6 Bylaws—Friends of the Kettering University Library and Scharchburg Archives (Flint, MI)

Bylaws of Friends of the Kettering University Library and Scharchburg Archives
Revised June 2006
Approved September 7, 2006

Article I. Name and Address

Section 1

The name of the organization shall be "Friends of the Kettering University Library and Scharchburg Archives" and the organization shall be known as ***"FOLA."***

Section 2

The post office address of the principal office is: Friends of the Kettering University Library and Scharchburg Archives, Kettering University, 1700 West Third Avenue, Flint, MI 48504; or such other places as the Board of Directors may from time to time designate.

Article II. Purpose

Section 1

The purpose of the Friends shall be to promote an interest in the Library among students, faculty, staff, alumni, and public; to provide a fuller understanding of the role of the Library & Archives in education; to encourage gifts and bequests in support of the Library & Archives; and to assist the Kettering University Library & Archives in its educational mission through exhibits, programs, publications, and other means.

Section 2

The monies raised by the Friends shall be donated to Kettering University to the benefit of the Kettering University Library & Archives. The Friends Board of Directors shall administer such funds.

Article III. Membership

Membership in the Friends is open to any person or organization interested in supporting the activities and programs of the Kettering University Library & Archives. Membership categories shall be set by the Board of Directors and may be modified by the Board. Memberships also may be awarded by vote of the Board, generally in consideration of services rendered or donations (monetary or non-monetary) made.

Article IV. Membership Meetings

Section 1

The annual meetings of the Friends shall be held 120 days **before or after** the close of the fiscal year at a time and place determined by the Board of Directors.

Section 2

Special meetings of the membership may be called by action of the Board of Directors or upon written request by 10 percent of the membership, but by not fewer than 25 members.

Section 3

The Board of Directors shall notify the members of the date, time, and place of the annual and any special meeting at least two weeks before the meeting.

Section 4

Proxies may be appointed in writing for attendance at any meeting of the membership.

Section 5

A quorum at all meetings shall be the membership present in person or by proxy.

Article V. Board of Directors

Section 1

The Board of Directors shall consist of seven to fifteen **elected** members.

Section 2

Prior to the first annual meeting, the Friends shall be governed by the Steering Committee, which shall act as the Friends Board of Directors. At the first annual meeting, the membership shall elect seven to fifteen Directors. Immediately following election, those selected shall draw lots with one-third of the Directors to serve one-year terms, one-third to serve two-year terms, and one-third to serve three-year terms.

Members shall elect Directors at each subsequent annual meeting; the number of Directors to be elected and the length of the terms (three years maximum) shall be determined by the membership.

Section 3

The University Librarian, Archivist of the University Archives, and the Provost and Vice President for Academic Affairs of Kettering University shall serve as ex-officio members of the Board of Directors.

Section 4

Nominations for Board membership shall be made by the Board of Directors and may also be made from the floor at the annual membership meeting. Nominees must indicate their willingness to serve.

Section 5

Should any duly elected member of the Board resign or be unable to complete his/her term, the vacancy created may be filled by appointment by the Board of Directors.

Section 6

The Board may remove any Director who has three or more absences from regular meetings of the Board of Directors.

Section 7

The FOLA Board may choose to appoint representatives from various constituencies to serve on the Board, with student representatives selected from both A and B sections. Such representatives will serve a one-year term, renewable at the FOLA annual meeting, and will be non-voting members of the FOLA Board.

Article VI. Duties of the Board of Directors

Section 1

Meetings of the Board of Directors shall be held at least quarterly.

Section 2

The administrative powers of the organization shall rest with the Board of Directors, who shall have the power to perform all acts not inconsistent with these Bylaws or with the policy and procedures of Kettering University.

Section 3

A Volunteer Trustee (as defined in section 110 of Act 162, Public Acts of 1982, as amended) of the organization shall not be personally liable to the organization or its members for monetary damages for breach of the Trustee's fiduciary duty arising under any applicable law. However, the Article shall not eliminate or limit the liability of a Trustee for any of the following:

1. A breach of the Trustee's duty of loyalty to the organization or its members.
2. Acts or omissions not in good faith or that involve intentional misconduct or a knowing violation of the law.
3. A violation of Section 551(1) of Act 162, Public Acts of 1982, as amended.
4. A transaction from which the Trustee derived an improper personal benefit.
5. An act or omission occurring before January, 1988.
6. An act or omission that is grossly negligent.

To the extent permitted by law, the organization assumes all liability to any person other than the organization or its members for all acts or omissions of a volunteer director (as defined in section 110 of Act 162, Public Acts of 1982, as amended) occurring on or after January 1, 1988, incurred in the good faith performance of the volunteer Trustee's duties as such.

Any repeal or modification of this Article shall not adversely affect any right or protection of any Trustee of the organization existing at the time of, or with respect to, any acts or omissions occurring before such repeal or modification.

Section 4

A quorum for any meeting of the Board of Directors shall be not fewer than one-half of the number of Directors.

Section 5

The Officers of the Board shall be Chairman, Vice Chairman, Secretary, and Treasurer, and they shall carry out the customary duties of those positions. They shall be elected at the first meeting of the Board of Directors following the annual meeting and shall serve one-year terms. No officer shall serve more than three consecutive terms except by unanimous consent of the Board.

Section 6

The Chairman, with Board approval, may appoint committees to handle defined subjects or projects.

Article VII. Administration

The Board of Directors may select and employ staff. The authority and duties of any such employed staff shall be spelled out in a position description which shall be reviewed no less often than annually. The Board shall review the performance of any such staff member(s) no less often than annually.

Article VIII. Fiscal Year

The fiscal year of the Friends of the Kettering University Library shall run from July 1 through June 30.

Article IX. Amendments

These Bylaws may be amended by a majority of members present in person or by proxy at annual or special meetings. The text of any proposed amendments must be provided to the membership at least two weeks before the meeting at which the vote is to be taken.

Article X. Dissolution

If, for any reason, the organization is dissolved, custodianship of all assets shall revert to the Kettering University Library and Scharchburg Archives Endowment Fund.

6-7 Bylaws—San Antonio (TX) Public Library Foundation

BYLAWS OF THE
SAN ANTONIO PUBLIC LIBRARY FOUNDATION

ARTICLE I: GENERAL

1.01 **Name.** The name of this Texas Non-Profit Corporation is the San Antonio Public Library Foundation (the "Foundation").

1.02 **Purpose.** The purpose of the Foundation is exclusively to support the San Antonio Public Library System and to increase the awareness and use of the Library through financial support and programmatic efforts.

1.03 **Office.** The principal office of the Foundation shall be located in the City of San Antonio, Bexar County, Texas. The Foundation shall have and continuously maintain in the State of Texas a registered office and a registered agent, whose business office is identical with the registered office.

ARTICLE II: EXECUTIVE COMMITTEE

2.01 **Management.** The business of the Foundation shall be managed by its Executive Committee. The Executive Committee may exercise all such powers of the Foundation and do all such lawful acts and things as are not prohibited by statute, by the articles of incorporation, or by the bylaws of the Foundation.

2.02 **Voting Members of Executive Committee.** Voting members of the Executive Committee shall be comprised of the following officers of the Foundation:

- ❑ Chairman of the Board
- ❑ Immediate Past Chairman
- ❑ Vice Chairman
- ❑ Secretary
- ❑ Treasurer

Nothing herein shall prevent any voting member from holding more than one office at the same time. In addition to officers of the Foundation, voting members of the Executive Committee shall be comprised of such other members as elected by the Board of Directors; provided that the Executive Committee shall have no greater than twenty-five (25) voting members.

2.03 **Term.** Voting members of the Executive Committee shall be elected for a period of one (1) year and hold office for no longer than six (6) consecutive one-year terms, not including time served in the offices of Vice Chairman, Chairman of the Board, and Immediate Past Chairman. Non-Voting Ex Officio Members of the Executive Committee shall serve for a period of one (1) year and hold office for not greater than five (5) consecutive one-year terms.

2.04 **Ex Officio Non-Voting Members.** Ex Officio Non-Voting Members of the Executive Committee shall be comprised of the following:

❑ President of the Library Foundation
❑ Director of the San Antonio Public Library
❑ Chair of the Library Board of Trustees
❑ Such other Ex Officio Non-Voting Members as may be appointed jointly by the current Chairman of the Board and Vice Chairman

Ex Officio Executive Committee Members shall be entitled to receive meeting announcements and to attend meetings, but shall not be permitted to vote. Ex Officio Members shall not be counted in determining the existence of a quorum.

2.05 **Change in Number.** The number of voting members of the Executive Committee in any fiscal year may be increased by action of the Board of Directors, but no change in number shall have the effect of shortening the term of any incumbent member.

2.06 **Quorum.** Seven voting members of the Executive Committee shall constitute a quorum.

2.07 **Election.** Voting members of the Executive Committee who are not officers shall be elected by the Board of Directors at its Annual Meeting. Ex Officio Non-Voting Members of the Executive Committee shall be appointed jointly by the Chairman and Vice Chairman.

2.08 **Removal from Office.** Any voting member of the Executive Committee may be removed with or without cause by action of the Board of Directors. One specified cause for removal shall be absence from three (3) consecutively scheduled meetings of the Executive Committee without valid excuse, as determined solely by the Executive Committee. Ex Officio Members of the Executive Committee may be removed with or without cause by joint action of the Chairman and Vice Chairman.

2.09 **Regular Meetings.** A regular meeting of the Executive Committee shall be held each month at such time and place as determined by the Executive Committee with written notice provided at least thirty (30) days in advance. The Chairman of the Board may cancel any regular meeting if the Executive Committee determines such meeting is unnecessary or impractical.

2.10 **Special Meetings.** Special meetings of the Executive Committee may be called by the Chairman of the Board or three voting members of the Executive Committee on three (3) days' written notice to each member. The attendance of a member at any such meeting shall constitute a waiver of notice of such meeting, except where a member attends a meeting for the express purpose of objecting to the meeting on the ground that the meeting is not lawfully called. Neither the business to be transacted nor the purpose of any special meeting needs be specified in the notice.

2.11 **Telephone Meetings.** The Executive Committee may hold meetings by conference telephone or similar communications equipment which allows all members to participate in any such meeting and participation in such a meeting shall constitute presence in person at such meeting, except where a person participates in the meeting for the express purpose of objecting to the transaction of any business on the ground that the meeting is not lawfully called.

2.12 **Action Without Meeting.** The Executive Committee may take action without meeting only with the written consent of three-fourths of all voting members of the Executive Committee. A signed consent, or signed copy thereof, shall be kept of record in the principal office.

2.13 **Majority Vote.** The act of a majority of the voting members of the Executive Committee at a meeting in which a quorum is present shall be the act of the Executive Committee. No action may be taken without the presence of a quorum.

2.14 **Vacancies.** Any vacancy occurring in the Executive Committee may be filled by appointment of the Chairman of the Board, provided that such appointment is approved by action of the Board of Directors at the meeting immediately following such appointment. A member elected to fill a vacancy shall be elected for the unexpired term of his or her predecessor.

2.15 **Other Vacancies.** The Executive Committee shall have the authority to establish all other committees deemed necessary for the management and operation of the Foundation. Appointment of members to such other committees shall be in the sole discretion of the Executive Committee.

2.16 **Minutes.** Minutes of all actions of the Executive Committee shall be kept of record in the principal office of the Foundation.

ARTICLE III: BOARD OF DIRECTORS

3.01 **Board of Directors.** The Board of Directors shall elect the officers, Executive Committee members, and members of the Board of Directors for the Foundation and shall conduct such additional business as is delegated to the Board of Directors by the Executive Committee.

3.02 **Number, Qualifications, Term.** The Board of Directors shall consist of no greater than one hundred and ten (110) persons. Each director shall be elected for a period of one (1) year and may hold office for no more than six (6) consecutive one-year terms, not including time served in the offices of Chairman of the Board, Vice Chairman, and Past Chairman. Members of the Board of Directors shall include the Chairman of the Board of *The Friends of the Library* (or his or her designee), and the Chairman of the Board of the Library Board of Trustees (or his or her designee), and two (2) additional members of the Library Board of Trustees.

3.03 **Change in Number.** The numbers of members of the Board of Directors in any fiscal year may be increased by action of the Board of Directors, but no change in number shall have the effect of shortening the term of any incumbent member.

3.04 **Quorum.** Thirty (30) members of the Board of Directors shall constitute a quorum.

3.05 **Election of Directors.** Directors shall be elected by the Board of Directors at its Annual Meeting.

3.06 **Removal from Office.** Any Director may be removed with or without cause by action of the Board of Directors. One specified cause for removal shall be absence from three (3) consecutively scheduled meetings of the Board of Directors without valid excuse, as determined solely by the Board of Directors.

3.07 **Regular Meetings.** A regular meeting of the Board of Directors shall be held every other month with one-month written notice, with the time and place of the meeting to be designated. The Chairman of the Board may cancel or change any regular meeting if the Executive Committee determines such meeting is unnecessary or impractical.

3.08 **Special Meetings.** Special Meetings of the Board of Directors may be called by the Chairman of the Board or fifteen (15) voting members of the Board of Directors on seven (7) business days' written notice to each member. The attendance of a member at any such meeting shall constitute a waiver of notice for such meeting, except where a Director attends a meeting for the express purpose of objecting to the meeting on the ground that the meeting is not lawfully called. The nature of the business to be transacted or the purpose of the meeting will be specified in the notice.

3.09 **Action Without Meeting.** The Board of Directors may take action without meeting only with the written consent of three-fourths of all voting members of the Board of Directors.

3.10 **Majority Vote.** The act of a majority of the directors present at a meeting at which a quorum is present shall be the act of the Board of Directors. No action may be taken without the presence of a quorum.

3.11 **Vacancies.** A vacancy occurring in the Board of Directors may be filled by appointment of the Chairman of the Board provided that such appointment is approved by action of the Board of Directors at the meeting immediately following such appointment. A Director elected to fill a vacancy shall be elected for the unexpired term of his or her predecessor.

3.12 **Compensation.** Directors shall not receive compensation of any kind for their service as Director. Nothing herein shall be construed to preclude any Director from serving the corporation in any other capacity and receiving compensation therefor.

3.13 **Minutes.** Regular minutes of the proceedings of the Board of Directors and of any committee to whom management authority has been delegated shall be kept and retained of record in the principal office.

ARTICLE IV: ADVISORY BOARD

4.01 **Advisory Board.** The Foundation shall include an Advisory Board of up to fifty (50) members. Members shall be non-voting, and their presence at any meeting shall not be counted for purposes of determining a quorum. Advisory Board members shall serve at the pleasure of the Chairman of the Board with the approval of the Executive Committee. Invitation of Advisory Board members to any committee meetings shall not be required, but may be extended at the discretion of the Chairman of the Board.

4.02 **Honorary Board.** The Nominating Committee subject to the approval of the Board of Directors shall name an Honorary Board who shall serve for a period of one (1) year and may be re-appointed to successive one-year terms. Persons eligible to be named to the Honorary Board shall be persons eminently qualified in one or more aspects of the Library Foundation's activities and interests. Election to the Honorary Board shall be reserved for persons who have demonstrated a continuing interest in the Library Foundation's affairs and its future and who have made outstanding contributions of time and/or assets to the Library Foundation. The Honorary Board shall be invited to attend all annual and regular meetings of the Board of Directors. Members shall be non-voting, and their presence at any meeting shall not be counted for purposes of determining a quorum. They may serve on committees at the request of the Chairman of the Board.

ARTICLE V: CERTAIN TRANSACTIONS, INDEMNIFICATION, AND EMERGENCIES

5.01 *Interested Directors, Officers, and Members.* Any contract or other transaction between the Foundation and any of its Directors, officers, or members (or any corporation or firm with whom such Director, officer, or member may be interested) shall be valid for all purposes notwithstanding the presence of such Director, officer, or member at the meeting authorizing such contract or transaction, and notwithstanding such person's participation in the meeting. The foregoing shall, however, apply only if (i) the contract or transaction is fair to the Foundation as of the time it is authorized or approved, and (ii) the Board of Directors is provided advance disclosure of the interests of any such Director, officer, or member in the contract or other transaction under consideration. However, the failure to disclose such interest will not invalidate any contract or transaction discussed herein.

5.02 *Indemnification of Directors, Officers, and Members.* The Foundation shall indemnify any person who was, is, or is threatened to be made a named defendant or respondent in a proceeding because of the person's position as Director or officer. This indemnification shall be made by the Executive Committee upon a determination that the person:

(1) Conducted himself/herself in good faith;
(2) Reasonably believed that, in the case of conduct in his official capacity as a Director, that his conduct was in the Foundation's best interest;
(3) Reasonably believed, in all other cases, that his conduct was at least not opposed to the Foundation's best interests;
(4) In the case of any criminal proceeding, had no reasonable cause to believe his conduct was unlawful.

The indemnification responsibilities stated herein are expressly subject to the provisions and limitations contained in the Texas Non-Profit Corporation Act (including provisions prohibiting indemnity for a person found liable on the basis that personal benefit was improperly received by him and cases in which the person is found liable to the non-profit corporation). The determination of whether a director or officer is entitled to indemnity must be made by a majority vote of a quorum consisting of Executive Committee members who at the time of the vote are not named defendants or respondents in the proceeding. If such a quorum cannot be obtained, the determination must be made as provided for in the Texas Non-Profit Corporation Act.

ARTICLE VI: NOMINATING COMMITTEE

6.01 *Purpose.* The Nominating Committee shall nominate persons to stand for election to the Board of Directors, Executive Committee (voting and non-voting members), and all offices of the Foundation.

6.02 *Members of Nominating Committees.* The nominating committee shall be comprised of the following members:

- ❑ Chairman of the Board
- ❑ Immediate Past Chairman
- ❑ Vice Chairman
- ❑ Three (3) members of the Executive Committee (voting or non-voting)
- ❑ Three (3) members of the Board of Directors who are not serving as Executive Committee members

The Chairman of the Board shall appoint those members of the Nominating Committee who are not specifically designated by this section. The Chair of the Nominating Committee shall be appointed by the Chairman of the Board with the approval of the Executive Committee.

6.03 *Term.* Members of the Nominating Committee shall hold office for a period of no longer than one (1) year, and the existence of the committee shall terminate upon the installation of the Chairman of the Board.

6.04 *Quorum.* Five members of the Nominating Committee shall constitute a quorum.

6.05 *Majority Vote.* The act of a majority of the members of the Nominating Committee at which a quorum is present shall be the act of the Nominating Committee. No action may be taken without the presence of a quorum.

6.06 *Meetings.* The time, place, and manner of meetings of the Nominating Committee shall be determined by the chair.

6.07 *Action Without Meeting.* The Nominating Committee may take action without meeting only with the written consent of all members of the Nominating Committee. A signed consent, or a signed copy thereof, shall be kept of record in the principal office.

6.08 *Report to Executive Committee.* The Nominating Committee shall report to the Executive Committee.

6.09 *Removal from Office.* Any member of the Nominating Committee may be removed with or without cause by action of the Board of Directors, provided that voting members of the Executive Committee shall have sole discretion to remove members who are absent without valid excuse from three (3) consecutively scheduled meetings.

ARTICLE VII: NOTICE

7.01 **Notice.** Any notice required to be given to any Director need not be by personal notice. Any such notice may be given (i) in writing, by mail, by e-mail, or by fax, addressed to such Director at his last known address; or (ii) any other method permitted by law. Any notice required or permitted to be given by mail shall be deemed complete at the time the notice is deposited in the United States Mail.

7.02 **Waiver.** A written notice of waiver signed by the person entitled to notice shall be deemed the equivalent of actual proper notice. Attendance of a person at any meeting shall constitute a waiver of notice for such meeting, except when the person attends the meeting for the express purpose of objecting to the meeting on the grounds that it is not lawfully called or convened.

ARTICLE VIII: OFFICERS AND AGENTS

8.01 **Number, Qualification, Term.** The Foundation shall have (i) a Chairman of the Board who shall be elected by the Board of Directors at its Annual Meeting and who shall hold office for a period of one (1) year, subject to a maximum of three (3) one-year terms; and (ii) one or more Vice Chairmen, a Secretary, and a Treasurer, each of whom shall be elected by the Board of Directors at its annual meeting, and each of whom shall hold office for a period of one (1) year, subject to a maximum of five (5) one-year terms; and (iii) such other officers as the Executive Committee may deem necessary, each of whom shall be appointed by the voting members of the Executive Committee, and each of whom shall hold office for such term as the Executive Committee may determine, provided that no officer shall hold office for more than five (5) one-year terms. Officers shall be selected from the Board of Directors or from the voting members of the Executive Committee.

8.02 **Compensation.** Officers shall serve without compensation.

8.03 **Chairman of the Board.** The Chairman of the Board shall be the chief executive officer of the Foundation and shall preside at all meetings of the Board of Directors and the Executive Committee. The Chairman of the Board shall see that all votes and resolutions of the Board of Directors and the Executive Committee are carried into effect. The Chairman of the Board shall perform such other duties and have such other authority and powers as the Executive Committee may from time to time prescribe.

8.04 **Vice Chairman.** The Vice Chairman shall exercise the powers and responsibilities of the Chairman of the Board in the event the Chairman of the Board is removed from office or upon the Chairman of the Board's death, resignation, or inability to discharge the duties of Chairman of the Board. The Vice Chairman shall continue to exercise the powers of the Chairman of the Board until the Chairman of the Board's disability is removed or an interim Chairman of the Board is elected. The Vice Chairman shall perform such other duties and have such other authority and powers as the Executive Committee may from time to time prescribe or as the Chairman of the Board may from time to time delegate.

8.05 *Secretary.* The Secretary shall attend all meetings of the Board of Directors and of the Executive Committee and shall record or cause to be recorded all votes and all proceedings in minutes of the Foundation. Such minutes shall be kept and retained of record in the principal office. The Secretary shall give, or cause to be given, notice of all meetings of the Board of Directors and the Executive Committee. The Secretary shall perform such other duties and have such other authority and powers as the Executive Committee may from time to time prescribe or as the Chairman of the Board may from time to time delegate.

8.06 *Treasurer.* The Treasurer shall have the custody of the corporate funds and securities and shall keep full and accurate accounts, receipts, and disbursements of the Foundation and shall deposit all monies and all valuable things in the name of and to the credit of the Foundation in such depositories as may be designated by the Executive Committee. The Treasurer shall disburse the funds of the Foundation as may be ordered by the Executive Committee, taking proper vouchers for such disbursements, and shall render to the Chairman of the Board and the Directors at the regular meetings of the Board an account of the Foundation's transactions and financial condition. The Treasurer shall perform such other duties and have such other authority and powers as the Executive Committee may from time to time prescribe or as the Chairman of the Board may from time to time delegate.

8.07 *Other Offices.* All other offices, including that of Immediate Past Chairman and Vice Chairman, shall be assigned and appointed by the Executive Committee which will specify the duties and responsibilities of such other offices.

8.08 *Removal from Office.* Any officer or agent of the Foundation may be removed by the Board of Directors whenever in its judgment the best interests of the Foundation would be served thereby. [Omitted reference to contract rights.]

ARTICLE IX: GENERAL

9.01 *Annual Meeting.* The annual meeting of both the Executive Committee and Board of Directors shall be held in the fall of each year at such time and place as may be determined each year by the Chairman of the Board. Written notice of the annual meeting and time and place thereof shall be provided at least thirty (30) days in advance.

9.02 *Books and Records.* The Foundation shall keep correct and complete books and records of accounts and shall keep minutes of the proceedings of all meetings of the Board of Directors and Executive Committee, and shall keep at its registered office or principal place of business, or at the office of its transfer agent or registrar, a record of all its members, giving the names and addresses of all members.

9.03 *Annual Statement.* The Board of Directors shall present at each annual meeting of the members a full and clear statement of the business and condition of the Foundation, including a reasonably detailed balance sheet and income statement.

9.04 *Checks and Notes.* All checks and demands for money and notes of the Foundation shall be approved by a signature of an authorized Foundation representative: Chairman of the Board, Treasurer, Designated Member of the Executive

Committee, Foundation President, and Executive Director in accordance with the following schedule:

$0–$5,000	One (1) signature required;
$5,001–$50,000	Two (2) signatures required, one staff and one Board Member;
$50,001 and above	Three (3) signatures required, one staff and two Board Members.

9.05 *Calender Year.* The Foundation shall operate on a calendar year for accounting purposes.

9.06 *Amendments.* The power to alter, amend, or repeal these bylaws, or adopt new bylaws, subject to repeal or change of action of the members, shall be vested in the Executive Committee.

9.07 *Resignations.* Any director, officer, or agent may resign by giving written notice to the Chairman of the Board or Secretary. Such resignation shall take effect at the time specified therein, or immediately if no time is specified therein. Unless otherwise specified therein, the acceptance of such resignation shall not be necessary to make it effective. Resignation or termination of any director, officer, or agent may be noted in the minutes of a meeting of the Board of Directors or Executive Committee in which event any written notice as required herein shall not be necessary, and the resignation or termination shall be effective on the date specified.

9.08 *Construction.* Whenever the context so requires, the masculine shall include the feminine and neuter, and the singular shall include the plural, and conversely. If any portions of these bylaws shall be held invalid or inoperative, then, so far as reasonable and possible (i) the remainder of these bylaws shall be considered valid and operative, and (ii) effect shall be given the intent manifested by the portion held invalid or inoperative.

9.09 *Headings.* Headings used in these bylaws have been inserted for administrative convenience only and do not constitute matter to be construed in interpretation.

9.10 *Gender References.* The use of the pronoun "his" or "her" in these bylaws is for convenience only and is not intended to in any way impair or restrict the action or ability of either gender.

ഈ ഈ

6-8 University of Pittsburgh's (PA) University Library System Marketing Communications Strategy/Plan

The University Library System at the University of Pittsburgh worked with a professional marketing firm, Krakoff Communications, Inc., to help devise a plan to market their library to their community of users and to the university itself. Following is their plan.

Situation Analysis

The mission of the University Library System (ULS) at the University of Pittsburgh is to provide and promote access to information resources necessary for the achievement of the University's leadership objectives in teaching learning, research, creativity, and community service, and to collaborate in the development of effective information, teaching, and learning systems.

To further the attainment of these goals, the ULS continues to be on the forefront of acquisition and library technology implementation. In fact, what sets the ULS apart from other university library systems are the depth, focus, and comprehensiveness of the programs, services, and special collections. During the Marketing Retreat, the comment was made that "We are innovative users not necessarily innovative creators of the technology. We are implementing what others are developing and talking about doing." This mindset of advancement through user-friendly applications needs to be communicated to all pertinent parties.

The ULS is faced with what most would consider a good problem to have—an identity disconnect coupled with an information conveyance void as a result of a multitude of programs and resources to aid specific populations within the University. As a result, a unified marketing strategy must be established to:

1. Brand these programs individually but under an umbrella, dominant ULS logo/brand.
2. Specify the end user/audience for each of these programs.
3. Determine a method or combination of methods through which to best deliver the information about each program to the appropriate end user.

Strengths of the ULS

- Pound-for-pound, one of the best in the United States
- Seamless access and delivery of resources
- Quality of staff
- Depth of subject-specific material, wealth of collections
- Variety in forms of information:
  - Print collections
  - Electronic collections
  - Microfilm
  - Other archives

Overall Problems/Challenges

- Target audience members unaware of the library's central role within the University, not thought of in high esteem
- General confusion/unaware as to the complete offerings of the ULS
- General confusion/unaware as to how to most-efficiently access the offerings

The challenge is to reassemble the fragmented programs/benefits of the ULS by creating a unified, comprehensive initiative to market specific programs and resources to appropriate end users.

Objectives

1. Increase awareness/usage of resources and services while promoting and leveraging investments.
2. Increase support/budget, which will help to increase donations.
3. Enhance professional perception and knowledge about capabilities and resources, both internally and externally.

Target Audiences

Target audiences can be grouped into internal and external categories and then further categorized for targeting purposes as follows:

INTERNAL

1. ULS Staff
   - Librarians/Staff
2. University of Pittsburgh Decision Makers
   - Chancellor/Provost
   - Deans/Director
   - Institutional Advancement
3. Faculty
   - Admin./Department Chairs
   - Professors
4. Undergraduate and Graduate Students
   - Grad Assistants/TAs
   - Student Groups
   - Graduate Professional Associations
   - Distance Education Students

EXTERNAL

1. Current/Potential Donors
   - Alumni
   - Retirees
   - Foundations
   - Friends of Library Groups
   - Corporations (Local, National, International)
2. Current/Potential Users
   - Peer Institutions/Graduate Students
   - Researchers
   - General Community/Business
   - Not for Profits
   - Retirees
   - Local/National and International Companies
   - Other Librarians
3. Decision Makers
   - Board of Visitors
   - Board of Trustees

4. Groups/Associations
   - Peer Institutions
   - Professional, Academic, and Library Associations

Best Case Scenarios
INTERNAL
1. ULS Staff
Desired Result: All staff members comprehensively informed about all new programs, collections, reference mechanisms, and associated technologies to better help students/researchers at any level. By understanding the "big picture," they will have a more positive outlook regarding their job.

2. University of Pittsburgh Decision Makers
Desired Result: Continually aware of the strides the ULS is making. Should be kept aware of prominent collections acquired, technological innovations, and ULS rankings and statistics as compared to other library systems nationally. This will help to increase funding and general awareness of the quality of the ULS.

3. Faculty
Desired Result: Readily incorporate library education and information into assignment plans and project sheets. General awareness of library capabilities and collections to accurately convey information to/answer questions from students—especially during their time of need, i.e., finals, midterms, etc. This will increase usage of ULS services and resources.

4. Undergraduate and Graduate Students
Desired Result: Comprehensive understanding of library functionality and available collections/reference mechanisms. Comfort with research as a result of breadth of materials and user-friendly delivery mechanisms.

EXTERNAL
1. Current/Potential Donors
Desired Result: Donations (both in amount of donors and amount of individual donations) increase.

2. Current/Potential Users
Desired Result: Feel as though the ULS is an integral part of our region/nation/world supporting the educational and pragmatic efforts of businesses and individuals throughout without hassle, roadblocks, or confusion.

3. Decision Makers
Desired Result: Equipped with the most up-to-date information about the ULS so recommendations can be made to senior University staff to impact funding/programs in the best interests of the students and the community.

4. Groups/Associations
Desired Result: Feel comfortable using the ULS as a resource and, more importantly, as a model for unparalleled ease-of-use programs and comprehensive acquisition plans.

Strategies
A mix of direct marketing, e-mail communications, internal advertising, and public relations efforts specific to each target group could be utilized to achieve all of the objectives stated above. From a graphics standpoint, a standard ULS look/logo (keeping within the identity rules of the University) will be established so every communication (printed or electronic) will have a consistent look.

The variation will be in the look of the programs that piece serves to publicize. For example, a HelpHub piece will look different than a ULS Special Collections piece but they will be instantly recognized as pieces associated with ULS through usage of the standard ULS umbrella logo and graphics standards such as placement of logo, general design of piece, etc. In addition, we recommend that targeted information be distributed to the various groups on a more frequent basis, mixing the delivery vehicle so that all audiences maintain a high awareness of the ULS and its services.

Below is an outline of how the ULS can accomplish the stated objectives while also achieving the desired results from each target group.

1. Increase awareness/usage of resources and services while promoting and leveraging investments.
The purpose of this campaign will be to reach all target audiences in as many ways as possible while conveying the message of "What Can the ULS Do for Me." These communication mechanisms, including printed newsletters, e-newsletters, printed postcards in mailboxes, or e-mail alerts will be benefit-specific for the target. They will also contain focused, organized, and concise messages so they are (1) read and (2) processed.

2. Increase support/budget, which will help to increase donations.
Through increased communication with current and potential donors about the ULS programs their funds are supporting, their dollars would be given more meaning so they feel connected to a specific collection or technological innovation. A bi-annual piece should be sent to all donors and prospects to educate them about where their funds are going, and, more importantly, why the projects their funds are supporting are integral to making the ULS and the University of Pittsburgh a researcher's destination. In addition, if they are kept informed about stages of implementation of programs they are helping to fund, they will start to personally identify with the project and feel a need to increase, continue, or begin donations in order to "finish what they started." Also, new sources for funding will be identi-

fied, e-mails and addresses will be collected, and regular, electronic communications will be developed.

3.   Enhance professional perception and knowledge about capabilities and resources, both internally and externally.

To accomplish this objective, we recommend playing up the prominence and prestige of the ULS among other comparable institutions including acquisitions rankings, technological advancements, ground breaking ease-of-use efforts, etc. This will help with internal comprehensive understanding and instill a sense of pride. An annual report for University "management" and administrators will be developed and disseminated. Externally, this piece will serve as intrigue and may increase traffic from curious locals or frustrated researchers or companies.

Tactics
A.   Printed Pieces
It is in these pieces where the graphics standard and the unified look (regardless of the message or target) will become apparent.

1.   Postcards/Mailers

A series of informational postcards can be developed and printed with message-specific copy to each target group. These postcards can be used as a stand-alone piece or can be inserted into a target-specific pocket folder packet.
Ideas for postcard content:

- User testimonials for each group (a large business, a student, an outside researcher, a grad student, a faculty member, etc.).
- Quick resource/services guide about the ULS (this can include who to go to for what, quick research how-tos, etc.).
- A program and promotional postcard can be developed to introduce the concept of a "Research Challenge." Although this concept is best for undergraduate students, graduate students could participate as well. The idea is that classes or individuals could compete to find some piece of information in a special collection that is not often searched or a collection that has been newly acquired. The winner is the one who finds it first and a prize can be given. If these become monthly or annual events this could prove to be an interesting PR piece as well.
- A "Delivery" focused piece, perhaps a spoof on all the food delivery flyers undergrads and grads get, that details the many convenient ways research materials can be delivered to them (e-mail, etc.).

2.   Folder

For cost effectiveness, we recommend printing an 8.5 × 11 multipurpose pocket folder introducing the new graphic standard for the ULS. The folder will feature general information on it about the ULS and be useful for ALL audiences. Target-specific information for each audience will then be inserted into the pocket and sent. Information that could be enclosed:

- Cover letter
- Appropriate postcard (testimonials, how-to info., etc.)
- Info for deans to use in promotions
- Updates on specific programs that donors have helped fund to keep them "in-the-loop" and feel part of the project
- Annual or periodic report to inform staff/faculty of new info
- List of all collections, services, and contact person for each or how-to access section for each

3.   Direct Mail: Discipline-Based Packets

A two-color or four-color-process discipline-based packet can be developed for all faculty members and delivered during the summer months or at the start of each term to help with lesson planning. A similar packet can be distributed to TAs. This piece will contain information about what specifically the ULS can do for you or your students in sociology, math, etc. Also should include a section on what the ULS can do for students in terms of papers, theses, projects, comparative research, etc., and a similar info sheet for faculty.

4.   Newsletters/E-mail Blasts

Internal and external newsletters should be printed 4 times a year and mailed to all target groups. The newsletter will contain a basic ULS update: new happenings, projects completed, projects in the works, new acquisitions, etc.

An e-newsletter will be emailed 4–6 times a year to complement the printed version and to keep people informed and aware of ULS activities. This can be tailored to all of the different target groups and will contain targeted information, unlike the hard copy newsletter.

The effectiveness of implementing this e-newsletter is based on the e-mails you have captured for all of your target audiences who are outside of the University system.

In addition, e-mail blasts will be sent out to different groups on an as-needed basis if there seems to be confusion about a new policy/process, or if general information about something needs to be disseminated quickly. The e-newsletter and e-mail blasts could be used to introduce the opt-in regular ULS information option.

B.   Educational Sessions and Special Events

There should be a library orientation for all new faculty, students, and transfers. In addition, we recommend working with faculty to implement project-specific, mini-orientations and then incorporating these sessions into the syllabus for the class. This could be carried into educational outreach to the other target audience members. For example, host a wine and cheese event for donors during which you showcase a technology or collection their funds helped to facilitate. Also, events could be planned for high-ranking officials/administrators at University of Pittsburgh and other institutions, business leaders, non-profit leaders, etc.

C. Publicity

Since all three objectives involve a better and broader communications effort, publicity will be a large component of the plan.

A comprehensive media list needs to be developed to include daily and weekly newspapers, magazines, radio, television, and Web. The list will be used to distribute press releases on a variety of topics. This list will also include internal media exclusive to the University of Pittsburgh.

There will be two components to the media plan: volume and quality. One press release per month will be distributed announcing something new at ULS, a new hire, a promotion, etc., to maintain regular appearances in the media. In addition, newsworthy feature stories should be pitched to key reporters/editors. For example, pitches could be based around:

- Each new collection or technological advancement
- Superior public funding stats and acquisition rates
- Introduction of "Ask a Librarian" to the regional libraries

Stories can also be ghost written and placed in numerous publications. One such example is the importance of past, present, and future in a researcher's and library's success. A story focusing on the importance of current and historical collections to comprehensive research would provide a perfect opportunity to showcase the old and new collections at ULS. In addition, it would provide for a nice segue from how these historically relevant resources continue to be used to the ever-changing methods of accessing them.

Also, some of the testimonials in the printed pieces may be success stories that can be shared with the media. Articles should be secured in the University Times and/or the Pitt News that would focus on one aspect, collection, or program in each issue. Maybe a regular column can be established in one or both regarding "how to" pieces on reference/research challenges.

D. Web/Electronic

The Web site could be redesigned to find out "up front" the interest of the visitor and quickly sending them to the information that is most important for them. In addition, a "facelift" for the Web could be performed during which the new umbrella ULS brand from the printed pieces could be incorporated on the Web. We recommend making the Web a place for further information.

The idea is to print short, inexpensive pieces to obtain interest, then sending them to the Web for more details and specific information. For example, a person receives a postcard detailing delivery methods for all types of research but maybe the recipient wants to know a bit more. On the bottom of the postcard it would say, For more information, go to this site. Once the recipient goes to the site, there will not only be more information about the postcard topic but there will also be an option to select to receive further library info and updates through e-mail. Finally, an area of the homepage could be changed to announce the next library training session or new program being introduced.

Evaluation

In order to track the success of this program we recommend that surveys be distributed to each end-user group at the beginning or completion of the academic year to assess their level of knowledge/comfort with specific programs and to gage their feelings about ULS. Then, these results should be compared to survey results of previous years to see if measurable improvements have been made. In addition, informal evaluation sheets could be made available at all librarian stations and ULS entry/exit desks. A suggestion box could also be located prominently in high-traffic areas to gage what the target groups think could be improved upon. Finally, as comments are made in passing to staff from visitors of ULS, these should be documented (both positive and negative) and shared at staff meetings.

Next Steps

Establish clear parameters for objectives, budget to be allocated to this effort; then a final plan with schedules, responsibilities, and line-item budgets can be developed, and the plan will be implemented.

୶ ୬

6-9   Friends of the Joseph T. Simpson Public Library (Mechanicsburg, PA) Strategic Plan for 2005–2007

The following detailed strategic plan was adopted by the Friends of the Joseph T. Simpson Public Library (Mechanicsburg, PA) Board of Directors on May 2, 2005, and includes three years of priorities and action items.

Mission:

The purpose of the Friends of the Joseph T. Simpson Public Library is to provide support and present a positive voice for the Joseph T. Simpson Public Library in our community.

Vision:

The Friends of the Joseph T. Simpson Public Library will promote the resources, services, and needs of the library through advocacy, education, and community support. We offer our continued commitment to help make our library the best it can be in serving our community.

Members of the Friends of the Joseph T. Simpson Public Library share a passion for libraries and a desire to help their library meet the challenges of the day, as well as remain vital far into the future. The primary purpose of a Friend of the Library group is to be of service to the library through the following activities:

1. **Money**—Friends of the Library raise funds for projects or acquisitions in excess of the general library budget.
2. **Services**—There is no limit to the services that a dedicated volunteer group can provide.
3. **Public Relations**—Each Friend is a walking public relations vehicle for the library to its community.
4. **Advocacy**—An informed, active citizen lobby provides the public library with its strongest allies.
5. **Community Involvement**—A Friend of the Library group is validation of the public library's importance to its community.

Abbreviations used in this document:

FOLUSA—Friends of Libraries U.S.A.

PaLA—Pennsylvania Library Association

PCBL—Pennsylvania Citizens for Better Libraries

Goals:

For 2005 through 2007, the Friends of the Joseph T. Simpson Public Library will focus on the following six goal areas:

1. Advocacy
2. Fund-Raising
3. Membership Recruitment and Retention
4. Organizational Structure
5. Community Relations and Marketing
6. Volunteer Recruitment and Retention

1. Advocacy

Advocacy Goal #1: The Friends of the Library will be positive advocates for the library and the Friends of the Library through their contacts with elected officials.

Advocacy Objective #1a: The Advocacy Committee will write an annual "State of the Library" letter from the Friends of the Library Board to elected officials. **ANNUAL PRIORITY**

Advocacy Objective #1b: The Friends of the Library will continue financial sponsorship of the library's annual Municipal and Officials Breakfast, and the Friends' President or his/her designated alternate will attend this event. **ANNUAL PRIORITY**

Advocacy Objective #1c: When requested by the library, Friends of the Library will contact elected officials either in writing, by phone, or personally to show their support of the library and request the support of the elected officials. **PRIORITY FOR 2006**

Advocacy Objective #1d: Support the Pennsylvania Library Association (PaLA) and Pennsylvania Citizens for Better Libraries (PCBL) in statewide advocacy efforts. **PRIORITY FOR 2006**

Advocacy Goal #2: The Friends of the Library will be positive advocates for the library and the Friends of the Library through their contacts with the community.

Advocacy Objective #2a: The Friends of the Library will have current statistics available to use in demonstrating library usage by the community and how additional funding would benefit library users. **PRIORITY FOR 2006**

Advocacy Objective #2b: When requested by the library, the Friends of the Library will submit newspaper editorials or letters to the editor on library matters. **PRIORITY FOR 2005**

2. Fund-Raising

Fundraising is an important component of Friends' activities throughout the course of the year. The more money the Friends of the Library can raise, the more they can contribute to the library to help with general library operations and capital projects. Fund-raising encompasses a number of activities including, but not limited to, the Holly Trail House Tour, book sales, merchandise sales, and bus trips.

Fund-Raising Goal #1: The Friends of the Library will continue offering the Holly Trail House Tour through 2007.

Fund-Raising Objective #1a: The House Tour Committee will continue to expand the house tour locations into other parts of the library's service area. **PRIORITY FOR 2005 AND 2006**

Fund-Raising Objective #1b: The House Tour Committee will continue to expand advertising and sponsorship options to increase tour profits. **PRIORITY FOR 2005 AND 2006**

Fund-Raising Objective #1c: The House Tour Committee will explore adding new features to the tour each year. **PRIORITY FOR 2005 AND 2006**

Fund-Raising Objective #1d: The House Tour Committee will explore developing a different type of tour in the future. **PRIORITY FOR 2006**

Fund-Raising Goal #2: The Friends of the Library will continue sponsoring book sales and explore new avenues of generating revenue related to the book sales.

Fund-Raising Objective #2a: Set goals for growth of the book sale in number of items for sale, number of sales, gross sale income, etc. **PRIORITY FOR 2006**

Fund-Raising Objective #2b: Investigate feasibility of selling selected books on the Internet. **PRIORITY FOR 2006**

Fund-Raising Objective #2c: Annually evaluate book sale pricing and adjust as necessary. **ANNUAL PRIORITY**

Fund-Raising Objective #2d: Travel to other book sales in the area for new ideas and methods of holding book sales. **PRIORITY FOR 2006**

Fund-Raising Objective #2e: Consider establishing a newsletter devoted to book sale news. **PRIORITY FOR 2006**

Fund-Raising Objective #2f: Continue investigating options for "recycling" book sale leftovers by sharing them with other organizations such as shelters, prisons, day care centers, schools, etc. **PRIORITY FOR 2006**

Fund-Raising Goal #3: The Friends of the Library will invite interested community residents to participate in the various volunteer opportunities available at BOOKS BY THE GROSS.

Fund-Raising Objective #3a: Consider perks for book sale volunteers. **PRIORITY FOR 2005**

Fund-Raising Objective #3b: Develop job descriptions which include physical requirement and minimum time commitment required for book sale volunteers. **PRIORITY FOR 2005**

Fund-Raising Objective #3c: Develop list of requirements for book sale volunteers and create an information sheet that is completed by each volunteer and kept on file. **PRIORITY FOR 2005**

Fund-Raising Objective #3d: Increase the number of volunteers involved with the book sales to spread the workload and help with identifying future leaders for the committee. **PRIORITY FOR 2005**

Fund-Raising Objective #3e: Create a handbook of operations for the Book Sale Committee which documents in detail all aspects of the book sales. **PRIORITY FOR 2005**

Fund-Raising Goal #4: The Friends of the Library will operate their traditional book sales at an off-site location near the library that is affordable, accessible, and safe.

Fund-Raising Objective #4a: Assess BOOKS BY THE GROSS location as it relates to affordability, accessibility, safety, convenience, and any other factors deemed relevant. **ANNUAL PRIORITY**

Fund-Raising Objective #4b: Maintain positive working relationship with John Gross and Co. employees. **ANNUAL PRIORITY**

Fund-Raising Objective #4c: Review lease agreement for BOOKS BY THE GROSS annually. **ANNUAL PRIORITY**

Fund-Raising Goal #5: The Book Sale Committee will evaluate the frequency of book sales and determine if more or fewer sales are warranted.

Fund-Raising Objective #5a: Consider sponsoring specialty sales during the year. Examples might include "Gift Quality" books for sale around the holidays or a "Books for Kids" sale at the library in conjunction with a special program going on at the library. **PRIORITY FOR 2006**

Fund-Raising Goal #6: The Book Sale Committee will continue "Members Only" Previews for designated book sales.

Fund-Raising Objective #6a: Research options related to previews sponsored by other Friends' groups. **PRIORITY FOR 2005**

Fund-Raising Goal #7: The Book Sale Committee will work closely with the Community Relations and Marketing Committee to promote and publicize the book sales.

Fund-Raising Objective #7a: Establish mailing lists, using both U.S. mail and e-mail addresses, to inform customers of book sale activities. **PRIORITY FOR 2005**

Fund-Raising Objective #7b: Develop method of tracking marketing efforts to determine impact on attracting book sale customers. **PRIORITY FOR 2005**

Fund-Raising Objective #7c: Develop methods to increase the quantity and quality of book donations received throughout the year. **PRIORITY FOR 2005**

Fund-Raising Goal #8: The Friends of the Library will continue sponsoring the sale of assorted merchandise at the library.

Fund-Raising Objective #8a: Sell existing supply of cookbooks. **PRIORITY FOR 2005 AND 2006**

Fund-Raising Objective #8b: Investigate a new edition of a Friends' cookbook after first edition is sold out.

Fund-Raising Objective #8c: Develop marketing and merchandising opportunities to sell the cookbooks. **PRIORITY FOR 2005 AND 2006**

Fund-Raising Objective #8d: Have several items available for purchase at all times such as, but not limited to, book bags, miniatures, note cards, and crocks. Investigate new merchandise opportunities that appeal to various ages and are at various price levels. **PRIORITY FOR 2005 AND 2006**

Fund-Raising Objective #8e: Fund the replenishment of library merchandise that is selling well as supply levels are depleted. **PRIORITY FOR 2005 AND 2006**

Fund-Raising Objective #8f: Develop marketing and merchandising opportunities to sell library merchandise. **PRIORITY FOR 2005 AND 2006**

Fund-Raising Goal #9: The Friends of the Library will sponsor periodic bus trips.

Fund-Raising Objective #9a: Sponsor a minimum of one bus trip per year. **PRIORITY FOR 2005 AND 2006**

Fund-Raising Objective #9b: Investigate other travel opportunities. **PRIORITY FOR 2005 AND 2006**

Fund-Raising Goal #10: The Fund-Raising Committee will investigate and explore new fund-raising ventures.

Fund-Raising Objective #10a: Explore feasibility of having a Silent Auction fund-raiser, perhaps in conjunction with the Annual Dinner. **PRIORITY FOR 2005 AND 2006**

Fund-Raising Objective #10b: Investigate raffle opportunities such as quilts, artwork, woodcarvings, etc. **PRIORITY FOR 2005 AND 2006**

Fund-Raising Objective #10c: Attend fund-raising events in the area that may be viable fund-raisers for the Friends of the Library to see what is involved in the event and if it is something that is feasible for the Friends of the Joseph T. Simpson Public Library. **PRIORITY FOR 2005 AND 2006**

3. Membership

Membership Recruitment and Retention Goal #1: The Membership Committee will explore new ideas for membership recruitment.

Membership Recruitment and Retention Objective #1a: Periodically conduct membership drives targeting nonmembers from a specific geographic area or a specific category (such as registered voters, library cardholders, school teachers, etc.). **PRIORITY FOR 2005**

Membership Recruitment and Retention Objective #1b: Conduct a membership drive called "Ask a Friend to Be a Friend" in which Friends of the Library board members and library trustees write personal notes to people they know asking them to join the Friends. **PRIORITY FOR 2005**

Membership Recruitment and Retention Objective #1c: Investigate feasibility of establishing a Junior Friends of the Library organization. **PRIORITY FOR 2006 OR 2007**

Membership Recruitment and Retention Objective #1d: Conduct a membership drive targeted to businesses in the library's service area. **PRIORITY FOR 2006**

Membership Recruitment and Retention Goal #2: The Membership Committee will explore new ideas for membership retention.

Membership Recruitment and Retention Objective #2a: Investigate options for using e-mail for communication with members. **PRIORITY FOR 2006**

Membership Recruitment and Retention Objective #2b: Continue annual membership renewal mailing to existing members. Beginning in 2006, mailing will occur in mid to late January with a membership year of January through December explained in the renewal mailing letter or flyer. A reminder mailing will be sent two months after the first mailing asking "Are We Still Friends?" to give people an additional opportunity to renew their membership. **PRIORITY FOR 2006**

Membership Recruitment and Retention Objective #2c: Maintain present members and strive to increase membership rolls by **15%** annually. **ANNUAL PRIORITY**

Membership Recruitment and Retention Objective #2d: Review membership dues levels every other year in the summer of even numbered years (2006, 2008, etc.) so that suggested price increases can be approved by the Board in August or September and the increased projected income from dues can be accurately calculated in the proposed budget for the following year. Prior to proposing any dues increases a review of membership dues for other Friends of the Library organizations will be conducted. **PRIORITY FOR 2006**

Membership Recruitment and Retention Goal #3: The Membership Committee will identify member "perks" that could be offered as part of membership.

Membership Recruitment and Retention Objective #3a: Investigate options related to member recognition. **PRIORITY FOR 2005**

Membership Recruitment and Retention Objective #3b: Develop a list of "perks" offered by other Friends' groups and evaluate their appropriateness for our members. **PRIORITY FOR 2005**

Membership Recruitment and Retention Goal #4: The Membership Committee, in conjunction with the Community Relations and Marketing Committee, will explore avenues to promote the Friends of the Library and membership in the Friends of the Library at community events.

Membership Recruitment and Retention Objective #4a: Identify opportunities for community outreach efforts such as at the Ox Roast, Jubilee Day®, and the Wildcat Festival where the Friends of the Library could purchase a booth space to hand out information about the Friends and the library.

Membership Recruitment and Retention Objective #4b: Display and distribute Friends of the Library membership applications at all Friends' sponsored events (such as book sales, annual dinner, etc.). **PRIORITY FOR 2005**

Membership Recruitment and Retention Objective #4c: Continue providing membership information and application through library's Web site. **PRIORITY FOR 2005**

Membership Recruitment and Retention Goal #5: The Membership Committee will maintain accurate and up-to-date membership data using a computer database.

Membership Recruitment and Retention Objective #5a: Evaluate existing computer hardware and software and make recommendations for necessary upgrades, as needed. **PRIORITY FOR MID TO LATE 2005**

4. Organizational Structure

Organizational Structure Goal #1: The Board will periodically review the mission, vision, and bylaws.

Organizational Structure Objective #1a: The mission and vision will be reviewed on an annual basis and updated as needed. **ANNUAL PRIORITY**

Organizational Structure Objective #1b: The bylaws will be reviewed in their entirety every five years, or sooner, if requested by the President or the Board. **PRIORITY FOR 2005**

Organizational Structure Goal #2: Develop a written procedure manual that outlines in detail the committee responsibilities and activities undertaken by the Friends of the Library.

Organizational Structure Objective #2a: After the annual business meeting in November but before the end of the calendar year, the President-Elect, with input from the existing President and committee chairs or cochairs, will determine if the current committee structure is adequate or if committee additions, deletions, or changes are needed for next year. **ANNUAL PRIORITY**

Organizational Structure Objective #2b: By the end of each calendar year, committees will update their sections of the procedure manual so that the chairpersons selected in January will start the year with up-to-date and accurate information. **PRIORITY FOR 2006**

Organizational Structure Objective #2c: Committees will develop job descriptions for all positions which include information on physical demands and minimum time commitments required. Descriptions should be reviewed and updated on an annual basis. **ANNUAL PRIORITY**

Organizational Structure Goal #3: The long-range plan will be reviewed annually.

Organizational Structure Objective #3a: The long-range plan will be reviewed annually by the Board of Directors at the annual business meeting in November. Priorities for the coming year will be determined at that time. **ANNUAL PRIORITY**

Organizational Structure Goal #4: A Public Relations and News Media Policy will be developed.

Organizational Structure Objective #4a: A Public Relations and News Media Policy will be established which designates the Friends' President or the Library Director as the designated spokespersons for the Friends of the Library on general library topics and the appropriate committee chairs or cochairs as spokespersons for an event such as the house tour or book sale. **PRIORITY FOR 2006**

5. Community Relations and Marketing

The Friends of the Library can be a community relations force in the community if armed with accurate information and a positive attitude toward the library. The Community Relations and Marketing Committee's responsibilities will often overlap with Fund-Raising and Membership Recruitment and Retention activities.

Community Relations and Marketing Goal #1: The Friends of the Library will continue efforts to broaden community awareness of the Friends and the library.

Community Relations and Marketing Objective #1a: Develop a Frequently Asked Questions (FAQ) flyer that answers such questions as: What do you do? How do you support the library? Why should I be a Friend? Aren't the Friends and the Library the same thing? **PRIORITY FOR 2006**

Community Relations and Marketing Objective #1b: Identify opportunities for community outreach efforts such as at the Ox Roast, Jubilee Day®, and the Wildcat Festival where the Friends of the Library could rent a table to hand out information about the Friends and the library. **PRIORITY FOR 2006**

Community Relations and Marketing Objective #1c: Promote the Friends of the Library and library services in general to residents and businesses in all five municipalities in the library's service area. **PRIORITY FOR 2006**

Community Relations and Marketing Goal #2: The Community Relations and Marketing Committee will develop printed materials that promote the Friends of the Library and their activities.

Community Relations and Marketing Objective #2a: Assist the Membership Committee in updating the membership application on an annual basis. **ANNUAL PRIORITY**

Community Relations and Marketing Objective #2b: Explore opportunities with the Cumberland–Perry Area Vocational Technical School for assistance with graphic design and printing. **PRIORITY FOR 2006**

Community Relations and Marketing Goal #3: The Community Relations and Marketing Committee, in conjunction with the Book Sale Committee, will work together to promote and publicize the book sales.

Community Relations and Marketing Objective #3a: Establish mailing lists, using both U.S. mail and e-mail addresses, to inform customers of book sale activities. **PRIORITY FOR 2005**

Community Relations and Marketing Objective #3b: Develop method of tracking marketing efforts to determine impact on attracting book sale customers. **PRIORITY FOR 2005**

Community Relations and Marketing Goal #4: The Community Relations and Marketing Committee, in conjunction with the Membership Committee, will explore avenues to promote the Friends of the Library and membership in the Friends at community events.

Community Relations and Marketing Objective #4a: Identify opportunities for community outreach efforts such as at the Ox Roast, Jubilee Day®, and the Wildcat Festival where the Friends of the Library could rent a table to hand out information about the Friends and the library. **PRIORITY FOR 2006**

Community Relations and Marketing Objective #4b: Display and distribute Friends of the Library membership applications at all Friends' sponsored events (such as book sales, annual dinner, etc.). **ANNUAL PRIORITY**

Community Relations and Marketing Objective #4c: Continue providing membership information and application through library's Web site. **ANNUAL PRIORITY**

Community Relations and Marketing Objective #4d: Develop a table top display to promote membership in the Friends of the Library, what membership includes, and how it benefits the Friends and the library. Have display available at community events and Friends' sponsored events. **PRIORITY FOR 2005**

Community Relations and Marketing Goal #5: The Community Relations and Marketing Committee, in conjunction with the Holly Trail House Tour Committee, will promote this annual fund-raising event.

Community Relations and Marketing Objective #5a: Obtain timely and appropriate publicity in advance of the Holly Trail House Tour. **PRIORITY FOR 2005**

Community Relations and Marketing Goal #6: The Community Relations and Marketing Committee, in conjunction with the Fund-Raising Committee, will promote opportunities to purchase Friends of the Library merchandise.

Community Relations and Marketing Objective #6a: Develop methods to marketing the cookbook resulting in increased sales volume. **PRIORITY FOR 2006**

6. Volunteer Recruitment and Retention

Volunteer Recruitment and Retention Goal #1: Maintain current and accurate records related to Friends of the Library volunteers.

Volunteer Recruitment and Retention Objective #1a: Update volunteer list annually and contact volunteers to determine if they wish to stay on the volunteer roster for the following year. **ANNUAL PRIORITY**

Volunteer Recruitment and Retention Objective #1b: Develop a volunteer application form that asks for committee interests and special skills, in addition to name, address, phone, e-mail, and municipality of residence.

Volunteer Recruitment and Retention Objective #1c: Create a volunteer orientation packet which outlines the duties of the job, requirements, and expectations.

Volunteer Recruitment and Retention Goal #2: Obtain job descriptions from each committee for every volunteer position available. Description needs to include information on physical requirements and minimum time commitment requested.

Volunteer Recruitment and Retention Objective #2a: Develop methods to determine how to best utilize volunteers based on their skills, abilities, and availability.

Volunteer Recruitment and Retention Goal #3: Assess volunteer satisfaction levels through feedback obtained after each Friends' event.

Volunteer Recruitment and Retention Objective #3a: Solicit feedback from volunteers on their experience helping with a Friends' event. Forward feedback to the appropriate committee for use in planning the next event.

Volunteer Recruitment and Retention Goal #4: Seek opportunities to expand the pool of volunteers willing to help the Friends of the Library.

Volunteer Recruitment and Retention Objective #4a: Identify opportunities for community outreach efforts such as at the Ox Roast, Jubilee Day®, and the Wildcat Festival where the Friends of the Library could rent a table to hand out information about the Friends and the library. **PRIORITY FOR 2006**

Volunteer Recruitment and Retention Objective #4b: Expand board committees to include more nonboard members so that new people can be considered for future board positions and future Friends of the Library leadership positions. **ANNUAL PRIORITY**

Volunteer Recruitment and Retention Objective #4c: Develop a diverse pool of volunteers of varying ages, from various municipalities, and with different skills to provide the broadest possible range of talents to help the Friends of the Library. **ANNUAL PRIORITY**

Volunteer Recruitment and Retention Goal #5: Create more community involvement in the library and its activities through increasing the number of Friends involved in helping with volunteer activities.

Volunteer Recruitment and Retention Objective #5a: In a timely fashion, contact members who have expressed an interest in volunteering on their membership application form. **ANNUAL PRIORITY**

Annual Priorities

Advocacy Objective #1a: The Advocacy Committee will write an annual "State of the Library" letter from the Friends of the Library Board to elected officials.

Advocacy Objective #1b: The Friends of the Library will continue financial sponsorship of the library's annual Municipal and Officials Breakfast, and the Friends' President or his/her designated alternate will attend this event.

Fund-Raising Objective #2c: Annually evaluate book sale pricing and adjust as necessary.

Fund-Raising Objective #4a: Assess BOOKS BY THE GROSS location as it relates to affordability, accessibility, safety, convenience, and any other factors deemed relevant.

Fund-Raising Objective #4b: Maintain positive working relationship with John Gross and Co. employees.

Fund-Raising Objective #4c: Review lease agreement for BOOKS BY THE GROSS annually.

Membership Recruitment and Retention Objective #2c: Maintain present members and strive to increase membership rolls by 15% annually.

Organizational Structure Objective #1a: The mission and vision will be reviewed on an annual basis and updated as needed.

Organizational Structure Objective #2a: On an annual basis, the Board will determine if the current committee structure is adequate or if committee additions, deletions, or changes are needed.

Organizational Structure Objective #2c: Committees will develop job descriptions for all positions which include information on physical demands and minimum time commitments required. Descriptions should be reviewed and updated on an annual basis.

Organizational Structure Objective #3a: The long-range plan will be reviewed annually by the Board of Directors at the annual business meeting in November. Priorities for the coming year will be determined at that time.

Community Relations and Marketing Objective #2a: Assist the Membership Committee in updating the membership application on an annual basis.

Community Relations and Marketing Objective #4b: Display and distribute Friends of the Library membership applications at all Friends' sponsored events (such as book sales, annual dinner, etc.).

Community Relations and Marketing Objective #4c: Continue providing membership information and application through library's Web site.

Volunteer Recruitment and Retention Objective #1a: Update volunteer list annually and contact volunteers to determine if they wish to stay on the volunteer roster for the following year.

Volunteer Recruitment and Retention Objective #4b: Expand board committees to include more nonboard members so that new people can be considered for future board positions and future Friends of the Library leadership positions.

Volunteer Recruitment and Retention Objective #4c: Develop a diverse pool of volunteers of varying ages, from various municipalities, and with different skills to provide the broadest possible range of talents to help the Friends of the Library.

Volunteer Recruitment and Retention Objective #5a: In a timely fashion, contact members who have expressed an interest in volunteering on their membership application form.

Summary of Priorities for 2005

Advocacy Objective #2b: When requested by the library, Friends of the Library will submit newspaper editorials or letters to the editor on library matters.

Fund-Raising Objective #1a: The House Tour Committee will continue to expand the house tour locations into other parts of the library's service area.

Fund-Raising Objective #1b: The House Tour Committee will continue to expand advertising and sponsorship options to increase tour profits.

Fund-Raising Objective #1c: The House Tour Committee will explore adding new features to the tour each year.

Fund-Raising Objective #3a: Consider perks for book sale volunteers.

Fund-Raising Objective #3b: Develop job descriptions which include physical requirement and minimum time commitment required for book sale volunteers.

Fund-Raising Objective #3c: Develop information sheet and requirements for book sale volunteers.

Fund-Raising Objective #3d: Increase the number of volunteers involved with the book sales to spread the workload and help with identifying future leaders for the committee.

Fund-Raising Objective #3e: Create a handbook of operations for the book sale committee which documents in detail all aspects of the book sales.

Fund-Raising Objective #6a: Research options related to previews sponsored by other Friends of the Library groups.

Fund-Raising Objective #7a: Establish mailing lists, using both U.S. mail and e-mail addresses, to inform customers of book sale activities.

Fund-Raising Objective #7b: Develop method of tracking marketing efforts to determine impact on attracting book sale customers.

Fund-Raising Objective #7c: Develop methods to increase the quantity and quality of book donations received throughout the year.

Fund-Raising Objective #8a: Sell existing supply of cookbooks.

Fund-Raising Objective #8c: Develop marketing and merchandising opportunities to sell the cookbooks.

Fund-Raising Objective #8d: Have several items available for purchase at all time such as, but not limited to, book bags, miniatures, note cards, and crocks.

Fund-Raising Objective #8e: Fund the replenishment of library merchandise that is selling well as supply levels are depleted.

Fund-Raising Objective #8f: Develop marketing and merchandising opportunities to sell library merchandise.

Fund-Raising Objective #9a: Sponsor a minimum of one bus trip per year.

Fund-Raising Objective #9b: Investigate other travel opportunities.

Fund-Raising Objective #10a: Explore feasibility of having a Silent Auction fund-raiser, perhaps in conjunction with the Annual Dinner.

Fund-Raising Objective #10b: Investigate raffle opportunities such as quilts, artwork, woodcarvings, etc.

Fund-Raising Objective #10c: Attend fund-raising events in the area that may be viable fund-raisers for the Friends of the Library to see what is involved in the event and if it is something that is feasible for the Friends of the Joseph T. Simpson Public Library.

Membership Recruitment and Retention Objective #1a: Periodically conduct membership drives targeting nonmembers from a specific geographic area or a specific category (such as registered voters, library cardholders, school teachers, etc.).

Membership Recruitment and Retention Objective #1b: Investigate a membership drive "Ask a Friend to Be a Friend" in which Friends of the Library board members and library trustees write personal notes to people they know asking them to join the Friends.

Membership Recruitment and Retention Objective #3a: Investigate options related to member recognition.

Membership Recruitment and Retention Objective #3b: Develop a list of "perks" offered by other Friends' groups and evaluate their appropriateness for our members.

Membership Recruitment and Retention Objective #4b: Display and distribute Friends of the Library membership applications at all Friends' sponsored events (such as book sales, annual dinner, etc.).

Membership Recruitment and Retention Objective #4c: Continue providing membership information and application through library's Web site.

Membership Recruitment and Retention Objective #5a: Evaluate existing computer hardware and software and make recommendations for necessary upgrades, as needed.

Organizational Structure Objective #1b: The bylaws will be reviewed in their entirety every five years, or sooner, if requested by the President or the Board.

Community Relations and Marketing Objective #3a: Establish mailing lists, using both U.S. mail and e-mail addresses, to inform customers of book sale activities.

Community Relations and Marketing Objective #3b: Develop method of tracking marketing efforts to determine impact on attracting book sale customers.

Community Relations and Marketing Objective #4d: Develop a table top display to promote membership in the Friends of the Library, what membership includes, and how it benefits the Friends and the library. Have display available at community events and Friends' sponsored events.

Community Relations and Marketing Objective #5a: Obtain timely and appropriate publicity in advance of the Holly Trail House Tour.

Summary of Priorities for 2006

Advocacy Objective #1c: When requested by the library, Friends of the Library will contact elected officials either in writing, by phone, or personally to show their support of the library and request the support of the elected officials.

Advocacy Objective #1d: Support the Pennsylvania Library Association (PaLA) and Pennsylvania Citizens for Better Libraries (PCBL) in statewide advocacy efforts.

Advocacy Objective #2a: The Friends of the Library will have current statistics available to use in demonstrating library usage and the need for additional funding.

Fund-Raising Objective #1a: The House Tour Committee will continue to expand the house tour locations into other parts of the library's service area.

Fund-Raising Objective #1b: The House Tour Committee will continue to expand advertising and sponsorship options to increase tour profits.

Fund-Raising Objective #1c: The House Tour Committee will explore adding new features to the tour each year.

Fund-Raising Objective #1d: The House Tour Committee will explore developing a different type of tour in the future.

Fund-Raising Objective #2a: Set goals for growth of the book sale in number of items for sale, number of sales, gross sale income, etc.

Fund-Raising Objective #2b: Investigate feasibility of selling selected books on the Internet.

Fund-Raising Objective #2d: Travel to other book sales in the area for new ideas and methods of holding book sales.

Fund-Raising Objective #2e: Consider establishing a newsletter devoted to book sale news.

Fund-Raising Objective #2f: Continue investigating options for "recycling" book sale leftovers by sharing them with other organizations such as shelters, prisons, day care centers, schools, etc.

Fund-Raising Objective #5a: Consider sponsoring specialty sales during the year. Examples might include "Gift Quality" books for sale around the holidays or a "Books for Kids" sale at the library in conjunction with a special program going on at the library.

Fund-Raising Objective #8a: Sell existing supply of cookbooks.

Fund-Raising Objective #8c: Develop marketing and merchandising opportunities to sell the cookbooks.

Fund-Raising Objective #8d: Have several items available for purchase at all time such as, but not limited to, book bags, miniatures, note cards and crocks.

Fund-Raising Objective #8e: Fund the replenishment of library merchandise that is selling well as supply levels are depleted.

Fund-Raising Objective #8f: Develop marketing and merchandising opportunities to sell library merchandise.

Fund-Raising Objective #9a: Sponsor a minimum of one bus trip per year.

Fund-Raising Objective #9b: Investigate other travel opportunities.

Fund-Raising Objective #10a: Explore feasibility of having a Silent Auction fund-raiser, perhaps in conjunction with the Annual Dinner.

Fund-Raising Objective #10b: Investigate raffle opportunities such as quilts, artwork, woodcarvings, etc.

Fund-Raising Objective #10c: Attend fund-raising events in the area that may be viable fund-raisers for the Friends of the Library to see what is involved in the event and if it is something that is feasible for the Friends of the Joseph T. Simpson Public Library.

Membership Recruitment and Retention Objective #1c: Investigate feasibility of establishing a Junior Friends of the Library organization.

Membership Recruitment and Retention Objective #1d: Conduct a membership drive targeted to businesses in the library's service area.

Membership Recruitment and Retention Objective #2a: Investigate options for using e-mail for communication with members.

Membership Recruitment and Retention Objective #2b: Continue annual membership renewal mailing to existing members. Mailing to occur in mid to late January with a membership year of January through December explained in the renewal mailing letter or flyer. A reminder mailing will be sent two months after the first mailing asking "Are We Still Friends?" to give people an additional opportunity to renew their membership.

Membership Recruitment and Retention Objective #2d: Review membership dues levels every other year in the summer of even numbered years (2006, 2008, etc.) so that suggested price increases can be approved by the Board in August or September and the increased projected income from dues can be accurately calculated in the proposed budget for the following year. Prior to proposing any dues increases a review of membership dues for other Friends' organizations will be conducted.

Organizational Structure Objective #2b: By the end of each calendar year, committees will update their sections of the procedure manual so that the chairpersons selected in January will start the year with up-to-date and accurate information.

Organizational Structure Objective #4a: A Public Relations and News Media Policy will be established which designates the Friends' President or the Library Director as the designated spokespersons for the Friends of the Library on general library topics and the appropriate committee chairs or cochairs as spokespersons for an event such as the house tour or book sale.

Community Relations and Marketing Objective #1a: Develop a Frequently Asked Questions (FAQ) flyer that answers such questions as: What do you do? How do you support the library? Why should I be a Friend? Aren't the Friends and the Library the same thing?

Community Relations and Marketing Objective #1b: Identify opportunities for community outreach efforts such as at the Ox Roast, Jubilee Day®, and the Wildcat Festival where the Friends of the Library could rent a table to hand out information about the Friends and the library.

Community Relations and Marketing Objective #1c: Promote the Friends of the Library and library services in general to residents and businesses in all five municipalities in the library's service area.

Community Relations and Marketing Objective #2b: Explore opportunities with the Cumberland–Perry Area Vocational Technical School for assistance with graphic design and printing.

Community Relations and Marketing Objective #4a: Identify opportunities for community outreach efforts such as at the Ox Roast, Jubilee Day®, and the Wildcat Festival where the Friends of the Library could rent a table to hand out information about the Friends and the library.

Community Relations and Marketing Objective #6a: Develop methods to marketing the cookbook resulting in increased sales volume.

Volunteer Recruitment and Retention Objective #4a: Identify opportunities for community outreach efforts such as at the Ox Roast, Jubilee Day®, and the Wildcat Festival where the Friends of the Library could rent a table to hand out information about the Friends and the library.

Roles and Responsibilities of the Board of Trustees, Library Director, and Friends of the Library

Adapted from Model State Friends' Cooperative Framework developed by Connecticut State Library, Association of Connecticut Library Boards, and Friends of Connecticut Libraries, included in Friends of Libraries Sourcebook, third edition, by Sandy Dolnick (ALA, 1996).

	Library Director	**Trustees**	**Friends**
Administrative	Administer daily operations of the library, including personnel, collection development, fiscal management, maintenance of buildings and grounds, and programming. Act as technical advisor to the board and ensure staff representation at Friends' board meetings.	Recruit and employ a qualified library director; maintain an ongoing performance appraisal process for the director.	Support quality library service in the community through fund-raising, volunteerism, and serving as advocates for the library's programs and services.
Library Policies	Apprise board of need for new policies as well as policy revisions; implement the policies of library as adopted by the board; keep Friends of the Library apprised of all library policies.	Identify and adopt written policies to govern the operations of the library, including personnel, general operating, and collection development policies.	Support the policies of the library as adopted by the library board; periodically review the bylaws, mission, and vision for the Friends of the Library.
Short-Term and Long-Range Planning	Coordinate and implement short-term and long-range planning process with board, Friends, staff, and community.	Ensure the library has a long-range planning process with implementation and evaluation components. Process should include input from Friends, community, and staff.	Provide input into the library's long-range planning process and support the library in carrying out their plan. Work with library director on long-range planning for the Friends of the Library.
Marketing and Public Relations	Coordinate and implement an ongoing marketing and public relations program.	Ensure that the library has an active marketing and public relations program.	Promote the library's programs and services to the public and the role that the Friends of the Library play in providing these programs and services.

	Library Director	Trustees	Friends
Fiscal Responsibilities	Prepare an annual budget for the library in consultation with the board; present current report of expenditures against budget at each board meeting; make the Friends of the Library aware of the special financial needs of the library.	Secure adequate funds to carry out the library's programs and services; assist in the preparation of the annual budget. Develop long-range financial projections.	Conduct fund-raising that complements the library's mission and provides funding for special library projects.
Legislative Responsibilities	Educate board and Friends regarding current local, state, and federal library laws and pending library legislation.	Be familiar with local, state, and federal library laws as well as pending library legislation. Serve as advocates for local, state, and national library issues; represent the library program to legislators.	Serve as advocates for local, state, and national library issues; represent the library program to legislators.
Meetings	Provide written reports at and participate in all board and Friends of the Library meetings; ensure that there is a staff liaison to the Friends of the Library.	Attend and participate in board meetings and see that accurate records are kept on file at the library; appoint a liaison to the Friends' board to attend their meetings.	Maintain a liaison to the board of trustees to attend all their meetings.
Networking	Affiliate with state and national professional organizations and attend professional meetings and workshops. Be active in community organizations, too.	Attend state sponsored trustee meetings and workshops, and support the efforts of the PaLA, PCBL, and FOLUSA.	Affiliate with state and national organizations such as PCBL and FOLUSA & attend their workshops. Support efforts of PaLA.

Index

About the Authors

Sally Gardner Reed is the executive director of Friends of Libraries U.S.A. and the acting director of the Association of Library Trustees and Advocates—a division of the American Library Association. She speaks nationwide and worldwide about the critical role Friends and Trustees play in ensuring that libraries are fully funded in the community and on campus. She is the author of eight books, including *Making the Case for Your Library* (Neal-Schuman, 2002). She works and resides in Philadelphia, Pennsylvania.

Beth Nawalinski is the Marketing and Public Relations Coordinator of Friends of Libraries U.S.A. Although Beth completed her undergraduate studies in nuclear engineering, she has pursued her career supporting literacy and libraries as Community Relations Coordinator with Barnes & Noble and, before coming to FOLUSA in 2002, as Public Information Specialist with the Norfolk (VA) Public Library. She resides in Downingtown, Pennsylvania.

Both are the authors, with Alexander Peterson, of *101+ Great Ideas for Libraries and Friends*, the predecessor of *Even More Great Ideas for Libraries and Friends*, also published by Neal-Schuman.